The Concept of Person in Judaism, Christianity and Islam

Key Concepts in Interreligious Discourses

Edited by
Georges Tamer

Volume 6

The Concept of Person in Judaism, Christianity and Islam

Edited by
Georges Tamer

DE GRUYTER

ISBN 978-3-11-075664-7
e-ISBN (PDF) 978-3-11-075671-5
e-ISBN (EPUB) 978-3-11-075683-8
ISSN 2513-1117

Library of Congress Control Number: 2023939544

Bibliographic information published by the Deutsche Nationalbibliothek
The Deutsche Nationalbibliothek lists this publication in the Deutsche Nationalbibliografie; detailed bibliographic data are available on the internet at http://dnb.dnb.de.

Printing and binding: CPI books GmbH, Leck

www.degruyter.com

Preface

The present volume in the book series “Key Concepts in Interreligious Discourses” (KCID) contains the results of a conference on the concept of person in Judaism, Christianity and Islam. The conference was held at the Friedrich-Alexander-Universität Erlangen-Nürnberg on February 13–14, 2019. It was partially sponsored by the Evangelische Kirche in Deutschland (EKD), which I wish to thank for the support given to us in the past to investigate interreligious discourses in the service of social cohesion and mutual understanding among people belonging to different religions.

The conference and book series “Key Concepts in Interreligious Discourses” (KCID) belong to the main projects of the Bavarian Research Center for Interreligious Discourses (BaFID). The main aim of the Center is the study of the fundamental ideas and central concepts in Judaism, Christianity and Islam in order to uncover their reciprocal connections and reveal deeply rooted similarities and differences between these three religions. In this way, BaFID endeavors to strengthen peaceful relations between religious communities by communicating research results. In addition to the published volumes, selections of particularly salient parts from each volume are made available online on BaFID’s website.

In this fashion, BaFID fulfills its aspirations not only by reflecting on central religious ideas amongst a small group of academic specialists, but also by disseminating such ideas in a way that appeals to the broader public. Academic research that puts itself at the service of society is vital for counteracting powerful contemporary trends of segregation rooted in ignorance, and to improve mutual respect and acceptance amongst religions. Such a result is guaranteed due to the methodology deployed by the research center, namely the discursive investigation of the concepts, as documented in the present volume on the concept of person. The contributions contained in this volume illuminate various aspects of this complex concept in Judaism, Christianity and Islam particularly from a metaphysical, existential, historical and philological points of view.

I wish to thank the publishing house Walter de Gruyter for competently taking care of this volume and the entire book series. I would also like to thank Catharina Rachik, MA, and Dr. Ghassan El Masri for preparing the volume, and Antonia Steins, MA, for proofreading its language.

Georges Tamer
Erlangen, May 2023

https://doi.org/10.1515/9783110756715-001

Table of Contents

Aryeh Botwinick
The Concept of Person in Judaism — 1

Edward J. Alam
The Concept of Person in Christianity — 45

Peter G. Riddell
The Concept of Person in Islam — 97

Ghassan El Masri
Epilogue — 157

List of Contributors — 171

Index of Terms — 173

Index of Names — 175

Aryeh Botwinick

The Concept of Person in Judaism

1 Methodological Preface

The very formulation of the topic of this paper which I was invited to contribute to this volume constitutes an anachronism. The categories of Biblical narrative are persons, events, and relationships. Conceptual elaboration, abstraction, and analysis are an important part of the legacy of Ancient Greece for Western civilization. So, it is part of the complex design of the subject matter of this essay that in order to elucidate the concept of a person in Judaism, I need to talk about such central topics in Jewish religious practice and evolving theology as the concept of the monotheistic God, repentance, and the messianic age. This represents the progression of topics that I cover in this essay.

Since Judaism as the subject matter of this essay constitutes a way of life and does not compose a philosophical treatise, the only approach for teasing out from it its concept of a person is indirect and inferential. I have chosen three central subject matters within the broad confines of Jewish tradition as the basis for my inferences and generalizations concerning its concept of a person. The first is the human paradigms of emulation and the human paradigms of avoidance that we are presented with within the Biblical text. The personality types that the Bible endorses are those that evince a closeness to God, so that God inevitably becomes an important topic for discussion in my analysis of their personalities. The second is the concept of repentance, which charts the paths of human beings' deconstruction and reconstruction of their sense of self and personal identity. Repentance in Judaism is supposed to be part of a lifelong dynamic of personal growth and self-transcendence – and that is the way I approach it in this essay. The Messianic age in Christianity and in right-wing versions of Judaism and Islam is a putative total eclipse and transformation of normal patterns of living. It signals the consummation of the particular monotheistic religion and the end of human history. Where and when strong messianism prevails, the human story is over. A strong vision of the messianic age in any monotheistic religion constitutes its epitaph of the concept of a person.

In order to maximize the coherence of my argument, I try to show in this Methodological Preface how my analytical approach to the concept of a person in Judaism is immediately appropriate – and matches – what it seeks to describe. For millions of people around the world, Judaism is a vibrant, utterly alive religion. This means that there is no final reading of its principles and tenets. Understand-

https://doi.org/10.1515/9783110756715-002

ing is always subject to new readings and new interpretations – which enrich the prevailing understanding and become the subject, in turn, of new interpretations. The relationship between understanding and interpretation is irredeemably – irrevocably – circular in character. We are the source of what we see and discover in ourselves – and in the world. The unbridgeable distance between God and human beings becomes the model for our understanding and reading of our relationship with ourselves, the world at large, and other human beings. My quasi-phenomenalistic reading of the Jewish concept of the person dovetails with what I find unique and highly instructive about its content.

The methodological position that I am advocating for in this preface has roots in the writings of Friedrich Nietzsche (1844–1900) and Hans-Georg Gadamer (1900–2002). In his great essay *On the Advantage and Disadvantage of History for Life,* Nietzsche writes:

> A historical phenomenon, clearly and completely understood and reduced to an intellectual phenomenon, is for him who has understood it dead. [...] History, conceived as pure science and become sovereign, would constitute a final closing out of the accounts of life for mankind. [...] History, so far as it serves life, serves an unhistorical power. [...] For with a certain excess of history life crumbles and degenerates, and finally, because of this degeneration, history itself degenerates as well.[1]

At least partially in response to Nietzsche's critique of historical knowledge, Hans-Georg Gadamer – one of the leading hermeneutical theorists of the 20th Century – "describe[s] the work of hermeneutics as a conversation with the text."[2] Given the fact that every crystallization of meaning out of a text is underdetermined by the text itself – that there are always more possibilities of meaning than we are able to extract through any one act of interpretation – Gadamer goes on to add that "A person who seeks to understand must question what lies behind what is said. He must understand it as an answer to a question."[3] The questions that we pose to texts will change with evolving historical and cultural circumstances. Gadamer argues that: "It is part of the historical finiteness of our being that we are aware that after us others will understand in a different way. And yet it is an equally well established fact that it remains the same work, the fullness of whose meaning is proved in the changing process of understanding."[4] Gadamer affirms that "[t]he standpoint that is beyond any standpoint, a standpoint from which we could conceive its true iden-

1 Nietzsche, Friedrich, *On the Advantage and Disadvantage of History for Life,* trans. Peter Preuss, Indianapolis: Hackett Publishing Company, 1980, 11–12.

2 Gadamer, Hans-Georg, *Truth and Method,* New York: The Seabury Press, 1975, 331.

3 Ibid., 333.

4 Ibid., 336.

tity, is a pure illusion."[5] The skeptical considerations adduced earlier in the paper also contribute to the realization that consensus and communion need to substitute for certainty in our interpretation of texts: "To reach an understanding with one's partner in a dialogue is not merely a matter of total self-expression and the successful assertion of one's own point of view, but a transformation into a communion, in which we do not remain what we were."[6]

We need to realize that words generally are metaphoric surrogates for our ignorance. We do not know how many conceptual investments have gone into fashioning a word that we now take to neutrally describe a thing. From the skeptical perspective of the underdetermination of words by things, all words are metaphors that represent extensions and variations upon a not-fully-known beginning. No one definition can ever qualify as the full literal disclosure of what a word means. Human beings generally do not have a full and clear inventory of how a word came to be formed – and an accurate and comprehensive summary of the whole list of prior conceptual investments that launched a word into circulation in one of the world's languages. That being the case, every attempt at definition and paraphrase of a word is a metaphor – an extension and special application of it – and not a direct translation of what the word taken by itself before any conceptual tinkering or investment signifies. In terms of the grammatical ontology of words, they are all metaphors. Since there is no original, conceptually uncontaminated, or conceptually un-infiltrated thing to latch on to, whether one speaks of clouds of glory, real booths, or negative theology one is in the domain of metaphor. None of these terms is grounded in certainty.

It is important to note that this very statement is contradictory. If I claim that the ontological status of every word that we use is metaphoric, this very formulation is self-contradictory because the meaning of the term metaphor is parasitic upon the meaning of its contrasting term realistic representation. In this implicit sense, I am committed to conferring reality upon the notion of a realistic representation of an object of thought and to the idea that our vocabulary consists of more than metaphors. So, by arguing as I do, I dramatize that I am in the throes of contradiction. I adopt a skeptical position by denying the independent reality of things. But skepticism itself is contradictory. To be a consistent skeptic, one would have to be skeptical of skepticism as well as of all other alternative positions in philosophy. I could always only be a mitigated skeptic, but not an extreme skeptic. By making my positions worse in relation to both negative theology and skepticism, however, I paradoxically improve them. As Karl Popper and others have ar-

5 Ibid., 339.
6 Ibid., 341.

gued based on the principles of Aristotelian logic, by admitting even one contradictory statement into the set of statements that I regard as true, I have forfeited the possibility of resisting contradictory statements or ruling them out.[7] Popper's aim in his essay on dialectic might officially be that we should become vigilant in noticing and removing contradictions in our arguments. However, following the logical argument based upon the principles of Aristotelian logic that he adduces in his essay on dialectic that once one contradiction is classified as irremovable no contradiction whatsoever can be banished or excluded from the set of statements that we take to be true, and if as I argue that negative theology and skepticism are both unavoidably contradictory, then the paradoxical inference can be drawn from them that they have ipso facto legitimated themselves. Since, according to Popper, arguing in Aristotelian terms, if no contradiction can be ruled out once one contradiction is accepted, then contradiction becomes the normal fate of argument, and statements and arguments espousing skeptical and negative theological positions must be affirmed as acceptable. I am also not debarred from considering my statement about the pervasiveness of metaphor as true.

What is the conceptual linkage between negative theology and skepticism? As I suggested earlier, negative theology – the formulation of its tenets – eventuates in a contradiction, and, following Karl Popper, once even a single contradiction is allowed, no possibility can be logically ruled out so that one willy-nilly finds oneself in a skeptical position. Negative theology, which says that our only way of conceiving God is to consistently disown the literalistic import of any attributes that we are tempted to ascribe to Him, simultaneously constrains us to a perpetual disowning of attributes while retaining some recognizable substantive entity called God whose attributes are being unceasingly deliteralized – swept away on a literal level. According to negative theology, we have God only for the sake of continually disowning Him on a literal level. Sustaining allegiance to God in a negative theological context thereby presupposes the normalizing of contradiction. Once contradiction is affirmed, no possibility can be ruled out and we are therefore ensconced in a skeptical position that is bereft of the resources for defending other minds and all the other traditional components of the common, everyday world.

Rabbi Akiva is regarded in the Talmud itself as the dean of the Talmudic rabbis[8] – as the teacher of all the leading teachers of the *Oral Law of Judaism*, which today we could subsume under the rubric of *Talmudic Studies*. The *Babylonian Talmud* in *Ned* 54a–54b seems to suggest that Rabbi Akiva adheres to the position of

7 Popper, Karl R., *Conjectures and Refutations: The Growth of Scientific Knowledge*, 2nd ed., London: Routledge and Kegan Paul, 1965, 312–335; see especially p. 317.
8 b Sanh 86a.

nominalism in philosophy. If this reading is correct, then no word can ever be taken to overlap with any one thing, and the slack that subsists between words and things remains indefinitely present. With sufficient ingenuity and persistence, we could always choose other words from those we originally selected to subsume or circumscribe the things we have in mind. If this is the case, then an infinite distance can be said to prevail between ordinary words and ordinary things. The case of *God* would not be unique. Infinity would be in the world, not just in *heaven*. The substratum of continuity defining human personhood would be as hard to figure out and theorize as the substratum of continuity inherent in the concept of God, which enables us to project the contradictory attributes of unlimited power and unlimited compassion unto God.

Given the volatility of our experience and the consequent, sometimes kaleidoscopic fungibility attendant to our use of words, it is impossible to conceive of words as essentially coinciding with particular things. Words are continually revised, expanded, foreshortened, or exchanged for other words in terms of managing and communicating our experience. Nominalism is a metaphysical and linguistic theory that is in sync with the possible, instead of aspiring to an impossible and utterly unstable overlap between words and things.

In general, we need to learn the art of creating and drawing distinctions, because hardly anything in the world is a direct reflection of what it truly is. Everything is tainted; everything is classified and categorized and harnessed for some human purpose. For example, in Jewish theology, the Sabbath evokes God's original world before the human interruption began. It brings us back to a self-erasing beginning – where the perpetual -weekly- movement back and forth between a non-traceable beginning and a non-consumable middle or end mocks our conceptual audacity and assertiveness, making only an interminable middle seem real.

Claims to knowledge, certainty, and truth are vulnerable to the charge that the evidence that we invoke to buttress them will always be willy-nilly infiltrated by categorial presuppositions and commitments that vitiate the objective corroboration that we seek. As Plato pointed out long ago in the *Meno*, to know anything, on some level we must already know it. Knowledge proceeds in the trajectory of circularity – not in an all-or-nothing engagement or conquest of the truth. Knowledge of God resides on the same plane as knowledge of physical objects. In both cases, there is an infinite distance between our vocabularies of conceptualization and the reliability and stability of the objects that they are presumably netting for us. The concept of God subsists at the outward perimeter of our ongoing activity to use language to fashion and inventory a world. Perhaps the most fruitful route to follow in order to achieve a consensus on the relevance and usefulness of the term God is to disseminate the teachings of skepticism as broadly as possible, so as to normalize and naturalize our invocation of the word *God* – to gain widespread recognition of the idea that it is not ontologically any more or less secure than the other terms in our vocabulary – and thereby to gain for it the status of the term *rational* in the full-fledged Maimonidean sense.

Given the confluence of the skeptical factors I have been cataloging, Gadamer reaches the conclusion that "Understanding and interpretation are indissolubly bound up with each other"[9]. This sentence can be taken as Gadamer's statement of the background assumption of hermeneutics. What the text provides us with – and what we bring to the text – are inextricably linked. If we do not have interpretative frameworks, there is no text. If we do not have an external text, there is nothing to interpret. The text is inevitably received, interpreted, and understood by our receptive *apparati*. The receptive *apparati* themselves were nurtured and cultivated through our encounter with earlier texts.

From almost every conceivable angle of vision, the *Hebrew Scriptures* and key passages of rabbinic thought in its legal and homiletical guises are about the pervasiveness of the metaphysical middle in human beings' perception and engagement with the world. The Bible does not envision either a firm beginning or a firm end to human life. Its major energies are devoted to projecting and sustaining the middle and to ensuring that this overall activity becomes the dominant focus of human life. The Biblical and rabbinic emphasis on the middle creates a very large space for viewing human beings in general and Jews in particular as harboring the potential for exercising tremendous freedom and responsibility in shaping, structuring, and assessing our lives. In many key respects, the understanding of God and the images of human nature are correlative in the Jewish religion. One achieves the deepest and most secure understanding of the concept of a person, the nature of human nature, by probing and exploring the concept of God.

The name of the first human being that God creates – Adam – very eloquently captures the contradicting nature – the duality – of human identity. The word *Adam* in Hebrew is etymologically linked to the Hebrew word *Adamah*, which means *earth*. Human beings are fashioned out of the lowliest elements. At the same time, the Bible in the creation story emphasizes that man is created *B'Tzelem Elokim* – in the image of God. The tension between limitation and aspiration defines, or, one might almost say, is constitutive of human identity. A kindred perception of infinite distances defining the landscape of the human psyche, the human self, is found in chapter 8, verses 4–6, of the Psalms:

> When I behold your heavens, the work of your fingers, the moon and the stars that you have set in place. What is frail man that you should remember him, and the son of mortal man that

9 Ibid., 360.

> you should be mindful of him? Yet, you have made him but slightly less than the angels, and crowned him with soul and splendor.[10]

The Bible mocks the notion of human selfhood as a stable container that easily reconciles the elements of tension and conflict within itself. The self is rather perceived as an arena or battleground in which antagonistic forces battle for supremacy, and victories on any side of an inner conflict remain tenuous and fragile. The self, the human person, retains more of the character of a posit or wager, rather than of a fixed entity that remains stable throughout a person's lifetime.

The Jewish understanding seems to be that neither overarching redemption nor passive withdrawal is appropriate for the human estate. We can neither fulfill all our aspirations nor can we overcome all our limitations. Establishing a program in which we struggle and grow but also backslide and continually reinterpret where we are and where we would like to be is more faithful to the human condition than any extreme position. Judaism consists of a continuous romance with the unromantic and un-glorious elements of human life. We strive to become who we are – but learning who we are itself forms a lifetime project.

The Hebrew Scriptures as a foundational text for all three monotheistic religions is a major source for us to consider in order to ferret out the concept of personhood in Judaism. The way I propose to do this is by concentrating on key biblical personalities and through a process of inference reconstructing the dominant motifs in their personalities. I think that the Bible communicates to us its teachings concerning human nature by establishing paradigms of emulation, such as Adam, Abraham, Isaac, Jacob, and Moses, and fixing paradigms of avoidance, such as Pharaoh, Korach, Nadav and Avihu, and the spies that Moses sent from the desert to scout out the land of Israel. In the first section of this paper, I would like to analyze Biblical religious sensibility especially as it relates to the formation of human personhood as reflected in the key Biblical personalities that I mentioned.

Throughout this paper, I will be alluding to Maimonides' (1135/38–1204) conceptualization of God in his Laws Concerning the Foundations of the Torah, the first section of his Code, called *Mishneh Torah*[11] which overlaps with his discussion of God in *The Guide of the Perplexed.*[12] Maimonides' theorizing of God can be seen as a fitting complement to the metaphysical sensibility suffusing the Biblical text it-

---

10 Scherman, Nosson (ed.), *The ArtScroll Tehillim*, trans. Hillel Danziger, Brooklyn, NY: Mesorah Publications, 1988, 13.

11 Maimonides, *Mishneh Torah*, vol. 1, *Sefer HaMada*, Commentary by Shmuel Tanchum Rubinstein, Jerusalem: Mossad Harav Kook, 1989.

12 Maimonides, *The Guide of the Perplexed*, trans. Shlomo Pines, Chicago: University of Chicago Press, 1963.

self – and it most certainly derives part of its inspiration from it. Maimonides' conceptualization of God as an infinite, conceptually inaccessible being creates an interpretative dynamic that locates finite versions of the attributes ascribed to God in the setting of human personality – and thus gives us further insights into the classic concept of Jewish personhood.

Another ideal context from which to theorize Jewish understandings of human nature is to consider how Jewish textual sources approach the project of periodically remaking ourselves, or some unsatisfactory aspects of self, encapsulated in the concept of *Teshuvah*, meaning repentance in English. Repentance involves some reinstatement of one's original vision of what one is striving to be – and therefore provides an ideal window for recapturing that vision. In the second section of the paper, I would like to address this theme.

The largest challenge to my reading of the concept of personhood in Judaism comes from the contemporary resurgence of a strong Jewish messianism which seems to want to abrogate any continuation of the middle as I have theorized it so far in this paper, and to very assertively reach the end-point of Jewish history with the expansion of the land of Israel to approximate to what this version of messianism takes to be the biblical boundaries of the land, and the establishment of hegemonic control over this expanded territory. To sustain my reading of the concept of personhood in Judaism, I need to show how the practice of a strong messianism by a minority of very vocal groups in Israel – supported by a minority of very conspicuous and assertive groups in the diaspora – distorts and undermines Jewish understandings of selfhood and the religious climate in which it lives out its being. In the third and final section of the paper, I would like to consider the question of whether and how classic Jewish texts envision an end to history. Is there an end to human history? If in reflective equilibrium one could say that classic Jewish texts respond ambivalently, or even negatively, to this question by retaining their grip on the metaphysical middle, then this would have drastically transformed how Jews conceive of their personal identity and what their mission as Jews and as persons in the world is.

2 The Dichotomy of Negative Theology vs. Gnosticism as a Shaping Influence on Jewish Personhood

A distinction between negative theology and gnosticism animates some of the most arresting passages in the Biblical text. For example, the Biblical descriptions of Moses' confrontations with his Jewish archenemy – Korach – and his non-Jewish archenemy – Amalek – receive heightened point and poignancy when viewed from the perspective of this distinction. In addition, our understanding of such central Biblical events as the theological transgression of the *Dor Ha-Pelagah* – literally, the generation of the dispersion; figuratively, the builders of the Tower of Babel –, the theological distinctness of the Post-Expulsion – from the Garden of Eden – stage of human life in relation to the Pre-Expulsion stage; the significance of the Biblical accounts of Creation and prophecy; the transgressions involved in fashioning the golden calf, of Nadav and Avihu, and the spies, as well as a number of striking metaphors in the Biblical narrative such as *Jacob's Ladder* and the *Burning Bush* is enhanced by invoking the categorial contrast between Gnosticism and negative theology. In this section, I would like to briefly explore the central Biblical events and symbols I have inventoried in relation to the overarching typology of negative theology versus gnosticism, which I believe is central in illuminating the Jewish concept of personhood. I shall not define these very broad and elastic terms at the outset but shall rather let their definitions emerge contextually in relation to the Biblical texts I will be examining.

I would like to focus first on the Bible's description of Moses in contrast to the way it characterizes his archenemy, Korach, who leads a religious and political rebellion against him recounted in the *Book of Numbers.*[13] Moses is called in the Biblical account an *Eved Hashem* – a servant of God.[14] *Eved* is the term used in the Bible to describe the servile status of the Jews in Egypt. Moses is resolutely not deified in the Biblical account of the *Exodus*, which pays close attention to the intra-family tensions and rivalries between Moses, Aaron, and Miriam and the vagaries of class position, such as Moses's adoption by Pharaoh's daughter, in charting his rise to religious and political prominence. The Bible very squarely situates Moses as being in the throes of what Harold Bloom (1930–2019) following Freud has called "a family romance"[15] which reaches a climax in the *Book of Numbers*. There, Miriam and Aaron speak against Moses "because of the Cushite woman" he had taken. The Bible very pointedly juxtaposes their rebuke of Moses with the statement that "Moses was very humble above all the men who were upon the face of the earth."[16] Moses feels powerless to speak out against them. As the parent-favored and sibling-resented youngest child, his preferred medium of communication is action – pick-

---

13 Num 16–19.

14 Num 12:7.

15 The Freudian notion figures prominently in Harold Bloom's tetralogy: *The Anxiety of Influence: A Theory of Poetry*, New York: Oxford University Press, 1973; *A Map of Misreading*, New York: Oxford University Press, 1975; *Kabbalah and Criticism*, New York: Seabury Press, 1975; *Poetry and Repression*, New Haven (et.al.): Yale University Press, 1976.

16 Num 12:3.

ing up the cues and signals of opportunity earlier than other people and responding to them more swiftly. There is an eerie congruence between the physical oppression of the Jewish people as a whole and the psychological oppression of Moses – with the configuration of Moses's oppression encoding for him a strategic way out which he is able to apply to relieve the condition of the people as a whole.

The humanization of Moses, which is symptomatic of the Biblical account of his career, is perceived by the rabbis as a disguised theological statement. The rabbis read the Biblical text as burning the most plausible bridge between humanity and God – namely Moses – to underscore that the distance between us and God remains unbridgeable. In the *Passover Haggadah's* recounting of the Exodus story compiled by later generations of rabbis, Moses is nearly omitted altogether so that the inscrutability of the Divine role in redemption is not marred by any overly intrusive human presence.

Moses's personification of a negative theological stance in relation to God receives classic expression in the subversive reading that Rashi provides for a famous Talmudic text. In explicating Moses's superiority over all other prophets, the Talmud says "All the prophets looked into a dim glass, but Moses looked through a clear glass"[17]. Rashi glosses this statement by saying that "[the other prophets] thought they had seen, but hadn't; whereas Moses saw through a clear glass and knew that he hadn't seen Him face to face."[18]

The Biblical prototype of a Gnostic believer is Korach. He rebels against the structure of authority instituted by Moses in the desert by saying to Moses and Aaron: "Ye take too much upon you, for all the congregation are holy, every one of them, and the Eternal is among them: why then lift up yourselves above the assembly of the Eternal?"[19] The Hebrew phrase – *U'Betocham Hashem* – is ambiguous. The word *Toch* in Hebrew can be translated – as the translation I have just cited suggests – as *among*. *Toch* can also be translated as *inside* – so that the phrase would now read *and the Eternal is inside them.* While I think the theological import of the passage remains the same, the Gnostic thrust of Korach's rebellion against Moses is most graphically communicated by the word *inside.* God is not outside the community of believers, so a stable and legitimate structure of authority to transmit and enforce his messages is needed. He is rather inside the psyches, if not the bodies, of believers – so that patterns of interaction can be more anarchic and spontaneous.

---

17 b Yeb 49 b.

18 Ibid; my translation.

19 Num 16:3. The translation comes from an edition of the Pentateuch published in Jerusalem in 1973 – no publisher listed. All subsequent translations of the Pentateuch in this paper come from this edition.

Moses, by contrast, serves as the personification of a negative theological set of understandings. The idea of negative theology – that we can only say what God is not; He is not any of those things that we think he literally is – for him contains an implied legitimation for rabbinic authority. The voluntarism encoded in negative theology – it is through our assertions of will that God emerges as an object of worship at all – sanctions for Moses the institution of a collectively ordered response to God's role in the world through the introduction of systems of authority and hierarchy.

Further Biblical exemplifications of the negative theology versus Gnosticism typology include the following:

1. Through a rabbinic prism, there is an interconnected invocation of how the expulsion from Eden and the Tower of Babel incidents in the Bible gesture toward Gnosticism. According to Maimonides, in the Garden of Eden, Adam and Eve had the capacity to discern truth from falsehood. This made the delineation of specific moral categories and explicit conformity to them entirely redundant. Whatever comes under the categories of truth and falsehood would be intrinsically coercive, and does not require, or perhaps even allow for, the interposition of separate assertions of human judgment to make particular courses of action binding upon individuals. The self-imposed mission of the tower builders was to recoup this privileged state of Divine knowledge, of knowing exactly what was true and false, and therefore binding, for human beings.[20]

2. The *Book of Genesis* in the Bible, which according to its title is supposed to begin by recounting the creation of the world, does no such thing. In the first instance, the grammar of the first three verses of *Genesis* belies this sort of content. The first two sentences of the Bible are sentential fragments that form the background to the third sentence which constitutes a bona fide sentence, containing a proper subject and predicate. It is as if the Bible wants to alert us that it is not beginning at the beginning – but rather *in medias res,* inserting itself into a narrative that was begun elsewhere. This impression is reinforced by various Midrashic – homiletic – statements found in the *Midrash* and *Talmud.* The rabbis say that prior to the creation of the currently existing world, God had created multiple worlds and destroyed them, until He finally created this one and let it stand until the Flood.[21] The rabbis also say that *shamayim* – the heavens – which God officially created on the second day of Creation is a composite word consisting of the two words *Aish*, meaning *fire*, and *Mayim*, meaning *water,* but nowhere in the *Genesis*

---

20 This is Rashi's exegesis of Gen 11:5 based upon Midrash Tanhuma.

21 Midrash Bereshit Rabbah, 3, 9.

narrative of creation is there a listing of the fashioning of fire and water. *Genesis* appears to be inserting us into the middle of a pre-existing account of creation.

3. The theme of the paramountcy of the middle seems to be picked up again in what the Bible has to tell us about the lives of Adam and Eve. According to rabbinic tradition, Adam and Eve are buried alongside the Patriarchs and Matriarchs – Abraham and Sarah; Isaac and Rebecca; and Jacob and Leah – in the sacred site of *Mearat HaMachpelah* in Bethlehem. The question that immediately presents itself is: What are their special attributes that evoke this type of extraordinary recognition? Aside from being the first man and the first woman in the Biblical account of creation, in what other unique ways do they impress themselves upon us? Abraham, for example, is identified with the virtue of kindness, in terms of his generosity to guests, among other behavioral manifestations. Aside from chronology, what else do Adam and Eve have to recommend them?

Gordon Tucker[22] has suggested that what Adam and Eve embody is the centrality of new beginnings in terms of how we design and manage our lives. After being created by God, Adam and Eve are placed in the most privileged and exalted of environments – the Garden of Eden. After disobeying God's prohibition against eating from the tree of knowledge, they are thrust 'East of Eden', never to return to it in their lifetimes. Once they become regular denizens of planet earth, they have twin sons, Cain and Abel, one of whom out of jealousy rises up and slaughters the other. Finally, in their third attempt to re-inaugurate their lives, with the birth of Seth, they succeed in establishing the genealogy out of which the rest of humankind emerges. The story of Adam and Eve is fully in sync with – it re-encodes on a human level – the story of God. God, as it were, engaged in multiple attempts to fashion an imperfect world, and Adam and Eve require multiple attempts to efficiently and successfully live in one.

Hannah Arendt (1906–1975), in *The Human Condition*, explores the etymological background in the Greek and Latin languages of the English verb *to act* and discovers that it resides in the notion of *to begin.*[23] To act means to seek out and engage in new beginnings. Without any guarantee of reaching a safe or stable destination, we human beings have the courage, the stamina, and the equilibrium to begin again and again. Re-establishing new beginnings restores us to some metaphysical middle, where the very augustness of the task keeps us motivated and involved.

22 Tucker delivered this reading of the careers of Adam and Eve at a talk I heard him deliver in Riverdale, New York in 1971.

23 Arendt, Hannah, *The Human Condition*, Chicago: University of Chicago Press, 1958, 9–11.

1. In the historical and hagiographical narrative that Judaism has initiated, which has been accepted by and large by both Christianity and Islam, the Patriarch Abraham is the discoverer of the monotheistic principle – that there is one infinite being whom we call God who is the creator and governor of the universe. The way the ancient rabbis present it – and the way Maimonides describes it in his *Code* –, Revelation is not the pivot of Abraham's discovery, but rather his coming up with the idea of God as a matter of theoretical investigation.

From sociological and historical perspectives as well as logical ones, monotheistic religion – with negative theology as its most cogent exegetical decoder – needs to be viewed as a secularist, skeptical response to the primitive animistic religion being practiced in the cultures in which monotheism emerged. Monotheism seeks to discredit the immanentist deities affirmed by animistic religion. It counterposes to them a single transcendent deity who both created and governs the world. This deity in his aloofness and loftiness can appropriately be viewed as flagging the limitations of human reason with regard to the search for ultimate explanations, rather than as a cognitively accessible and substantively recognizable and identifiable God.

The God of monotheistic religion has to be understood in terms of what he is blocking and ruling out, not in relation to what he is ostensibly affirming. He is blocking the divinization of natural and historical forces – rather than presenting himself as their literal replacement. In terms of the strategic factors at stake here, he cannot do what they do in the manner in which they do it without becoming them and forfeiting his status as the one transcendent, infinite God.

It is Abraham's discovery of the monotheistic principle that engenders the inner struggle that culminates in the *Akeidah*, the attempted sacrifice of his 'one son' – either Isaac, in Jewish tradition, or Yishmael, in Islamic tradition. The turmoil that is taking place in the psyche of Abraham might be translatable into the following terms: Can God command something fundamentally irrational and immoral, such as the slaughter of one's own son? If God is reified rationality, is he authentic? God has to command him to do something fundamentally irrational and 'unreconstructibly' immoral in order to attest to his identity as God. What ensues is an inner struggle in the soul of Abraham which the Midrash Rabbah, Rashi, and Maimonides capture magnificently. God specifically tells Abraham "V'Haaleihu Sham L'Olah" – not, "V'Hakreveihu Sham L'Olah" – "Raise him up as a sacrifice," not "Slaughter him as a sacrifice." As Rashi formulates it, Abraham could have simply placed his son on the altar to demonstrate his devotion to God, and then immediately removed him.[24] Given that his life's achievement of the creation of mon-

24 See Rashi's commentary on Gen 22:2.

otheism hung in the balance, he had to enact both sides of the struggle with equal vigor and conviction. The result would inevitably be a condition of irremediable post-traumatic stress suffered by his son – Isaac in the Jewish version. It is in this context that we can begin to grasp the surprising moral turns assumed by Isaac's son Jacob.

2. A central question we need to address in grappling with the personality of the patriarch Jacob is how the Bible could classify him as "an ethically perfect man residing in the tents of Torah", when in one incident after another the Bible recounts his deceitful, manipulative, and self-serving deeds? He expropriates the special advantages accruing from being the firstborn from his brother Esau, as well as outmaneuvering him in gaining their father Isaac's special blessing which he explicitly wanted to confer on Esau, and also comes up with ethically questionable biological and genetic stratagems to rip off a large portion of his father-in-law Laban's cattle for himself – and yet the Bible anoints him as the embodiment of moral and intellectual virtue? Is the *Torah* in these instances being self-deluded? Is it engaging in a deliberate debasement of language? What is the most charitable way in which we can strive to comprehend the *Torah's* text?

One possible approach to pursue here is that Jacob represents the third generation after his grandfather Abraham's discovery of the monotheistic principle. The monotheistic principle which emphasizes God's infinity and absolute difference from all things human gives rise to an irresolvable dilemma. God's infinity would seem to imply that the whole Divine vocabulary is metaphorical. No translation manual is conceivable between how the terms *power* and *knowledge* shape up in a finite human setting and what they signify in relation to an infinite being called God. We can only affirm, if we so choose, *that* he is – but not *what* he is on a literal level.[25] On the other hand, however, we can say that the very term *infinity* serves to rescue on a literal level the intelligibility of the word *God.* If God is truly infinite, then we cannot even assert that he is infinite. The adjective *infinite* debars us from using it in relation to God. If the adjective *infinite* connotes that the central theologically descriptive terms of *omnipotent* and *omniscient* cannot be applied literally to God. If we don't know what *power* and *knowledge* signify in relation to the infinite God, then we know something terribly momentous about God by calling him *infinite.* The usage of the term *infinite* in relation to God itself transgresses against the term *infinite.* If the language of infinity is applied authentically, consistently, to God, then we must take into account the possibility that the logic of the

25 Hobbes, Thomas, *Leviathan*, ed. Michael Oakeshott, Oxford: Basil Blackwell, 1946, 17: "And therefore the name of God is used, not to make us conceive him, for he is incomprehensible; and his greatness, and power are unconceivable; but that we may honor him."

term – the rules that govern the combinations and permutations that remain possible for the infinite being called God – includes inconceivable distances *and* literal nearness to finite human beings being conjointly applicable to Him. The philosophical rejection of literal descriptions and the non-philosophical religious person's embrace of them might both be reconcilable in relation to him. How is Abraham to act when he receives God's ostensible command to sacrifice his son Isaac, Jacob's father as according to Jewish tradition, on Mt. Moriah?

The Biblical account of the binding of Isaac on the altar is responsive to both readings of the monotheistic principle. On the one hand, the inscrutable, unreachable God issues a command to kill Isaac, and Abraham sets out to fulfill it. But he is giving a particular translation to a literally unfathomable command – and he needs to take responsibility for the fact that he might be misrepresenting it. Maybe God wants to see whether Abraham recognizes the limitless character of his freedom, and on that basis, he rejects what he had initially taken as God's command. Or, if Abraham adopts the second approach to the concept of God, then God's demand that he sacrifice Isaac as cruel and inhuman as it might appear is literally intelligible – and, after all, given the logically exotic character of the term *infinite,* it can be reconciled with the finite.

The need to sacrifice Isaac and the need to save him are both registered in Abraham's behavior. He lays Isaac down very reverentially upon the altar – and, after the sudden appearance of an angel, goes after a ram that is caught by its horns in the thicket in order to substitute it for Isaac as a sacrifice to God. Human ambivalence in the face of the infinity of God is thus inscribed in the *Akeidah* narrative.

Jacob grows up with this dual legacy of his grandfather Abraham, who is an adventurous theological innovator and political organizer who tries to get as many people as possible to imbibe his teaching about God – and his father Isaac, who is a shriveled and distinctly unadventurous human being forced to live most of his adult life in the shadow of his father's religiously motivated attempt to kill him. The point of equilibrium that Jacob establishes for himself includes an implicit reconceptualization of how the discovery of the principle of the infinite God needs to be understood. Overtly, he shifts his attention to coping with the challenges of a this-worldly existence, instead of re-drawing the map of Divinity. We can presume that on a theological level, Jacob intuits that given the premise of God's infinity saying that he is nowhere to be found in the finite world is ontologically equivalent to saying that he is everywhere. Saying that God is nowhere in the finite world can be understood as meaning that there is no exclusive, restricted space that belongs to God. In fact, He suffuses every nook and cranny of existence. He is everywhere, the two extremes, in this case, converge, as they do in many other regions of human experience. Saying that God is nowhere is ontologically equivalent to saying that He is everywhere. Total distance collapses upon total nearness – so that monotheism ends up overlapping with pantheism or panentheism – with human freedom being the exception to God's overweening presence and control.

If God is nowhere/everywhere – if he is the place of the world and the world is not his place – then whether to call the world 'world' or to call it 'God' is an arbitrary, nominal, decision. Our naming imparts to the world either a resolutely religious or a resolutely secular character – or covertly points to the coincidence of the two levels. The term *God* highlights for us the inscrutability of the world and indirectly alerts us to the need for evolving guidelines concerning how to function within the limits of the opacity of the world. Based upon the Biblical text, Jacob seems to operate on a level of seeking out immanentist guidelines to discover, on an ongoing basis, the appropriate content and limits of human action. Therefore, in accordance with the Biblical description, Jacob is a righteous individual who immerses himself in the study of the Torah. His brother Esau is a cunning hunter, a man of the field, who – in the absence of more productive and purposeful things to do – engages in hunting. In his relationship with Esau, Jacob is testing the moral and practical limits of how one relates to a brother of this sort. Is it permissible – and is it workable – to outwit him as in the case of the birthright and the blessings of his father? The distance/nearness of God does not relieve us of the need and the responsibility of rendering judgments and decisions concerning which guidelines to follow in a real-world situation of this sort. The world/God is the context in which we have to act. It does not generate any foregone, certain conclusions for us.

What I have just said about Esau is equally true about Laban. Laban's biography is replete with deceit, chicanery, and power plays. After working for him for twenty years under largely desperate, impoverished conditions, is it morally acceptable and practically workable to evolve a stratagem that while not fully honest does not constitute outright theft to force Laban to compensate Jacob for his unrelenting commitment and work on his behalf? In the God/world of our common habitation, he has to figure this out on his own.

The rabbis refer to Jacob as the *Bechir D'Avot* – the most select and elite of the patriarchs.[26] My reading of the *Jacob-Narrative* in *Genesis* affords us a new perspective from which to comprehend the rabbinic statement. Jacob emerges as the most select of the patriarchs because, under the conjoint challenge posed by the careers of his father and grandfather, he charts a new path for construing

26 *Midrash Bereshit Rabbah,* 76:1.

the monotheistic principle that assigns priority to the human initiative over certainty and fixity in orienting human beings concerning how to live in the world.

In my reading of the *Jacob-Narrative* in *Genesis*, the context that Jacob establishes for the keeping of the *Torah* and the fulfillment of *mitzvot* is that even with the binding character of the *Torah* text and the accompanying requirement to follow rabbinic interpretations of it established and solidified as a covenantal relationship between God and the Jewish people at Mount Sinai, we are never on 'automatic pilot' about what to do next in the course of our lives. The vicissitudes of our personal lives and historical circumstances are such that we confront ever-renewing challenges about the translation of these ostensibly categorical teachings. God – theologically and metaphysically speaking – is not the emblem of certainty, but of openness and irresolvability in our lives. The symbol of God highlights and heightens the tensions of what it means to be a human being. He does not offer us a safe and secure exit route out of them.

The dream of *Jacob's Ladder* in the *Book of Genesis* also seems to be emblematic of a negative theological sensibility, in contrast to a Gnostic one. As he sets out from Beersheva on his way to Haran to escape the wrath of his brother Esau, Jacob dreamed: "And behold a ladder set up on the earth and the top of it reached to heaven and behold angels of God going up and down on it"[27]. Rashi immediately latches on to what is peculiar in this verse: "It states first ascending and afterwards descending!"[28]. The natural sequence of conventionally-conceived angels would be to go down – to accomplish whatever their earthly mission is –, and then to go up – to return to their regular abode in the heavenly precincts. Jacob imagines angels that move in a reverse order – first up and *then* down. We might say that the disruption of the angels' natural sequence is suggestive of the negative theological inversion with regard to celestial matters generally. For angels in relation to us who have no literal grasp of either them or their movements, it is always a matter of going up for the sake of coming down. We humans who can only relate to angels metaphorically and never literally; after the manner of God himself, we first have to engage in our maneuvers of figuring out what they signify for us in relation to the rest of the Divine economy and then imaginatively projecting what an appropriate symbol for them might look like before they can engage in their hoped-for downward movement. We, in effect, have to take the initiative to ascend to them imaginatively and theoretically before they can descend to us. As Reb Chaim Vo-

27 Gen 28:12.

28 *Genesis with Rashi*, Rosenbaum and Silvermann trans., 132.

lozhiner (1749–1821) projects God in his book, *Nefesh HaChaim*,[29] so it is with angels as well. Just as Reb Chaim Volozhiner says that the upper, celestial, Divine worlds are controlled by the lower human worlds – the *L'Maala* – the Above – is always a function of the *Mimecha* – the below, meaning the actions undertaken by human beings, by us; what is taking place in the heavenly spheres is a shadow of what is being transacted and enacted in the earthly spheres[30], so, too, the movements and interventions of the angels constitute the repercussions and continuations of our initiatives. The dream of *Jacob's Ladder* in effect forms a precursor text for Reb Chaim Volozhiner's teaching.

To elaborate further: There are three striking interconnected features in this passage that I would like to emphasize. The first, as I have just outlined, is that though the ladder is clearly intended to represent a heavenly connection, the first image that the text communicates is *not* of angels descending from heaven and mingling with human beings – reassuring us of Divine support and consolation, but of angels, not human beings, going up to heaven. The descent of the angels constitutes the second movement of the dream. This suggests that the dream is not about what we think it is about – God relieving us of anxiety and cementing his relationship with us. The dream in its choice of phrasing and use of language rather seems to have a different focus: Not who we human beings are and what our needs might be, but who the God is to whom we are attempting to relate.

The second feature of the dream that I would like to emphasize follows immediately from the first. If the dream is not about us but about the nature of God, the dream is symbolically communicating to us that the God that forms our Divine counter-player is the God that we can approach from our limited earthly perspective. It is the *Artzidika*, the earthly God – the God that is cut from our earthly limitations – that forms the subject of our desired connection. This is the God that is riddled with the paradoxes that I have been referring to in this paper. This God is framed in the same way as in the dream of *Jacob's Ladder* in the supreme statement of *Kabbalat Ohl Malchut Shamayim* – acceptance of the yoke of heaven – in Judaism, namely the first verse of the *Sh'ma: Shma Yisrael Hashem Elokeinu Hashem Echad* – in English, *Hear O Israel the Lord is our God the Lord is one. It is our God*, the God that is projected on the basis of our limitations – who is one – ineffably, indescribably one. It is the one to whom the descriptive, quantitative one remains inapplicable that is the true God. It is the God who falls outside the pale of intelligible statement that is our God. It is the God about whom the only literal

29 Volozhiner, Reb Chaim, *Sefer Nefesh HaChaim Im Beur Yirat Chaim and Ruach Chaim Al Masechet Avot*, ed. Yisroel Eliyahu Weintraub, Israel: Benei-Brak, 2009.
30 Ibid., 26.

thing that we could say is that he is our God who is one. In the end, the possessive adjective recasts and overshadows the noun that it is qualifying.

The third thing that I want to say about *Jacob's Dream* is that given all the factors that I have pointed out, the latent content of Jacob's dream is that no Divine assurance is ever possible. We have to imagine and project the ascent to heaven of the angels before we can even begin to project their return to planet earth. The concept of God is a self-contained human construction before whom we stand in awe because of its potential otherness which would make it morally and religiously binding upon us. The infinitely regressive character of human theorizing – every premise, no matter how broad and deep it is, conjures up the prospect of still broader and deeper premises lying behind it – suggests that faith in the idea and possibility of faith is what keeps faith alive. Because of the logical constraint that requires us to be skeptical of our own skepticism, faith is nurtured and sustained through our practice of skepticism. Both faith and skepticism are manifestations of faith and expressions of skepticism.

3. Joseph, who is Jacob's favorite son, does his father one better in terms of exploiting immanentism as the means for crafting and advancing his life as a Jew. He not only reflects upon the constellation of possibilities residing in the dynamic of hostile forces arrayed against him in his family, but he also seems to have figured out, early on, how to harness those forces to rise to an ascendant position within his large and influential family. Joseph's dreams not only disclose the lofty and highly ambitious material, social, and political aspirations that he is nourishing, but they become direct instrumentalities in their own realization. Through their provoking of even greater jealousy, resentment, and hostility from his brothers than Joseph had experienced already, Joseph's dreams, communicated to his brothers and father, contributed significantly towards instigating a chain of events that led to their fulfillment. In a deep, unconscious sense, Joseph had imbibed from his father, Jacob, that the structure of a virtuous and successful human life is marked by indirection and obliqueness. Abraham's discovery of the monotheistic God was a directly contributing factor to his grandson Jacob's discovery of how the resources of anti-transcendentalism, what we might call *immanentism*, could contribute to compensating for and overcoming some of the anxieties and feelings of guilt induced by the expansion of human freedom bequeathed by monotheism. Along this same path of a strategic response to thwarting and immensely frustrating circumstances, Joseph realizes in his teenage years that a proactive and not merely reactive immanentism – figuring out how brotherly hostility might not only be contained but actually harnessed to facilitate the detested brother's even more spectacular rise in the world than he might have originally envisaged – becomes Joseph's adaptation of his father's immanentist model for achieving fame

and glory in the world. In a crucial sense, Joseph realizes that having and propagating the dream could itself be a source of its fulfillment.

4. In Moses' first encounter with Revelation as he tends to the flock of his father-in-law Jethro at the mountain of God, Horeb,[31] a phrase occurs whose metaphorical import seems to be distinctly – if not paradigmatically – negatively theological. The Bible states: "And the angel of the Eternal appeared unto him in a flame of fire out of the midst of a bush and he saw and behold the bush burned with fire and the bush was not devoured."[32] The burning bush which is supposed to be the symbolic medium heralding the presence of God does not get extinguished in relation to its source as if to underscore the primacy in Divine matters of representational mechanisms over that which they represent. In negative theology, the symbols have an opacity and a perdurability which confers upon them the status of semi-independent entities that do not fully refer to that which they are officially supposed to represent. The bush does not get consumed in relation to God because none of our metaphors are able to pierce the Divine Essence and disclose the elements of literalism attached to the notion of God. The burning bush serves as a metaphorical stand-in for the endless fertility and 'insurmountability' of metaphor when it comes to speaking about and relating to the monotheistic God.

5. The Biblical account of creation insinuates to us that the God who creates is of a negative theological character. What runs like a leitmotif throughout the story of creation are the pervasive roles of speech and naming as instrumentalities for God's creation. The prefatory phrases "God says" and "God calls" or "names" appear in relation to each of the six days of creation. On the seventh day, when God rests and ceases to create, these terms do not appear. The verb that substitutes for them is "bless". What sort of creation is it in which the creator merely speaks and names? We could say that these descriptive epithets conjure up a scene of irrevocable belatedness – where what is occurring is so alien and distant from our understanding that only terms that already bear a derivative trace that evokes human modes of creating are being used as metaphorical screens behind which the inscrutableness of the process of creation can be preserved. We create by naming, grouping, and classifying. God creates in the same way not because there is continuity between his mode of creating and ours but because the discontinuity is so overwhelming that the only palliative that will work is a metaphoric extension of our vocabulary of creation to God. God the Creator that the Bible presents is as Hobbes (1588–1679) and Nietzsche never tired of exploring and exploiting al-

31 Horeb is another name for Mt. Sinai.

32 Exodus 3:2. I am grateful to Stephen Schneck for emphasizing to me in personal conversation the importance of this passage for the larger theme of the paper.

ready a very keen model of the human capacity to create which is figured in such a way as to preserve the sanctity and remoteness of the Biblical concept of creation.

The Biblical vocabulary of creation encodes for us not only our inability to grasp the nature of God but also the metaphysical implications of such a position. The infinite regress in our explanatory quest in searching for the reasons and causes of things is finally blocked by postulating the monotheistic God as First Cause who bears no resemblance to that which He created and can therefore serve as a satisfactory ultimate cause. However, we are only able to ward off an infinite regress in our explanatory quests by postulating an entity as First Cause that is thoroughly unintelligible and unassimilable to regular human conceptual and logical frameworks. This means that in relation to our desire to rationally penetrate the human world the infinite regress is restored. We want to make sense of multiple discrete objects and phenomena in the world by grouping them under a much more limited number of words and concepts. We seek to anchor those words and concepts in turn by grounding them in words and concepts of still higher levels of abstraction and generality than our original set of words and so on indefinitely without finding a satisfactory arrest. This suggests that in the end, the words that we use have an ontological primacy over the things that they ostensibly group and subsume. There is thus an intimate metaphysical connection between the logical unapproachability of God and identifying creativity with acts of naming. The Biblical description of divine creation already presupposes a metaphysically fallen world.

6. One of the Bible's major paradigms of avoidance – the kind of person that the Jew should assiduously avoid becoming – is Pharaoh, the Egyptian king who enslaved and persecuted the Jews. The personality that Pharaoh exhibits in the pages of the Biblical text resembles that of Amalek. He mistrusts the idea of the infinite, monotheistic God because one cannot trace His causal background to the everyday, commonly shared world. For Pharaoh, just like for Amalek, the real is the realm of the given, not the made, or the rationally constructed or acknowledged. It has a definitiveness and a finality that make it indisputably real. It has lost all connection with the contingent and the hypothetical. The real is no longer merely possible – but necessary, irrevocably, indisputably *there*. The literal God as an inflated *being* is a romantic extravagance for those who hanker after the fungibility and volatility of the possible. Those who have outgrown such childhood hankerings after the indisputably given can live comfortably with the tensions imposed by affirming the monotheistic God.

7. The credo that the Jewish people counterpose to Pharaoh's animistic religion and idol worship is encapsulated in the phrase *Naaseh V'Nishmah* – meaning *We will do and we will listen* – which they collectively utter at the foot of Mount Sinai

upon entering into a covenantal relationship with God.[33] The 'listening' that the word *Nishmah* refers to is not just a physiological act of picking up soundwaves – but comprehending with the inner ear, or understanding. From a Jewish monotheistic perspective, doing, by definition, almost always comes before knowing. The attempt to know something always evokes the specter of having to go further back to unearth the premises behind the premises behind the premises etc. that make one's argument possible and cogent. Since the prospect of an infinite regress is logically unavoidable, understanding, which generally remains partial, has to be reclassified as a form of doing – a sealing off of inquiry at a necessarily arbitrary point. Invoking God as the First or Final Cause does not work because if we could figure out how the infinite intersects with the finite, then the infinite regress is resumed and the concept of "God" does not offer us the repose we seek. If we cannot work through how the infinite intersects with the finite, then the concept of God just highlights the built-in limitations of the human condition without offering us a release from them. The religious person and the secular person both end up in an analogous inextricable metaphysical middle, poised to receive more insight and more knowledge – but at least dimly aware of the endlessness of the task. Both the religious and the secular person live lives governed by authority and tradition – with each party because of its rhetorical obfuscations feeling at least dimly superior to the other.

8. The Bible's tests for determining the veracity of prophets subsequent to Moses reflect a negative theological understanding of the nature of God. In the *Book of Deuteronomy*, the Bible states:

> But the prophet who shall presume to speak a word in
> my name which I have not commanded him to speak
> or that shall speak in the name of other gods
> even that prophet shall die. And if thou say in
> thine heart How shall we know the word which the
> Eternal hath not spoken? When a prophet speaketh
> in the name of the Eternal if the thing follows not
> nor come to pass that is the thing which the Eternal
> hath not spoken but the prophet hath spoken
> presumptuously thou shalt not be afraid of him.[34]

The Bible lists only two tests for distinguishing the false from the true prophet. The first has to do with whom the prophet cites as authorizing his message – whether the Biblical monotheistic God or 'other gods'. The other has to do with whether his

33 Exod 24:7.
34 Deut 18:20–22.

forecast is borne out by events or not. In other words, the only tests to apply to validate the credentials of a prophet are the scheme of authority relations he invokes to situate himself as a prophet and the events that follow upon his prophecy. The tests for prophecy are all this-worldly in character: The prophetic tradition cited by the prophet of which he claims to be a member and the efficacy of his predictions in the real world. Given the infinite God's unbridgeable distance from things human, it is only by consulting this-worldly phenomena, rather than presumed otherworldly corroborations, that a prophetic mission can be validated. For all practical purposes, the prophet exercises his vocation in this world, and it is only by invoking empirical criteria of these two sorts that we can legitimate his role. Rashi very artfully delineates the scope of these two sets of criteria. When a prophet issues commands in the present, one must inspect his self-proclaimed pedigree. When he offers prognostications concerning the future, one must consult results. The most striking aspect of the Biblical account of the verification of prophecy is how the word *prophet* is already largely functioning in its extended metaphorical sense of someone who makes reliable predictions concerning the future, rather than in its strict, literal sense of someone who possesses a direct, commanding relationship with God.

9. An additional reading of Adam and Eve's transgression in the Garden of Eden that is partially inspired by Maimonides' reading cited earlier follows another route to make his point, and thereby reinforces our understanding that the Biblical God is negative theological, rather than Gnostic, in character. In the story of Adam and Eve's transgression in eating from the Tree of Knowledge, the relationship between what we might call negativity and positivity is so radically asymmetrical, and so fraught with ambiguity, that it ends up prefiguring the relationship between descriptions of God and God himself from a negative theological perspective. God issues a prohibition to Adam and Eve not to take from the Tree of Knowledge. They ostensibly know what they are supposed to refrain from doing. However, the question remains what positive configuration of human attributes is either compatible with, or supportive of, conforming to this prohibition? Regarding this question, the Bible remains strategically silent. When one ponders this question, one becomes aware that sustaining this prohibition is compatible with and nurtured by what looks like untold, infinitely imaginable configurations of human personality attributes and character traits. However, the negative formulation – the prohibition against eating from the Tree of Knowledge – is not translatable into a definitive positive ordering of attributes and traits. We can be many, infinitely diverse selves and still preserve our loyalty to the negative prohibition. On the level of imagery and metaphor, the Bible thus reinforces for us the idea central to negative theology that there is an infinite, unbridgeable gap – an infinitely un-

bridgeable gap – between negative formulations and their positive objects and correlatives.

As long as language was devoid of negative constructions – when everything was formulated in positive terms – one could harbor the illusion that we have unmediated access to an objective world, that words are transparent reflections of what is ineluctably out there. Introducing negativity – the prohibition against eating from the Tree of Knowledge constitutes the first negative construction in the Biblical text – represents the human fall from grace, as it were, because it illustrates beyond hope of reprieve how language everlastingly folds in upon itself without achieving a final resolution of the real. Our inability to find an unquestionable positive correlative to a negative prohibition – all versions of this seem subject to revision, expansion, and supersession – keeps us forever within the domain of words, unable to find a secure outlet in some configuration of worldly reality.

The infinity of the distance between negative prohibition and positive translation becomes more dramatically evident when we realize that even transgressing the negative prohibition is compatible with at least some versions of a positive translation – acceptance – of that prohibition. If violating the negative prohibition serves as a spur to *Teshuvah* (repentance), then the greater insight into the limitations of the self – the deepened humility – occasioned by an act of repentance is in a paradoxical but still fully intelligible way traceable to the negative prohibition. Adam and Eve's transgression in the Garden of Eden falls into this category. Their unfamiliarity, until this point, with the grammar of negativity makes them ill-equipped to fully appreciate and properly respond to the Divine prohibition. The positive translation of a negative prohibition into the paradoxical but still intelligible state of the penitent transgressor underscores for us more generally the elusiveness of the boundaries for achieving an appropriate positive translation of a negative prohibition. The elusiveness of those boundaries, in turn, itself becomes a metaphor for the underdetermination of words by objects.

10. Yosef Duber (1820–1892), the grandson of Reb Chaim Volozhiner (1794–1821), and the author of a commentary on halakhic themes and Torah texts called the *Beit Halevi*, formulates a question that should be most disturbing from the perspective of negative theology: If we follow the principle of *Klal Lo Yasiguhu* – if our ostensibly referential God-talk and all attempts at material concretization of God's presence are to be construed metaphorically – then in what sense is the building of the *Mishkan*, the sanctuary in the desert, less of a sacrilegious act than the fashioning of the golden calf? Don't they both constitute forms of idolatry, an inability to live with the extraordinary tension that monotheism imposes, which leads to a reification and sanctification of human handiwork? The *Beit Halevi* answers in a spirit that Maimonides would have instinctively understood:

> Since their essential transgression with the golden calf was that they wanted to rely on their own wisdom – to do in accordance with their own understanding something concerning which they were not commanded – therefore in the building of the sanctuary which came to atone for the golden calf the Biblical text states concerning each aspect of their work, "in accordance with God's command." The import of this recurring phrase is that even though Bezalel [the chief human architect of the *mishkan*] knew how to combine the words through which heaven and earth were created and knew secrets and hidden meanings in his work, nevertheless his whole intention was only to fulfill the command of God. They [Bezalel and his co-workers in building the *mishkan*] only intended to fulfill God's will and commands [as conveyed by the legitimate authority structure of the Jewish nation of their time], not because their own reason dictated that they should do what they did. It was this that atoned for the sin of the golden calf.[35]

11. The transgression of Aaron's sons Nadav and Avihu recounted in Lev 10:1–7 is qualitatively continuous with the sin of the golden calf. At the time of the consecration of the sanctuary in the desert, Nadav and Avihu "offered strange fire before the Eternal, which he commanded them not"[36]. In their intoxication with God, Nadav and Avihu embellished the sacrifice that they were asked to perform by placing additional fire on the altar. To the traditionally sanctioned outpourings of emotion toward God, Nadav and Avihu added their own personally-generated and driven outpourings of emotion. Parallel to the case of the golden calf, theologically considered there seems little to choose from between a *Mishkan* – a sanctuary – and a golden calf. Correspondingly, in the case of Nadav and Avihu, very little seems to be at stake between one more placement of fire on the altar and one less placement. Both Biblical events, however, seek to underscore for us how we cannot have an unmediated relationship with the word of God. It is the breaching of what is postulated as unbridgeable theological distance and tendering the claim to intimacy with and knowledge of God that the Torah text finds objectionable. To relate appropriately to God, we have no recourse but to follow what is transmitted to us by duly acknowledged structures of authority.

12. The transgression of the spies who issued a discouraging and demoralizing report about the prospects of the Jewish nation conquering the land of Canaan can also most persuasively be construed in a negative theological vein: The lack of faith that the Jewish community displayed at that moment was in the negative theological God. Monotheistic theorizing eventuates in contradiction. God can be invoked as the ultimate explanatory factor responsible for what takes place in the universe only at the cost of explanatory unintelligibility. God's total difference from all things human enables Him to serve as the ultimate explanatory factor for

35 Duber, Yosef, *Beit Halevi*, Warsaw: 1884; reprinted in Israel, 1973, 54.
36 Lev 10:1.

what takes place in the universe – but that very difference debars Him from explaining anything in a humanly comprehensible way. Ultimacy is achieved at the cost of explanatory illumination which drove the quest toward ultimacy in the first place. The concept of God, instead of functioning as a response to skepticism, just posts a limit to human rational capacities and in this crucial sense institutionalizes skepticism. The version of skepticism that it institutionalizes in order to remain consistent has to be in the form of a generalized agnosticism which incorporates skepticism of skepticism into its formulation of the protocols of skepticism. A generalized agnosticism underscores the centrality of an openness toward an indefinitely unfolding future which will help us recast and revise our perceptions and judgments uttered in the present. While we cannot count on the incompleteness of our understanding being conclusively remedied, we can confidently expect in the course of the passage of time re-castings and revisions that will shift the burden of inconclusiveness elsewhere than where we first diagnosed it.

From this perspective, the transgression of the spies and of the Jewish community of that generation that responded so uncritically to their report of impending disaster if a conquest of the land were attempted was in not appreciating the extent of the openness of the future. The factors of impregnability that the spies pointed to – e.g., "The cities are fortified and very great"[37] – were taken to be enduring and inalterable, instead of being perceived as subject to the vicissitudes and ravages of time. From the Biblical vantage point, the failure of the spies and the community that supported their judgment constituted in the end a failure of faith. It was not simply a lack of faith in the covenantal promise of inheriting the land, but a shallow and distorted appreciation of what that promise consisted of. That promise merely augured space for human interventions that in the end would facilitate conquest and habitation of the land. That promise in no way guaranteed direct and immediate access to the land with all barriers removed. All the initiatives relating to the conquest of the land would have to come from the human side in a climate where the usual murkiness and ambivalence surrounding the signs and portents that orient us in taking our initiatives have not been removed.

From the perspective that I am advancing here, theologically speaking, the transgression in the incident of the spies was of a piece with the transgression involved in fashioning the golden calf. In both cases, there is a rush on the part of the Jewish community in the desert to annul theological distance and to purge ambiguity by reifying the Divine Presence and trying to make it accountable to human standards of clarity and promptness. The incident of the spies – just like the making and worshipping of the golden calf – constitutes milestones along the path of

37 Num 13:28.

the Bible's oblique disclosure of what it means to be a follower and servant of the monotheistic God.

13. In the *Book of Numbers*, there is a remarkable formulation that goes unremarked by many rabbinic commentators. The verse says: "And the children of Israel shall lay their hands upon the Levites"[38]. The *Torah* in this context is speaking about the preparations and the investiture of the Levites to get them ready to perform their holy functions in the Sanctuary. One would have expected the *Torah* to deploy a vertical image to capture such investiture: that some kind of charismatic spirit or illumination descends from heaven that instills the Levites with their special holiness. No such image is to be found in the *Torah* text in relation to the Levites. Instead, the *Torah* depicts a process of horizontal and even circular investiture. Investiture with special holiness comes from other members of the Jewish community; a horizontal motion. What is especially noteworthy is that it is the very people whom the Levites themselves elevate into various degrees of holiness – through their blessings of the congregation in the Temple, their officiating over and participating in the sacrifices, and in their role as the religious counselors and decision-makers in the community – who themselves become invested with holiness through the very actions of the people whom they help to elevate in holiness. This suggests that for the *Torah*, holiness is a circular process that does not officially begin or end anywhere. It is reciprocally sustained through the interaction of Levites and ordinary Jews. Holiness itself is a function of that reciprocity – that mutual interaction. Holiness in Judaism is not something substantive and is not traceable to any one source. It is known only by its manifestations, by its fruits – which are discernible only in human interaction.

All of my citations – from the careers of Abraham and Jacob to those of Pharoah and Amalek, to the process depicted in the Bible for investing the Levites with their special degree of holiness – emphasize Judaism's preference for the metaphysical middle as the ideal terrain upon which to live out our lives. Paradoxically, but very pertinently from Judaism's perspective, it is by invoking the most exalted symbol of transcendence imaginable – namely, the monotheistic God – that we establish for ourselves the most equitable path for engaging and sustaining the middle.

---

38 Num 8:10.

3 *Teshuvah*/Repentance as a Re-Appropriation of the Middle of Human Life

One of the major metaphysical puzzles surrounding the concept of *Teshuvah* is how a new thought or intention in the present can nullify what has taken place in the past, so that through the act of repentance one's sins are, as it were, wiped away. Invoking Elizabeth Anscombe's (1919–2001) classic distinction[39], inspired by Ludwig Wittgenstein (1889–1951) in the *Philosophical Investigations*[40], between brute fact and institutional fact affords us a path through the metaphysical labyrinth generated by the concept of *Teshuvah.* Strictly speaking, the only things that are past, that are irrevocably over, are brute facts. On a particular occasion in the past, certain neurophysiological processes transpired within me and muscular energy was released the most apt description of which at the time was that I became angry. However, the set of institutional contexts under which a particular sequence of brute facts might be subsumed is potentially infinite. The set of brute descriptions of a particular event is sufficiently indeterminate to square with an indefinite range of institutional characterizations of the same event. In an institutional sense, therefore, no action is ever completed since the class of possible descriptions of what happened remains open. As I grow and gain deeper insight into myself, the institutional context of anger might appear hopelessly inadequate to capture my full sense of what had happened, and I might turn to other institutional contexts, such as one that assigns a crucial role to experimentation in thought and deed for an ongoing process of growth and self-discovery, as being truer to the brute facts than the original description. Whereas under the old description of anger my action had a fixed, finished aspect, under the new description of growth the action takes on the quality of a fresh beginning, whose precise emotional and even intellectual import cannot be assessed until further actions on my part reveal the emergence of a new pattern of meaning and possibility. One could also say that my earlier outburst served as a platform that enabled me to realize that I did not want to be the sort of person who was subject to periodic outbursts and that therefore, the occasion of anger itself was the first phase of my reorientation toward the path of *Teshuvah.*

The *Cheftza*/thing-*Gavra*/person distinction, which Rabbi Chaim Soloveitchik (1853–1918) of Brisk has made central in his reading of Rabbinic texts and Jewish

---

39 Anscombe, G. E. M., "On Brute Facts", *Analysis* 18 (1958), 69–72.

40 Wittgenstein, Ludwig, *Philosophical Investigations*, trans. G. E. M. Anscombe, 3rd ed., London: Macmillan, 1969.

law,[41] can also afford us an insight into the dynamics of *Teshuvah.* In a *Gavra* sense – a person moving through time –, *Teshuvah* looms as an impossibility. How can a later action that a person engages in – doing *Teshuvah,* repenting what he had done in the past – rectify an action or a set of actions that had been previously committed? On what logical or metaphysical basis can the future redefine and, as it were, 'cause' the past to assume the new configuration that it has as a result of *Teshuvah?*

In response to this, one can say – following Anscombe – that it is part of the *Cheftza* – of the substantive character of an action – to offer resources for its own re-conceptualization. It is only on a brute level – on the level of the expenditure of neuro-physiological energies – that any action is ever completed – is ever over. On the level of interpretation – of potential reconceptualization – no action is ever complete. We can always go on re-imagining what the action signifies in our lives. When an action becomes a basis for its own supersession through an act of *Teshuvah,* apparently part of the background to the action was its catapulting us to a level where we want to move beyond the action. The action as a spur, as an instigator, as a transformational agent was an integral part of what the action was about. Action – doing – connotes motion, movement – including the possibility of a dismantling of itself at the same time that it is being enacted, so that *Teshuvah,* whether articulated in a particular case or not, becomes an integral part of the *Cheftza* of an action.

Teshuvah in the technical, neutral sense in which Maimonides deploys the term can also refer to someone repenting from the good deeds that he has done, considering them in retrospect to have been a waste of time and energy, that they got him nowhere, and he wishes that he had never done them.[42]

An additional sense of the term *Teshuvah* for Maimonides is the manner in which people who have achieved intellectual insights and developed their character in a way that they approve of use these achievements as a plateau or platform upon which to attain deeper insights and further development of their character. Where we are at any given moment in our lives can nudge us to aspire to and achieve greater depth of intellectual insight and character formation beyond what we had cultivated heretofore. This, too, Maimonides refers to as *Teshuvah* – and he considers himself in this sense to be a *Baal Teshuvah,* a penitent human being. This is part of what the term *Teshuvah M'Ahava* (repentance from love) connotes

---

41 Soloveitchik, Chaim, *Chidushei Rabbeinu Chaim Halevi Im Gilyonot Chazon Ish*, Israel, n.d. For a translation into English of some key passages of Reb Chaim's work, see Hughes, Yonoson, *Understanding Reb Chaim*, Israel, 2010.

42 Maimonides, *Mishneh Torah, Hilchot Teshuvah* chap. 3, par. 3. The converse of this ruling is stated in chap. 3, par. 14.

for Maimonides. *Teshuvah* from Maimonides' perspective is coextensive with a human life – in all its phases of growth and despair.

Given the *Cheftza* aspect of human action as I have analyzed it, *Teshuvah* can only be theorized as a neutral process. Given the dangling threads and open possibilities that surround every interpretation that we provide for our own actions, what Maimonides delineates as *Teshuva*, including *Charata Al H'Avar* – regret for our past actions, which incorporates *Viddui* on our transgressions, explicit acknowledgement of our past sins –, *Kabbala Al H'Atid* – a resolution to avoid these same transgressions again –, and movement onto a new plane of thought, action, and value upon which to conduct our lives[43] become a major dynamic in accounting for the structure of human living generally. *Teshuvah* as a neutral process can lead to degeneration as well as to improvement. These contradictory movements in turn are open to continual reconceptualization, depending upon where we stand in particular moments in our lives.

What reinforces the idea of *Teshuvah* as a neutral process in Maimonides is also the fact that according to him – with his adherence to the principles of negative theology, which emphasize that we can only state what God is not, but not what He is –, we can never know where we stand in relation to God's scorecard on our actions. Maimonides in *Hilchot Teshuvah*, Chapter 3, Paragraph 2 says that one *Mitzvah* can sometimes outweigh many misdeeds – and one transgression can overwhelm and render secondary the performance of many commandments. Only God, he *Kale Deot* – the God of knowledge, is privy to the algorithms by which He assesses our actions. *Teshuvah* then cannot be enacted through calculation: We know exactly where we went astray and we repent. *Teshuvah*, therefore, is not just a narrowly normative category which a Jew needs to invoke whenever an alarm bell goes off in his consciousness that he committed a transgression. This aspect is true in the sense that it might be true – but it hardly exhausts the content of *Teshuvah*. *Teshuvah* equally importantly functions as a descriptive category that captures how we as human beings are morally and psychologically wired – the internal dynamic that enables us to move from one mode of relating to the world and other people to another mode.

As I read it, Maimonides' theorizing of *Teshuvah* parallels his theorizing of prayer. Since the whole Biblical and rabbinic vocabulary describing God is *Mashol U'Melitza*[44] – consists of metaphors and figures of speech – to whom are we praying when we pray? Maimonides does not flinch from this challenge. He theorizes

43 Maimonides, *Mishneh Torah, Hilchot Teshuvah*, chap. 1–2.

44 Maimonides, *Mishneh Torah. Book One: The Book of Knowledge: The Laws concerning the Foundations of the Torah*, chap. 1, par. 12.

prayer from an anthropocentric perspective. We need to view prayer in terms of what it does for us – not in terms of what it does for God. He is perfect and beyond our conceptual reach – and therefore does not need our prayers. It is we who need to pray. Being in a prayerful stance nurtures our sense of our own vulnerability, and therefore makes us more compassionate toward ourselves – which is a crucial precondition for enabling us to be more compassionate toward others. The *Jerusalem Talmud* at the end of the tractate of *Peah* poses the rhetorical question: "If a person does not relate compassionately toward himself, how can we expect him to relate compassionately toward others?"[45] Prayer is an integral part of the ethic of self-care. It helps us to become aware of our own neediness and motivates us to do things about it, and therefore equips us to be more empathetic with and responsive to the needs of others.

Analogously, with regard to *Teshuvah:* The *Kale Deot*, the *Omniscient God*, acts in His own inscrutable ways, and there are no mappable rational sets of calculations that enable us to correlate God's demands upon us with our failures and shortcomings and our attempts to rectify them through engaging in acts of *Teshuvah.* The insights that we gain into our own failures and shortcomings through acts of *Teshuvah* is our most assured route for being able to improve ourselves and therefore also for refining our relationship with God. The categorial levers to turn to achieve the most satisfactory relationship with other human beings and with God are self-scrutiny and self-elevation.

The way that God remains out of bounds in relation to us even on the one day of the year when *Teshuvah* is supposed to reign supreme is poignantly captured in the *You Set Man Apart from the Beginning*-prayer that we recite in *Ne'ila* at the climax of *Yom Kippur.* The first sentence of the prayer reads as follows: "You set man apart from the beginning and you considered him worthy to stand before you, for who can tell you what to do and if he is righteous what can he give you?"[46] Given the infinite distance that separates us from God, one of the most coherent and fruitful ways to describe *Teshuvah* is that it defines an ongoing strategy for Jews and human beings generally to recoup lost ground when we have gone astray in our actions and seek to return to a path of virtue and wholeness, and to move beyond the plateaus that we have achieved earlier.

For Maimonides, we become authentic *Baalei Teshuvah* – people committed to the project of repenting and revising our actions – the moment we begin to appre-

---

45 See the classic commentary of Rabbi Obadiah of Bartenura on the ninth *Mishnah* of the eighth chapter of *Peah* who paraphrases the conclusion of the *Jerusalem Talmudic* tractate of *Peah* along these lines. See the one-volume edition of *Mishnayot* published by Horeb in New York, 1924, p. 31.

46 Zlotowitz, Meir/Gold, Avie (eds): *The Complete ArtScroll Machzor: Yom Kippur,* trans. Nosson Scherman, Brooklyn, New York: Mesorah Publications, 1991, 723.

ciate the resources for self-improvement that reside in the concept of action itself. Doing – acting – connotes restlessness – motion. This restlessness affects the conceptual framings of our actions themselves. If we are dissatisfied with something we have done and notice how our very engagement in the critically vulnerable action itself provides us with the impetus to achieve its transcendence and supersession, we become *Baalei Teshuvah.* The discontinuity with our past identity and scheme of aspirations that *Teshuvah* represents is also simultaneously the high moment of continuity, as we come to realize that part of the conceptual background to the action or actions that we seek to disown is the establishment of a platform upon which to reinstate that unity of the self on a higher level than was attained before. The depth meaning of Maimonides' theorizing of the concept and practice of *Teshuvah* is the coincidence it seeks to disclose between the moment of discontinuity with the moment of continuity in the development of the self, so that wholeness is restored in the very instant when the unity of the self seemed hopelessly fractured.

There is a *Halakhic – Jewish legal* – counterpart or analogue to the concept of *Teshuvah.* It is the category of *Breirah.* In the Talmudic lexicon, the term *Breirah* constitutes a play on words. *Breirah* literally means *choice. Huvrar,* which is a cognate term to *Breirah,* means *clarified.* The Jewish legal category of *Breirah* establishes the legal fiction that once the outcome of a particular choice situation is known that knowledge is read back into the original choice situation itself and directly affects how Jewish law treats the case at hand. For example, before the *Sabbath,* one has to fix the geographic locale of where one wants to spend the Jewish religious day of rest, in effect establishing his boundary of movement – what in Jewish law is called one's *tehum* for the *Sabbath.* If one wants to relocate by foot to a different town or a different city on the *Sabbath,* Jewish law provides the recourse of engaging on Friday in an *Eruv Tehumin* – literally, a mixture or integration of boundaries –, which involves a Jewish ritual allowing one to extend his boundary of movement on the *Sabbath.*

A classis *Talmudic* example of an Eruv *Tehumin* is the following: If a Jew wanted to attend a lecture on the Sabbath by a *Chochom,* a rabbinic scholar, that would be given in a town adjacent to the one in which he lives, but he is not sure which town, in laying down his *Eruv Tehumin* he needs to recite the following formula: "If the scholar comes to the east, I want my eruv to the east to be valid. If he comes to the west, I want my eruv to the west to be valid."[47] The *Halachic* institution of

47 b Bei 37 b, 38 a. The *Talmud* concludes on 38a that with regard to rabbinic, in contrast to *Biblical* law – the laws pertaining to *Breirah* are rabbinic in origin – the principles of *Breirah* apply. The text cited above is reiterated in the following *Babylonian Talmudic* tractates: b Er 36 b; b Hul 14 b; and b Yom 56 b.

Breirah stipulates that in this case, we follow the principle of *Huvrar HaDavar L'Mafreah* – that the future point of arrival of the *Chochom* is read into the original declaration that the person made a day earlier on Friday when he ostensibly established the *eruv.* The idea enshrined in the category of *Breirah* is that the future can be seen as 'causing' the past – as reconstituting the nature of the original action. *Teshuvah* encodes the same logic as *Breirah.* The later realization that we need to repent prompted by the original action is read back into the original action as part of the *Cheftza* of action, so that an act of *Teshuvah* can legitimately rectify it, since it is not considered 'past', but integral to the original action.

There is a striking analog to *Breirah* and *Teshuvah* in one component of modern physics which transfers from Newtonian physics to Einsteinian physics. These are the *Boltzmann Equations* which are equally applicable whether one is seeking to calculate the movement of the whole glass to the broken fragments – a movement from past to future –, or the movement of the broken fragments to reconstitute the whole glass – a movement from future to past. Thus, from the perspective of modern physics, just as for the concepts of *Breirah* and *Teshuvah,* the arrow of time moves in a dualistic direction – from future to past as well as from past to future.[48]

Another complementary perspective to bring to bear in considering the phenomenon of *Teshuvah* is that *Teshuvah* can be viewed as being predicated upon the unreality of time. This idea is encapsulated in some famous paradoxes about time that might have influenced Maimomides' formulations in the *Laws of Teshuvah.* One of the oldest and most enduring of these paradoxes is the logical impossibility of singling out and identifying the present. The conceptualized, demarcated present already represents a move beyond the present. As soon as you flag the present as the present, you have already moved beyond the present. We always only confront the past or the future – but never the present. However, since these three temporal terms are all relativized in relation to each other, if we do not have the present, we do not have the past or the future either. Before a moment can be past or future, it first has to be – or had to be – present. But if it cannot be present, it cannot be past or future either. Hence, the proposition that follows from this train of argument emphasizes the unreality of time.[49]

---

48 I am indebted to my distinguished brother-in-law, Yaacov Marsh OBM, for pointing this out to me.

49 Paradoxes about time are famously associated with St. Augustine. In *Confessions* (book xi.14), he asks: "What is time? If nobody asks me I know; but if I were desirous to explain to one who should ask me, plainly I know not." See my discussion of the paradoxes surrounding time in my book, Michael Oakeshott's *Skepticism*, Princeton: Princeton University Press, 2011, 186. See Footnote 74 thereon.

Reb Chaim Volozhiner (1749–1821) in *Nefesh Hachaim* and in his commentary on *Avot* – and his mystical predecessors and *Baalei Musar* – those rabbis who emphasized ethical refinement and purification as the central teaching of Judaism, and as the appropriate context in which to pursue its other goals – successors, all contain a motif that overlaps with what I am talking about. This is the idea that *Olam Habah* – literally, *The World to Come* – is *now.* Our experience in performing a *Mitzvah* is not *Ma'ein Olam Habah* – a prefiguration of *Olam Habah* –, it *is Olam Habah* in the sense that "The reward associated with the concept of Olam Habah are the actions of the person himself which have caused the proliferation of holy upper worlds which the person then basks in after his soul has departed from his body".[50] The human being through his own actions in this world creates *The World to Come.* It is not something that simply awaits him; it is something that he fashions.

The epistemology of time that Reb Chaim Volozhiner and some of his most eminent predecessors and successors subscribe to is that time is unreal. If time is unreal, then it is legitimate for us to substitute another metaphor for the metaphor of time that we cannot cash in on. This metaphor that Reb Chaim Volozhiner chooses is *Olam Habah*, which defies human rational understanding by identifying human this-worldly actions as the causal factor in the creation of the other-worldly *Olam Habah.* If we cannot descend to a literal level in our perception and categorization of time, then *Olam Habah* becomes a valid term to use in our delineation of 'time', as we experience the exhilaration of performing *Mitzvot* as the significant calibrating factor in our lives.

Eliyahu Eliezer Dessler in *Michtav M'Eliyahu* capitalizes on the reversibility of time to deepen our appreciation of and emotional involvement with the Passover holiday that celebrates the exodus from Egypt. Rav Dessler speaks about the collapse of the spatial and temporal dimensions upon each other – so that the redemption from Egyptian bondage in a graphic spatial sense is experienced anew each year on the 14th day of Nissan in the Jewish lunar calendar – and for the remainder of the holiday. The same redemptive effects that transformed the lives of those leaving Egypt transform our lives – or have the potential to do so. The spatially bounded events are there to be psychologically and imaginatively re-engaged and re-appropriated again and again. This is a species of Nietzschean *Eternal Recurrence.*[51]

---

50 Volozhiner, Chaim, *Nefesh HaChaim with the Commentary Yirat Chaim by Yisroel Eliyahu Weintraub*, Bnei-Brak, Israel, 2009, 69.

51 "The question in each and every thing, 'Do you want this once more and innumerable times more?' would weigh upon your actions as the greatest stress. Or how well disposed would you have to become to yourself and to life to *crave nothing more fervently* than this ultimate eternal

The theoretical collapse of the spatial into the temporal and the temporal into the spatial dimensions of human life is an achievement of Einsteinian physics. Rav Dessler chronicles their halachic pre-figurations and implications.

In *The Guide of the Perplexed*, Maimonides looks at *Teshuvah* from a different vantage point than the way he relates to it in the *Mishneh Torah*. In *Hilchot Teshuvah*, Maimonides theorizes *Teshuvah* from an internal, first-person perspective: Why do I as a human being and as a Jew need to invoke the category of *Teshuvah* on a regular basis to make sense of and restore order to my life? In *The Guide of the Perplexed*, he looks at *Teshuvah* from an external, third-person vantage point: What communal and societal utilities accrue from widespread adherence to the halakhic category and institution of *Teshuvah?* He answers by saying that if an individual believed that the 'fractures' in his life that were introduced by his sins could never be overcome or healed, "he would persist in his error and sometimes perhaps disobey even more because of the fact that no stratagem remains at his disposal. If, however, he believes in repentance, he can correct himself and return to a better and more perfect state than the one he was in before he sinned."[52] Since from an interpretive perspective no action is ever complete and the class of possible interpretations of what happened on any given occasion remains open, we are all being indirectly encouraged by the concept of *Teshuvah* to go on with our own lives and contribute to sustaining and improving the life of our societies.

One major result that emerges from our discussion of *Teshuvah* is the light it sheds on how closely *Teshuvah* overlaps with our discussion of the God-human being encounter in Judaism in the first part of this paper and its implications for understanding the concept of Jewish personhood. We now notice that personal identity needs to be construed in analogy with the negative theological delimitation of God. Just as we can only say what God is not, so, too, with regard to human actions – and a fortiori with regard to persons, who are summations of their actions – we can only say what they are not. Given the distinction between physical movements and interpretive frameworks, our ascriptions of positive content can proceed to infinity. The content of any human action or any person re-

---

confirmation and seal?", From Aphorism 341 in Friedrich Nietzsche, *The Gay Science* [italics in original]. The editing and translation of this passage were done by Walter Kaufmann in Kaufmann, Walter (ed..), *The Portable Nietzsche*, transl. Walter Kaufmann, New York: Penguin Books, 1954, 102.

52 Moses Maimonides, *The Guide of the Perplexed*, trans. Shlomo Pines, Chicago: University of Chicago Press, 1963, Part III, chap. 36, 40. See the commentary on this text in my book, *Skepticism, Belief, and the Modern: Maimonides to Nietzsche*, Ithaca, New York: Cornell University Press, 1997, 129–131.

mains inexhaustible and permanently frustrates the attempt to achieve closure on the question of who or what persons or actions really are.[53]

4 What Steadfast Commitment to the Metaphysical Middle of Human Life Suggests to Us About the Choice Between a Strong and a Weak Messianism

My theoretical and theological analyses of how and why Judaism expresses its preference for the metaphysical middle in its concept of human personhood would naturally lead us to expect that Judaism would also adhere to a weak version of messianism, rather than a strong one.[54] This expectation is sorely disappointed by the sociological reality that a very vocal and active minority of Jews in both Israel, the United States, and in the diaspora generally are advocates of a very strong and aggressive messianism that makes a mockery of the conception of the middle as the key to Jewish personhood. Using Maimonides, who was one of the most influential expositors and codifiers of Jewish thought and law in the history of Judaism, as my background text, I will try to show how a fervent belief in messianic redemption that is expressed in his writings is counterbalanced by a very disciplined and restrained application of this belief to the immediacies of historical and religious experience.

In Chapter 11, Paragraph 1, in his *Laws Concerning Kings and Wars*, Maimonides says "Whoever does not believe in King Messiah, or does not eagerly await his coming not only denies the teachings of the other prophets but those of the Torah itself and of Moses our Teacher".[55] This very rigorous embrace of a conception of messianism as closing historical time is immediately counterbalanced in the first paragraph of Chapter 12 of the same Laws by an insistence on the largely metaphorical character of most of the *Biblical* and *Talmudical* descriptions of the Messianic Age:

> One should not think that in the days of the Messiah any of the laws of nature will be suspended or any innovation occur in creation – but rather the world will follow its accustomed

53 For further elaboration of the theme of this paragraph, see my discussion of 'Self-Transformation' in my book, *Skepticism, Belief, and the Modern: Maimonides to Nietzsche*, 129–131.
54 Benjamin, Walter, *Illuminations: Essays and Reflections*, ed. Hannah Arendt, trans. Harry Zohn, New York: Schocken Books, 1969, 254.
55 My translation.

> course. That which is stated in Isaiah that the wolf will dwell with the lamb and the leopard will lie down with the kid [Is. 11:6]needs to be understood as a parable and riddle. What the verse signifies is that Israel will be living securely with the evil of the nations of the world who are compared to wolves and leopards.[56]

And they will all return to the true religion and will not plunder or destroy. And the Jews and the heathens will both earn a comfortable living in a legitimate way, as the verse states, 'And the lion like the ox will eat straw.' Similarly, all passages similar to these dealing with the Messianic Age have to be construed as metaphors. And at the time of King Messiah it will become evident to all what the metaphor was referring to and what content was being hinted at.[57]

In Paragraph 2 of the same chapter, Maimonides writes: "In all these matters and those similar to them no one will know how they take place until they actually occur, for these matters are hidden from the prophets. The scholars as well do not have traditions in these matters. They are guided by the interpretations they come up with in their reading of the relevant verses."[58] In the conclusion of this paragraph, Maimonides states that 'one should wait and believe in the general idea of messianic redemption', without being able to figure out how it would be translated in practice.

On a rhetorical level, Maimonides uses the same idiom of analysis with regard to the theological category of resurrection of the dead that he employs in his treatment of messianism. In his *Treatise on Resurrection*, Maimonides says that "We are only compelled to interpret a speech whose literal meaning is impossible, like the corporealization of the God. As for the possible, it may remain in accord with it [i. e., the literal text]."[59] Since the ideas of resurrection and messianism are not incoherent, like the idea of God outside of a negative theological framework, but merely bordering on the impossible or actually impossible, the theologically appropriate way to react to them is to say that 'No one will know how they will take place until they actually occur'.

What is driving Maimonides' continual return from different angles of vision to the themes of the 'unknowableness' – we do not know when it will happen – and simultaneously the ordinariness – nothing changes in the order of reality –

---

56 Maimonides, *Mishneh Torah – The Book of Judges:* "The Laws of Kings and Wars," annotation Shmuel Tanchum Rabinowitz, Jerusalem: Mossad Harav Kook, 1975, 412; translation from the Hebrew by the author.

57 My translation.

58 My translation.

59 Maimonides, "Treatise on Resurrection" (1191), trans. Hillel G. Fradkin, in: Ralph Lerner, *Maimonides' Empire of Light: Popular Enlightenment in an Age of Belief*, Chicago: The University of Chicago Press, 2000, 172.

or in the rhythms and substance of Jewish religion – the performance of *mitzvot* is still the watchword of our religion? I think that an important clue for addressing this question can be found in Chapter 11, Paragraph 3 of the *Laws of Kings and Wars* where Maimonides says: "And the essence of the matter is this: This Torah and its laws and ordinances are eternal – and one cannot add to them or diminish them."[60] What is driving key aspects of Maimonides' formulation of his conception of messianism is what he takes to be the need to sustain for all eternity the viability and relevance of *mitzvot. Mitzvo*t, after all, represent partial redemptions of the different phases, moments, and moods of life from eating to sleeping to developing one's mind and managing one's emotions, and Judaism seeks to refine and elevate how we do all of these things. Partial redemptions through one's commitment to and practice of mitzvot constitute the preferred order of Judaism – not total redemption, which harbors the potential of subverting and undermining one's allegiance to mitzvot because one has entered a stage of full-scale liberation from human needs and responsibilities.

In b Sanhedrin 97b, we find the following piece of *Biblical* exegesis: "What is meant by the verse [in Habakuk 2,3] 'but at the end it shall speak [*we-yafeah*] and not lie?'" – R. Samuel, the son of Nahmani in the name of Rav. Yonathan, said: "Blasted be the bones of those who calculate the end. For they would say, since the predetermined time has arrived, and yet he has not come, he will never come. But [even so], wait for him, as it is written, though he tarry, wait for him."[61] Maimonides codifies this exegesis of Rabbi Samuel the son of Nahmani in his *Laws of Kings and Wars*, Chapter 12, Paragraph 2: "And one should not calculate the end. The rabbis have said: Blasted be the bones of those who calculate the end. Instead, one should wait and believe in the general idea [not the details] of redemption, as we have previously explained."[62]

There are at least two ways of interpreting the *Talmud*'s animadversion toward those who calculate the end, which Maimonides cites. One could read the resistance to calculations of the end as undertaken from a third-person perspective, by members of the broad citizenry or audience. One could also read the rejection of calculations of the end as extending to a first-person perspective undertaken by political actors powerfully driven to usher in the Messianic Age. It seems quite clear that Maimonides reads the Talmudic statement as encompassing first-person calculations of the end as well as third-person calculations. His codifying twice

---

60 My translation.

61 Hebrew-English Edition of *The Babylonian Talmud: Sanhedrin*, trans. H. Freedman, London: The Soncino Press, 1987. In footnote 5 on p. 97b, the editor/translator of the Soncino edition of Sanhedrin says, "The verse from Habakuk is rendered, 'he will blast him who calculates the end.'"

62 My translation.

within the confines of two chapters in his Code the prohibition against immersing oneself in the details of messianic deliverance rather than just affirming the general principle makes it fairly evident that he reads the Talmudic statement in b Sanh. 97b as intending to restrain political action governed by messianic impulses, and not just to restrain the calculations of ordinary civilians and third-party spectators.

The Talmudic source for Maimonides' approach to messianism which affirms widespread acceptance of the general principle of messianic redemption but is critical of a human initiative to translate this vision of the end of history into action is to be found in a statement of the Amora Samuel, who is one of the dominant voices in the whole Babylonian Talmudic canon: "Samuel said: There is no difference between this world and the days of the Messiah except [that in the latter there will be no] bondage of foreign Powers, as it says (Deut 15:11), For the poor shall never cease out of the land ['never,' i.e., not even in the messianic era.]"[63] For Samuel, the fact that the Bible says that class inequalities will persist indefinitely is a clear indication that the Hebrew Scriptures support only a very attenuated version of the messianic age. Maimonides cites Samuel's view as the normative view of Judaism in two places in his *Mishneh Torah:* The first is in the *Laws of Repentance* Chapter 9, Paragraph 2 – and the second is in the *Laws of Kings and Wars*, Chapter 12, Paragraph 2, which I have already alluded to earlier in the paper. It is important to note that in this second citation Maimonides emphasizes that the main function of King Messiah is "to bring [literally: to place] peace" in the world, as the verse says, "'And he will restore the hearts of fathers to their children and the hearts of children to their fathers'" (Malachi 3:24). Maimonides is very explicit in his theorizing of the messianic age that he is codifying the law in accordance with Samuel's formulation that the main goal and achievement of King Messiah – when he is successful – is to create peace between Israel and her neighbors.

Given the multiplicity of views about the messianic age and about its emergence and duration that one finds in the *Talmud*, what motivates Maimonides to consider Samuel's minimalist conception as authoritative? Perhaps, one factor might be the following: The *Babylonian Talmud* in Bekh 49b says that "Wherever Rab and Samuel differ in ritual law the ruling adopted is that of Rab and in civil cases the ruling adopted is that of Samuel." Samuel's saying that the only difference between ordinary, historically grounded Jewish history and the messianic age is the oppression of the nations which will cease suggests that the traditional

63 Hebrew-English Edition of Isidore Epstein (ed.), *The Babylonian Talmud: Berakoth*, trans. Maurice Simon; London: The Soncino Press, 1984, 34 b. Samuel's statement concerning the thinness of the messianic age is cited in the following additional tractates of the *Babylonian Talmud:* b Shab 6 3a and 151b; b Pes 68a; b Sanh 99a and 91b.

mechanics and dynamics of the political economy will continue into the messianic age. Samuel's pronouncement then looms as a somewhat disguised statement of the scope of Jewish civil law that in the messianic age it will be as broad ranging as it was in earlier historical epochs. This meta-statement about the scope of Jewish civil law itself forms part of the content of that civil law which the Talmudic consensus codifies as Samuel's area of expertise. This linkage between Samuel's conception of the messianic age and his recognized area of expertise in Jewish law might serve as an additional justificatory factor in terms of how Maimonides theorizes the messianic age.

In two very specific and dramatic details, Maimonides, relating to the organization of Jewish life in the messianic age, shows how minimalist and un-traditionally messianic his conception of the messianic age is. Under the auspices of a contemporary messianic movement, to attempt to expand the borders of the Jewish state so that they approximate one's conception of what the original borders were in the time of Joshua is clearly prohibited. In Chapter 5, Paragraph 4 of the *Laws of Kings and Wars*, Maimonides says: "It is a positive command to destroy the seven nations [that originally inhabited the land of Canaan], as it is said, 'But thou shalt utterly destroy them'"[64]. If one does not put to death any of them that falls into one's power, one transgresses a negative command, as it is said: "Thou shalt save alive nothing that breatheth"[65]. But their memory has long perished."[66] The crucial words in the paragraph that I have just cited from Maimonides are, "But their memory has long perished"[67]. This sentence indicates that the sanction for total devastation of an enemy who opposes total re-conquest of the land of Israel with its original borders has long been superseded. After the initial period of conquest and settlement of the land of Israel during the reign of Joshua, the closest disciple of Moses, Jews seeking to re-settle the land of Israel need to follow the normal protocols of war in Judaism which consist in making overtures toward peace and reconciliation at the outset, and limiting violence to the furthest extent possible.[68]

A second textual space where Maimonides gives dramatic expression to his messianic minimalism is in his *Introduction to Perek Chelek*, where he says "and

64 Deut 20:17.

65 Deut 20:16.

66 *The Code of Maimonides: Book Fourteen: The Book of Judges*, trans. Abraham M. Hershman, New Haven: Yale University Press, 1949, 217.

67 Ibid.

68 See Maimonides, *Laws of Kings and Wars*, Chapters 5 and 6.

the messiah will die and his son and grandson will reign after him".[69] From this text, I think that one can validly infer that the messianic era in Judaism lasts for three generations, and after that normal history is restored. There is no entry into a higher sphere of being or personal transformation that is guaranteed to endure. The contingency, fragility, and vulnerability normally associated with human life are restored. As Maimonides says about the messianic era, and this would be a fortiori applicable to the post-messianic era – "*Olam K'Minhago Nohaig*" – the world moves in its accustomed course.

5 Conclusion

What emerges from our analyses of Divine-human encounters in the Hebrew Bible, the category and practice of *Teshuvah*, and rabbinic visions of the messianic age is a conception of human life as an endless project with no fixed, known outcomes. The postulation of infinite distance between human beings and God which lies at the core of the Abrahamic rebellion against polytheism also suffuses the Jewish conception of human nature. The performance of *Mitzvot* – adherence to Biblically and rabbinically mandated commandments and prohibitions – reinforces the idea that life is lived in the here and now – the immediate present. In Judaism, all of the futures that the religion envisions and all of the pasts that it evokes have roots and repercussions in how we organize and structure our lives in the present. The Eternal is translated into an everlasting 'now' of commandments and prohibitions that both summarize and prefigure the theological trajectory of the tradition. Faith is sustained through a regimen of religious practice informed by the theological notions discussed in this paper. By living in the metaphysical middle – the daily present –, we harbor the best prospect of transforming our theological vision into some version of reality, so that interpretation – in the present – and understanding – of the past – truly become one. Religiously predicted outcomes like the messianic age and the resurrection of the dead will become known to us, as Maimonides either implies or openly says, only when they historically occur. In the meantime, the major principle that we have to guide us is stated in Rabbi Tarfon's *Mishnah* in *Avot:* "You are not required to complete the task – yet you are not free to exempt yourself from it."[70] Our preoccupation with deepening and extending the metaphysical middle of our lives becomes

---

69 Maimonides, *Hakdamot L'Peirush HaMishnah:* Introductions to the Commentary on the Mishnah, ed. Mordechai Dov Rabinowitz, Jerusalem: Mosad HaRav Kook, 1961, 131; my translation. I am indebted to Zeev Harvey for highlighting this passage for me.

70 Avot, 2:21. My translation.

our greatest source of spiritual and emotional satisfaction and intellectual enlightenment.

The image of the self that emerges from our discussion is one that nurtures ist continual replenishment, not overlooking the possibilities for ongoing growth. The *Tzaddik*, the righteous person, in Judaism resists rigid self-definition and self-enclosure. From a Jewish-rabbinic perspective, every achievement of the self, every successful enactment of an act of self-realization, must be viewed as a platform for attaining and enacting further moments of growth. The self consists of the conceptual and emotional infrastructure that allows us to navigate through time – to fill up the moments of our lives with the delineation of new challenges on religious and metaphysical as well as practical levels, and with the development of theoretical and psychological strategies for dealing with them.

The movement through time constitutes the ultimate project of the self. Judaism's emphasis on *Mitzvot* – conformity to Divine commandments and prohibitions as filling up the life of the Jew – has a built-in procedural bias. The revulsion against passivity and resignation becomes the occasion for an unremitting internal battle. In Judaism, the impetus is always present to transform moments of disorientation, uncertainty, and irresolvability into new crystallizations of action. The agenda of *Mitzvot* in Judaism is dictated as much by the openness and heterogeneity attached to the passage of time as by more specific factors, such as the commemoration of the Exodus from Egypt celebrated annually during the spring on the Passover Holiday.

In Judaism, as much as possible of the life of the individual Jew is mediated through the self – with the concepts and value hierarchy of the religion taking an ongoing detour through the self as the appropriate means for absorbing their content and proceeding to a virtuous and successful translation of them.

Sinfulness, one might say, is the non-personally grounded version of the teachings of Judaism. It is the attempt to practice the *Mitzvot* in an overwhelmingly mechanical and detached way that constitutes a core evasion of the human being. Sinfulness means allowing oneself to be sucked in by rhythms of life, not of one's own choosing – or personal recognition that they are bound up with the activity of living itself. A leading source of human self-rejection is our not realizing that the symbols, rituals, and conceptualizations that are integral to our identity could also propel us to undertake new initiatives in the structuring and organizing of our lives. These symbols, rituals, and conceptualizations could themselves become the chief elements in the meanings that we find in our lives, and thereby preempt the path toward self-rejection. Not offering ourselves the opportunity to find and relish these meanings is a major cause of alienation and self-hatred. Becoming who we are is the single most important imperative of human life. The action of accepting and embracing the metaphysical distances that I have described and working with the traditional materials that have been generated by human beings over the generations to fill them in with content harbors the promise of being a major source of human well-being and achievement.

Bibliography

Anscombe, G. E. M., "On Brute Facts," *Analysis* 18 (1958), 69–72.
Arendt, Hannah, *The Human Condition*, Chicago: University of Chicago Press, 1958.
The ArtScroll Tehillim, trans. Hillel Danziger, ed. Nosson Scherman, Brooklyn, NY: Mesorah Publications, 1988.
The Babylonian Talmud: Berakoth, trans. Maurice Simon; ed. Isidore Epstein, London: The Soncino Press, 1984.
The Babylonian Talmud: Sanhedrin, trans. H. Freedman, London: The Soncino Press, 1987.
The Babylonian Talmud: Yebamoth, trans. Israel W. Slotki, London: Soncino Press, 1984.
Benjamin, Walter, *Illuminations: Essays and Reflections*, ed. Hannah Arendt, trans. Harry Zohn, New York: Schocken Books, 1969.
Bloom, Harold, *A Map of Misreading*, New York: Oxford University Press, 1975.
Bloom, Harold, *The Anxiety of Influence: A Theory of Poetry*, New York: Oxford University Press, 1973.
Bloom, Harold, *Kabbalah and Criticism*, New York: Seabury Press, 1975.
Bloom, Harold, *Poetry and Repression*, New Haven (et.al.): Yale University Press, 1976.
Botwinick, Aryeh, *Michael Oakshott's Skepticism*, Princeton: Princeton University Press, 2011.
Botwinick, Aryeh, *Skepticism, Belief, and the Modern: Maimonides to Nietzsche*, Ithaca, NY: Cornell University Press, 1997.
Duber, Yosef, *Beit Halevi, Warsaw*, 1884; reprinted in Israel, 1973.
Gadamer, Hans-Georg, *Truth and Method*, New York: The Seabury Press, 1975.
Hobbes, Thomas, *Leviathan*, ed. Michael Oakeshott, Oxford: Basil Blackwell, 1946.
Hughes, Yonoson, *Understanding Reb Chaim*, Israel, 2010.
Kaufmann, Walter (ed. and trans.), *The Portable Nietzsche*, New York: Penguin Books, 1954.
Maimonides, *The Code of Maimonides: Book Fourteen: The Book of Judges*, trans. Abraham M. Hershman, New Haven: Yale University Press, 1949.
Maimonides, *The Guide of the Perplexed*, trans. Shlomo Pines, Chicago: University of Chicago Press, 1963.
Maimonides, *Hakdamot L'Peirush HaMishnah* [Introductions to the Commentary on the Mishnah], ed. Mordechai Dov Rabinowitz, Jerusalem: Mosad HaRav Kook, 1961.
Maimonides, *Mishneh Torah. Volume 1. Sefer HaMada*, Commentary by Shmuel Tanchum Rubinstein, Jerusalem: Mossad Harav Kook, 1989.
Maimonides, *Mishneh Torah: The Book of Judges*, annotation Shmuel Tanchum Rabinowitz, Jerusalem: Mossad Harav Kook, 1975.
Maimonides, "Treatise on Resurrection" (1191), trans. Hillel G. Fradkin, in: Ralph Lerner, *Maimonides' Empire of Light: Popular Enlightenment in an Age of Belief*, Chicago: The University of Chicago Press, 2000.
Maimonides, *Hakdamot L'Peirush HaMishnah:* Introductions to the Commentary on the Mishnah, ed. Mordechai Dov Rabinowitz, Jerusalem: Mosad HaRav Kook, 1961
Mishnayot, New York: Horeb, 1924.

Nietzsche, Friedrich, "The Gay Science", in: Walter Kaufmann (ed. and trans.), *The Portable Nietzsche*, New York: Penguin Books, 1954, 93–102.

Nietzsche, Friedrich, *On the Advantage and Disadvantage of History for Life*, trans. Peter Preuss, Indianapolis: Hackett Publishing, 1980.

Oakeshott, Michael, *Skepticism*, Princeton: Princeton University Press, 2011.

Popper, Karl R., *Conjectures and Refutations: The Growth of Scientific Knowledge*, 2nd ed., London: Routledge and Kegan Paul, 1965.

Soloveitchik, Chaim, *Chidushei Rabbeinu Chaim Halevi Im Gilyonot Chazon Ish*, Israel, n.d.

Volozhiner, Chaim, *Sefer Nefesh HaChaim Im Beur Yirat Chaim and Ruach Chaim Al Masechet Avot*, ed. Yisroel Eliyahu Weintraub, Bnwei-Brask, Israel, 2009.

Volozhiner, Chaim, *Nefesh HaChaim with the Commentary Yirat Chaim by Yisroel Eliyahu Weintraub*, Bnei-Brak, Israel, 2009, 69.

Wittgenstein, Ludwig, *Philosophical Investigations*, trans. G. E. M. Anscombe, 3rd ed., London: Macmillan, 1969.

Zlotowitz, Meir/Gold, Avie (eds): *The Complete ArtScroll Machzor: Yom Kippur*, trans. Nosson Scherman, Brooklyn, New York: Mesorah Publications, 1991.

Suggestions for Further Reading

Arieti, Silvano, *Abraham and the Contemporary Mind*, New York: Basic Books, 1981.

Baeck, Leo, *Judaism and Christianity: A Modern Theologian's Discussion of Basic Issues Between the Two Religions*, trans. Walter Kaufmann, Philadelphia: The Jewish Publication Society, 1960.

Heschel, Abraham J., *God in Search of Man: A Philosophy of Judaism*, London: John Calder, 1956.

Kaplan, Lawrence J. (ed.), *Maimonides Between Philosophy and Halakhah: Rabbi Joseph B. Soloveitchik's Lectures on The Guide of the Perplexed*, Jerusalem: Ktav Publishing; Urim Publications, 2016.

Moore, Adrian William, *The Infinite*, London: Routledge, 1990.

Edward J. Alam

The Concept of Person in Christianity

If anthropology, as Immanuel Kant says, is the most appropriate name for the science of man, what, we may ask, is the most appropriate name for the science of person, and should we confine this science, whatever we end up calling it, to the study of human persons alone? Any thorough study of the concept of person must take seriously the possibility of admitting that there may be persons other than human persons, assuming, that is, that such a study broadens its scope to include the vast intellectual history of speculating on this concept, and is not limited to the period we call modernity and late or post modernity, wherein any suggestion of angelic or divine persons falls flat at best or is taken to be downright unscientific or superstitious at worst.

1 Concept Qualifications

But even a superficial perusal of the history of the concept of person in the literature of the monotheistic religions reveals that the concept is more often qualified by these latter adjectives than by the term 'human'. In fact, the very concept of the human person is unintelligible in these traditions without considering the notions of angelic and divine persons alongside it. Are angels persons? Is God a person or, as in Christianity, persons? These are all fundamental questions which must be addressed in any serious historical enquiry into the meaning of the concept of person in the monotheistic religious traditions in general, and in Christianity in particular.

Now, although questions concerning whether our non-human animal 'relatives', or even 'our friends' in the plant kingdom are persons[1] are interesting questions *per se*, it is impossible to find any consistent or serious 'monotheistic' position arguing ontologically that they are. But this does not mitigate the obvious and irreplaceable value and importance of these other non-personal life forms in the overall meaning of creation; in fact, by underscoring the radically *relational* nature of all existing things and emphasizing their interdependence, what opens

---

1 Though I would not take the following quote from Richard Powers' best-selling 2018 novel, *The Overstory*, as a literal truth, I would still insist that it conveys a deep insight into the unity, relatedness, and, indeed, sacredness of all creation: "*A chorus of living wood sings to the woman:* If your mind were only a slighter greener thing, we'd drown you in meaning." See Powers, Richard, *The Overstory*, New York: W. W. Norton & Company, 2018, 4.

https://doi.org/10.1515/9783110756715-003

up is a way of seeing that every link on the hierarchical chain of being is indispensable for the overall unity and beauty of what we may then call a cosmos.[2]

Our topic, the concept of person in Christianity, is beset with difficulties from the beginning for a plethora of complex reasons, one of which is the obvious fact that Christianity is not monolithic. Which or whose Christianity shall we address in such an enquiry? Clearly, the first millennium presents fewer problems then the second, since the Christian leaders and their people from the first major urban Christian population centers of Antioch, Alexandria, Rome, Constantinople, and Jerusalem, in addition to the Christian communities tied to these traditional Christian centers in other parts of Asia, Africa, and Europe, all generally agreed on a set of fundamental teachings. This relative unity[3] between Eastern and Western Christianity during the first eight centuries of Christianity, evidenced by agreement on the first seven Ecumenical Councils (at least between Rome and Constantinople),[4] comes as a breath of fresh air when compared to the legions of fragmentation that take place in the second millennium, especially after the Reformation, making the question of "which or whose Christianity" impossible to tackle in a short chapter such as this. My choice to consider primarily Eastern Orthodox and Western and Eastern Catholic Christianity (along with their philosophers and theologians) is based on my judgment that these expressions of Christianity best embody, historically and doctrinally, what has been and still is mainline Christianity.

But this question is hardly the most challenging in such an enquiry. The much more perplexing problem and, again, one that is seriously compounded in the millennium (particularly in the second half), is an epistemological one. Not only the question of the role that ideas or concepts play in the act of knowing, but the prior question of what constitutes an idea or a concept both take center stage in modern philosophy – so much so that all philosophy virtually becomes a matter of epistemology. I shall briefly address this Cartesian epistemic shift later in this essay, but want to clarify now what I mean by the term concept since my title is the concept of person in Christianity.

2 For a broad and profound treatment of the evolutionary history of the cosmos rooted in an ever-increasing complex *relatedness* of biological, physical, and chemical laws of nature, see Polkinghorne, J. (ed.), *The Trinity and an Entangled World: Relationality in Physical Science and Theology*, Grand Rapids: Eerdmans, 2010. In this context, it would be helpful to review the relatively new academic discipline of "big history" proposed by David Christian about thirty years ago.

3 I say "relative" because compared to the fragmentation that takes place in Christianity after the Reformation, the differences and divisions, though substantive, do not seem so serious.

4 The same cannot be said, of course, for Antioch and Alexandria, where Christological differences caused great divisions.

First, I will use the terms concept and idea interchangeably as referring to an abstract mental entity which may or may not be associated with a corresponding mental image, and which may or may not correspond to an actual existing entity outside the mind. I will claim that the idea or concept of person does correspond to actual existing things (persons) outside the mind and that when we know other persons, the direct object of our knowledge is the person outside the mind and not the mental idea or image of the person in the mind. I acknowledge, nonetheless, that the mental idea plays a role in the knowledge and cognition of the extra-mental reality, but claim that this role is secondary, not primary. If the idea or the concept of another person becomes the primary and direct object of our knowledge, then our knowledge becomes seriously flawed, illusory, and corrupt and the limits of this knowledge are multiplied beyond measure. Even when the other person is the direct object of our knowledge, this knowledge is severely limited, but at least it can be considered genuine knowledge and not an illusion. In other words, when it comes to any and all extra-mental reality, I want to acknowledge that the idea or the concept of a thing plays a role in the act of knowing that thing, whatever it may be, but that the direct knowledge of that thing is the extra-mental reality itself, and not the idea or the concept of that thing in the mind. To make the idea of the extra-mental reality the direct object of knowledge, rather than the extra-mental reality itself, is a Cartesian shift in epistemology that complicates any and all discourse and confuses the already complex and difficult questions about the relationship, causal and otherwise, between language and thought for good. Moreover, this makes the already difficult task of interpersonal communication, or any communication for that matter, much more difficult – resulting in a vicious circle since individuals (I will claim) cannot become persons except through intimate communication with other persons. One critical point here is that accurate or meaningful knowledge of the concept of person, apart from the historical question of the concept of person, comes ultimately by way of direct knowledge of other persons in real (not virtual or merely mental) personal relationships. I shall focus almost entirely on the central role of interpersonal relations, and the centrality of dialogical relation-ality, when I attempt an exposition of the modern movements of Christian Personalism in both philosophy and theology towards the end of this essay. But I have gotten ahead of myself and I am already begging the question; I must back up a bit and, in preparation for this exposition, present a general historical account of the complex linguistic apparatus in which such an inquiry into the concept of person in Christianity must take place. I shall then attempt to present a very general account of the evolution of the concept in Christian history.

Before examining the etymologies of the key terms in Greek and Latin, there is one final, but crucial, preliminary point to make, which I will present in the form of a question: what kind of concept is the concept of person? If the key concept were, for instance, 'goodness', or 'the good', we would immediately identify it today as a moral concept and then the important debate would begin over whether this concept has changed over time. Some concepts, of course, do not change over long periods of time, such as those concepts that have emerged in highly specialized and continuing disciplines (geometry for instance), and thus retain stable and largely universal meanings. The same could be said for prepositions and conjunctions in complex languages, which is what gives mathematical logic its force and precision.[5] If the concept of person is to be understood as a moral concept, then it clearly cannot have a fixed and timeless meaning because morality and social life are so deeply imbedded in one another and it is obviously the case that social life changes. This does not mean, however, that moral concepts change "because" social life does, but rather that "moral concepts change 'as' social life changes."[6] But is the concept of person a moral concept? Clearly, the concept has moral and ethical implications, but it is not a moral concept in the sense that 'the good' or 'right' and 'wrong' are moral concepts. It is also clear that it is not an immutable, timeless, and stable concept in the same way as a 'circle' or the preposition 'or'. In many ways it is a theological and philosophical concept, which, at one level, means it is a dynamic and fluctuating concept because theology and philosophy as disciplines are not firm and permanent in the way that geometry is. From another angle, however, certain metaphysical and theological concepts do have durable and perpetual connotations; thus, to the degree that person is this kind of concept, it is possible to identify its enduring characteristics even over the course of its long and complex evolution. This complex story must begin by examining the etymologies of the key terms in Greek and Latin and then continue by tracing, in a general way, the development of the concept up to the present day.

2 Etymologies of Key Terms

Focusing on the Greek and Latin terms is not meant to downplay the importance of the original Hebrew and Aramaic terms, or to forget what is too often forgotten regarding the very early dissemination of Christianity into Mesopotamia, Africa, India, and China;[7] nor is it meant to ignore the central role of the Semitic languag-

5 MacIntyre, Alasdair, *A Short History of Ethics*, New York: Routledge Classics, 2002, 2.

6 Ibid., 1.

7 The Syriac Christians who thrived in China under the Tang dynasty from the seventh through the tenth century, and who managed to forge a fruitful dialogue with Chinese religion and philos-

es, particularly Syriac and Arabic, in transmitting to the Latin West not only most of the ancient Greek philosophical and scientific knowledge but also many of those unique synthetic insights that resulted in the dynamic marriage of Christian faith and pagan wisdom. Great progress has been made on these two fronts in the last six or seven decades, but much more linguistic, historical, philosophical, and theological work still needs to be done. Nonetheless, analysis of the Greek and Latin terms is still indispensable and must take pride of place in an enquiry such as this, especially when we consider that for the subsequent linguistic, social, political, philosophical, and theological history of Christianity, even up till the present, these parent languages and their offspring have been and still are the most influential in establishing what has come to be the common and accepted meanings globally in both technical theological and ordinary colloquial discourse in Christianity.[8]

The educated classes of Christians fluent in Latin and/or Greek and conversant in Greek philosophy played an important role in developing the proper theological terminology to best express the fruit of what was then emerging from the interplay between philosophizing and prayerful reflection upon the Christian faith recorded in Holy Scripture. While this terminological development was well underway as early as the end of the first century, it did not reach linguistic and philosophical/theological maturity until well into the fourth and fifth centuries at four decisive Ecumenical Councils.

In the years leading up to these councils, substantial theological work had been taking place, but due to the dangerous political and legal status of Christianity under the Roman Empire at this time, the work progressed slowly and without consistent momentum. Among the prominent and prolific early Christian thinkers and writers who would play a major role in this terminological development, Tertullian (155–240) of Carthage stands out, as he was the first to create a theological language in Latin that captured the meanings of the key Greek terms associated with the central mystery of the Christian Faith, the Holy Trinity. When Tertullian finally uses the phrase, *"una substantia – tres personae"* (one substance – three persons) to point to the mystery of the Trinity, a formula that would forever mark the subsequent development of all Christian theology, he drew upon earlier treatises written around the time of his own birth, most notably the work of Justin

---

ophy are typically identified as Nestorian Christians, though what this precisely meant, Christologically speaking, is still a matter of debate. In other words, Nestorianism never meant just one thing.

8 I mean here that English is the international language today and that it is a language influenced by the Greco-Latinate sources, and that it is increasingly becoming, for better or worse, *the* language in which the global religion of traditional and non-traditional Christianity is being disseminated.

Martyr (ca. 100–c. 165).[9] Martyr seems to have been one of the first Fathers of the Church to give a profoundly new meaning to the Greek word *prósōpon* (*πρόσωπον*) or *persona* in Latin, which in its most basic and ancient meaning is best rendered into English as "role" or "mask".[10] In his reading of Sacred Scripture, Justin began to see how the sacred authors, following the ancient literary device of prosopographic exegesis[11] employed by the great poets and philosophers (primarily the Stoics) of Antiquity, introduced different *prosopa* or "roles" to give dramatic life to the events they were narrating. Platonists, too, influenced by the Stoic prosopographic interpretation of Homer, used this same literary device in their reading of Plato's dialogues in order to designate the characters who best represented Plato's own philosophical positions. Not only Justin and Tertullian, but Hippolytus, Clement of Alexandria, Origen, and others, frequently did something similar in their exegesis of Sacred Scripture by designating certain passages in which the different persons of the Trinity were speaking. But it seems that only in Tertullian did the "literary metaphor. . . rise to the level of theological significance,"[12] allowing for the possibility of seeing God as a being in dialogue with himself (three persons-in-dialogue). Although the theological potential of this insight was enormous, it would take centuries before it could really bear fruit.[13] For one thing, the Eastern fathers thought that such expressions were too close to the heretical position of Sabellian Modalism in which the divine persons were spoken of as mere masks or modes of the One God who converses with himself in three roles. Clearly, however, Tertullian understood the literary device as a metaphor and saw and taught that, when it came to the sacred authors of Scripture, "the dialogical roles introduced by [say] the prophets [were] not mere literary devices. The 'role' truly exists; it is the prosopon, the face, the person of the Logos who truly speaks .... and joins

9 See Joseph Ratzinger's excellent journal article: Ratzinger, Joseph, "Concerning the notion of person in theology" *Communio* 17 (1990), 439–454.

10 Ibid. 440–441.

11 For the groundbreaking work into this literary device, known as "prosopographic exegesis", and its relevance to and importance in the history of the dogma of the Trinity, see Joseph Ratzinger's brilliant summary of Carl Andresen's "Zur Entstehung und Geschichte des trinitarischen Personbegriffs", ZNW 52 (1961), 1–38 in Ratzinger's *Dogma and Preaching: Applying Christian Doctrine to Daily Life*, San Francisco: Ignatius Press, 2005, 182–186.

12 von Balthasar, Hans Urs, *Theo-Drama: Theological Dramatic Theory, Volume III*, trans. Graham Harrison, San Francisco: Ignatius Press, 1992, 210–211.

13 I shall attempt to show below that after St. Thomas Aquinas reconsidered the Aristotelian category of "relation" anew in the light of the dogma of the Trinity, this potential was partially realized.

in dialogue with the prophet."[14] Tertullian takes Justin's insights[15] to heart when reading and interpreting certain passages of the Bible, ('Let us make man in our image and likeness') where God speaks in the plural, dialogically as it were. Following Justin and other early Christian writers, Tertullian transforms the word prosopon from merely role or mask to the actual face of a real person; perhaps we could say he recognizes how the sacred writers intentionally introduce the masks only to finally take them off – for the very purpose of ultimately revealing the real unique faces of the substantially existing persons par excellence.

With time, and building solidly upon this development, the notion of relation came to be closely associated with the term person, as we see in both St. Augustine's monumental work on the Trinity, as well as in St. Basil the Great's foundational Trinitarian insights. However, it is not entirely clear to me precisely when and how this identification of relation with person takes place at this time, since although Augustine read Aristotle's Categories (wherein relation as a serious philosophical category is first identified and addressed)[16] as a young man, and was duly impressed by Aristotle's logical analysis of the existing world, he did not interpret it as a metaphysical work, as some of the Platonists did or, as we shall see later, as many of the very first Syriac and Arabic translators and St. Thomas Aquinas did. In fact, as I will address in some detail below, the *Categories* came to be the most studied and commented upon of all Aristotelian texts in the Latin West. In this herculean attempt to classify and describe literally everything that exists, Aristotle presented his famous ten categories, the third of which, namely relation, is most noteworthy for our purposes. By the late patristic period, the term relation becomes closely associated with the term person and is considered, in some circles, to be another major category alongside the two enormous Aristotelian categories of substance and accident.[17] I shall return to this crucial issue below when I address the influential role of Jewish and Islamic philosophy and theology on the development of Christian doctrine.

The other key ancient Greek term to consider in an inquiry into the concept of person in Christianity, which was also in use long before Christianity, is *hypostasis* (*ὑπόστασις*), which meant something akin to solid reality, what we might call today, objective or concrete reality. Although the very earliest meaning seems to have referred to the solid substratum that remains after a process of precipitation, Aris-

---

14 Ratzinger, Joseph, "Concerning the notion of person in theology", *Communio* 17 (Fall, 1990), 439–454, p. 442.

15 Insights that come primarily from his reading of Justin's *Dialogue with Trypho.*

16 This could have been due to the fact that he struggled with the Greek text and/or read it in isolation from Aristotle's other works, which at that time were not available in Latin translations.

17 Ratzinger, "Concerning the notion of person in theology", 442–444.

totle used it to oppose the notion of illusion; and the Stoics used it to refer to a kind of universal underlying substratum, material and unformed, of fully formed individual things.[18] Although the term, as I note below, will eventually be used in the definitive orthodox doctrinal formula of the Trinity, it was originally introduced into doctrinal Trinitarian discourse by a certain unorthodox group (the Arians) in order to bolster their Platonist-inspired belief that both the Divine Son and the Holy Spirit were subordinate to the Divine Father.[19] It was sometimes translated into Latin as *substantia* (substance) and used primarily by Christian writers before the fourth century to mean substantial reality or sometimes even being, though the Greek word for being, *ousia*, from the Greek verb to-be, was translated into Latin as *essentia* (essence). Now because in its grammatical structure the Latin word *essentia* exactly resembles the Greek term *ousia*, in that both words are abstract forms of present participles of the verb "to be", it was natural to translate *ousia* as *essentia*, but, as a number of important linguists, philosophers, and theologians have clearly shown, this caused considerable confusion not only for choosing the right words to best capture the mysteries of the Christian faith, but for the entire history of metaphysics in the West.[20] *Hypostasis* will be reflected upon anew during the High Middle Ages in the light of the rich Aristotelian category of relation, thereby deepening and enriching the general concept of person in unprecedented ways. I shall also address this in some detail when I examine the contribution of St. Thomas Aquinas to the evolution of the concept of person.

3 Early Ecumenical Councils

For the purposes of this reflection, it is safe to say that, by the early fourth century, the key terms, essence, substance, nature, being, person, and *hypostasis*[21], had all already been assembled and sufficiently reflected upon so as to prepare for what

---

18 Von Balthasar, *Theo-Drama: Theological Dramatic Theory, Volume III*, 210. The Stoics defined the substratum as: *hyphystamene prote ousia.*

19 Ibid.

20 For an outstanding contribution to the history of the concept of "essence" from a linguistic, historical, and philosophical angle, accompanied by a deep knowledge of, and sensitivity to, the importance of orthodox Christian doctrine, see: Zubiri, Xavier, *On Essence*, Washington, D. C.: The Catholic University of America Press, 1980.

21 Though there is some evidence that this term was not introduced into the theological debate until the middle of the fourth century. The Greek term for both essence and substance is *ousia*. These key English terms come from the first Latin translations of *ousia* – a term so rich and meaning that Latin needed two different terms to capture all that it entails. In this, essence and substance are not just synonyms but together capture both the *mode and act of being*.

came next: an edict of toleration that legalized Christianity in 311, which made the first Ecumenical Council possible in 325, and then another decree in 380, which made Christianity the official religion of the empire and which set the stage for the second Ecumenical Council of 381. These Ecumenical Councils provided the first-ever platform for patriarchs, bishops, and theologians of the major Christian urban centers to discuss important theological questions. Moreover, and because they were supported and partially organized by the temporal rulers, all of whom were at least nominally Christian, they also provided a political framework that is sensitive to the practical social and political implications of theological debates and decisions.[22] The fifth century would bring two more Ecumenical Councils (Ephesus in 431 and Chalcedon in 451) after which the fundamental dogmas would be defined and, generally accepted, at least in the major urban centers where the Ecclesial authority was most recognized and intense, namely Rome and Constantinople.

In general, the fourth century councils revolved around Trinitarian disputes and controversies, while the fifth century meetings were preoccupied mostly with the related Christological debates. Christian philosophers and theologians were compelled to play sophisticated games on this rich Greek linguistic apparatus as they struggled to give expression to the central Trintarian and Christological mysteries of the Christian faith; their efforts at sorting out and defining these concepts and terms was to influence the history of theology and philosophy (primarily metaphysics) in unparalleled ways. When the debates were over, the final formula in Greek emerged as *mia ousia – treis hypostases,* translated into Latin as *una essentia – tres personae.* Significantly, rather than the Greek term, *prosopon*, the council opted for *hypostasis* to avoid the 'mask' or mere 'role' connotations originally associated with the Greek *prosopon,* in order to avoid the lurking theological tendency of the time to describe the divine persons of the Holy Trinity at this time as masks or roles or modes of the numerically one divine essence or being (*ousia*) and not three real subsisting realities that individually, equally and totally, but distinctly, possessed that same essence. This lurking tendency was ultimately rejected and marked as the as the dangerous heresy of Sabellian Modalism or Monarchianism – because it struck at the very heart of the Christian belief that God was a real community of distinct persons who eternally and infinitely exchanged knowledge and love among themselves, or better yet, were the very embodiment and defini-

22 Although the idea to distinguish between the political and religious realms had emerged from the teaching of Jesus himself, ("Give to Caeser what is Caeser's and to God what is God's") its radical novelty took a long time to penetrate actual Christian societies. Nonetheless, the distinction had been made and it began to play itself out in a significant way during these Ecumenical Councils.

tion of knowledge and love – a belief that established the essential foundation for all Christian theological thought and life. The Latin term, *persona*, which had been the first translation of *prosopon*, was allowed to stand, however, as it remained virtually free from any modal or 'mask' associations – primarily due to the arduous work of Tertullian who had transformed it in the light of Justin Martyr's reading of Sacred Scripture, and also because as early as the first century BCE, Cicero had already adopted persona as a philosophical concept. It is significant to note here, however, that in adopting persona as a philosophical concept, he preserved some of the early dramaturgical 'role' connotations that it had carried as a direct translation of the Greek *prosopon*, but not as mere 'role', as in 'mask' per se, but as in the permanent roles of real individuals who are obliged to carry out their social obligations in the real 'on the stage' of life.[23]

An unintended consequence of using *hypostasis* rather than *prosopon* in the authoritative Trinitarian definitions is the confusion it would ultimately introduce into all subsequent Christology. I mentioned above that the Arians had first introduced the term *hypostasis* to support their heterodox Trinitarian theology, and that the term was eventually adopted by orthodoxy after substantial qualification and then used precisely to resist Arianism. But few saw what this would mean for Christology. For one thing, in rejecting Arian Trinitarian theology, but accepting the term *hypostasis*, the orthodox Fathers of the Church unwittingly accepted a certain Arian Christological structure, which would manifest itself in the official Christological pronouncements in the following century. Another difficulty would be the need to fit Christological definition into the general "nature" vs. "person" distinction that emerged as a standard and orthodox way of approaching the Trinitarian mystery. The doctrinal history here is extremely complex and way beyond our present scope,[24] but it is necessary to be aware of the general doctrinal developments during these early centuries to understand how the concept of person in Christianity would later evolve.

After the Christological councils of the fifth century, the orthodox doctrine of the Hypostatic Union was to lay the theological foundation for all subsequent developments in Christology; it stated that two different natures, or essences, divine and human, were profoundly and forever united in the one divine person (*hypostasis*) of Christ. To put it another way, if in the Holy Trinity three who-s possessed one what, three divine persons each equally and totally possessed the numerically one and same divine nature, or essence, then in Christ, one who possessed two

23 Zubiri, Xavier, *Theological Dramatic Theory, Volume III*, 209.

24 One of the best accounts of this development can be found in Grillmeier, Aloys, *Christ in Christian Tradition*, London/Oxford: Moybrays, 1975.

what-s, one divine person possessed two natures, a divine nature and a human nature. Although the Chalcedonian formula became (and still is) the orthodox Christological doctrine, the effort, once again, to adjust Christological language into the terms and concepts of the defined Trinitarian doctrines created colossal philosophical and theological problems that would have to be worked out in later generations.[25] I will address in some detail this "working out", as it will play a major role in the story I am attempting to tell about the concept of person in Christianity.

4 Existential Implications

Looking back today from our secular or post-secular worldviews, perhaps we may incline toward interpreting these theological disputes, both at and after the Ecumenical Councils, either as pedantic hair-splitting among elitist, eccentric theologians or linguistic manipulation by powerful politicians for political gain, or some combination of both. Admittedly, there may be some truth to such an assessment, but it is hardly the case that this is ultimately what was at play during these epic meetings. For one thing, literally everyone at the time, Kings, Popes, Princes, and all ordinary people, regardless of how comprehensively Christianity had replaced the formerly prevalent paganism at this time,[26] really believed in some kind of afterlife wherein one's state of life in this world was somehow related to one's state in the next; these Trinitarian and Christological doctrines were directly related to such eschatological concerns. For instance, if Christ were not a divine person, but a mere human person, albeit a human person having a special relationship with the divine (some form of Nestorianism or Arianism), then it would be impossible to assert that his life, death, and resurrection had any supernatural or infinite efficacy. A merely human Christ could serve as a good role model or hero to imitate and thereby inspire people to live noble and moral lives, but how this would relate to questions about an afterlife would still be ambiguous and incomplete. A mere human person could not even save the living from eternal death, let alone bestow new life on those who had already died. Likewise, in the light of the commonly accepted orthodox Christian conviction that 'what has not been adopted has not been redeemed',[27] if Christ had not really "become"

25 See the excellent survey by Meyendorff, John, *Le Christ dans la théologie byzantine*, Paris: Cerf, 1969.
26 I use the term 'paganism' to designate the traditional religions of Rome, and fully acknowledge, as I mention in other parts of this essay, that there is such a thing as 'pagan wisdom'.
27 The saying is attributed to St. Athanasius of Alexandria and is found in a two-part work he wrote titled *Against the Heathen* and *The Incarnation of the Word of God.*

human (Monophysitism), no real redemption could have taken place. Some of my non-Christian (and even a few "Christian") colleagues have pointed out to me here that to speak about salvation in the tonality of 'being saved' restricts soteriology unnecessarily. They have suggested that it is much better to refer to nurturing the connectivity with the divine that is always already present deep within every person regardless of their creed. Such nurturing, they propose, does not require a divine savior per se, but only the right knowledge (gnosis) of how one's own unbalanced, incomplete, state of existence might be recovered and brought back to balance. Death, they assume, may be transcended by identifying more and more with spirit and mind through a series of techniques and disciplined concentrations, which ultimately lead to re-connecting with the divine spark within. While I have taken my colleagues' constructive criticism seriously, it seems to me that it does not take the majesty of death, with all of its arrogance, darkness, and finality, seriously enough. Moreover, it presupposes a mind/body, spirit/matter dualism, which imagines that the core of the human being subsists in some kind of purely spiritual self, which has been polluted by matter and the body, and will eventually be set free through the proper kind of intellectual and spiritual gnostic enlightenment. To be sure, there are plenty of important Neo-Platonic Christian mystics who are sympathetic to some versions of this position. One of the most important, Meister Eckhart, for instance speaks about the divine spark or ground of the soul which, when we intellectually become aware of it, has life-changing salvific effects. But this divine spark or ground of the soul is, for him, indeed a divine person, the Person of the Logos, who, by becoming flesh, re-kindles that barely burning spark, so that it may burn bright eternally, and who, by facing and defeating the ultimate enemy of death, overcomes its evil power, which continually threatens to extinguish this spark forever. Without the divine Logos, who unites his divinity with our humanity, the spark will go out, or worse, will continue to flutter for all eternity in the deepest darkness of isolation and separation from its body.

In any case, as alluded to above, the question about what happens after death was a central one in all ancient civilizations and although the answers varied greatly, and were continuously marked by ambiguity, there was considerable agreement that actions on earth prepared human beings in some way for a future state of either reward or punishment in another world. The idea that there is absolutely no afterlife and that human actions in the present have nothing to do with one's state after death is virtually non-existent in the ancient world, and even today, it is still a minority view – despite the success of modern agnosticism, atheism, scientism, and materialism. The Jewish answer before the time of Christ is also varied and somewhat unclear, but it begins to pave the way toward a clearer, more historically concrete, personal, and intimate answer to this perennial mystery called death – an answer that I will claim reaches a highpoint in Christianity. In the much celebrated poem of the Torah, sometimes referred to as the *Song of Moses*, which Jews still read today between the feasts of Rosh Hashanah and the festival of Tabernacles, and especially in certain sayings among the Hebrew prophets, most notably in Daniel, Isaiah, and Ezekiel, veiled and not so veiled references to a world to come (*Olam Ha-Ba*), wherein the righteous shall inherit eternal life, are clearly discernible.[28] And during Second Temple Judaism, this ultimate redemptive idea becomes more and more connected with belief in a Messianic Age, which is to be inaugurated by an actual historical person. The major point I have been making here is that eschatology is at the center of these long and sometimes bitter Christological disputes that took place in the early centuries, and that to interpret all the doctrinal controversy as driven primarily by worldly concerns is to grossly misinterpret it.

Likewise, with respect to the related Trinitarian debates, if God were not ultimately a community of really distinct persons knowing and loving one another infinitely and eternally – a God that freely creates human beings in his communal image and likeness – then it would be difficult to explain and sustain real authentic community in this world, let alone in another world, and genuine human communal existence would be in danger of losing its ultimate meaning. The eschatological and soteriological dimensions of the Christian faith were highly dependent on Trinitarian theology from the beginning, as Christians came to see early on (St. Augustine) that the entire history of salvation is a gradual revelation of the divine relations (persons), making all history, sacred or secular, ultimately a matter of personal relationships. Once again, the doctrinal disputations over the proper Trinitarian formulas were not pedantic, superfluous, or driven by worldly concerns, but were ultimately motivated by a search for meaning in the next life, a big part of which was to be saved from the tragedy of the present life.

Different heresies brought different challenges, but at the end of the day, to repeat yet once again, tough and resilient insistence on "orthodoxy" was ultimately motivated by a desire to understand the ultimate meaning of history and by very practical and real eschatological concerns that are related to, and perhaps the origins of, what we today would call existential self-understanding. Surely, to speak of self-understanding in the late fourth century is going way out on an anachronistic limb that could break at any moment, but a recent rereading of Augustine's *Confessions* has convinced me that the *Confessions* may be the very "first genuine au-

---

28 Dan 7:13, for instance, refers to a time when a new "divinized" community will perfectly fulfill the will of God. Also, see Zech 8:4–8, and 14:10–11.

tobiography in human history"[29] precisely because he may be one of the very first writers in antiquity to mean almost exactly what we mean today when we use the personal pronoun "I".[30] Without the insights of the theological syntheses achieved in the fourth century that Augustine inherits, I doubt whether this would have been possible, though the ground for such a profound, intimate, and relational use of the term person, and thus of the first personal pronoun, was long in the making, as a careful study of the biblical record, especially of the Psalms, the Prophets, and the Song of Songs, when compared to other ancient literature, clearly demonstrates.

This is not to say that we cannot find what the eminent Christian personalist, Emmanuel Mounier,[31] calls "gropings" for an authentic and decisive notion of the person, both divine and human, in other ancient literary traditions; we certainly can. In India, Vedanta philosophy long debated the issue of the personal vis-à-vis the impersonal, focusing in particular on the mysterious personal mode of Krishna's revelation to Arjuna in the Mahabharata's *Bhagavad-Gita* – a revelation that seems to issue from a kind of Personality of the Godhead revealed through a series of mysterious avatars. And one could make a strong case for a brand of personalism in the genuine continuity perceivable from Homer via Sophocles all the way to Shakespeare, though it is highly probable that Shakespeare himself was creating this continuity by projecting back into his reading of Greek tragedy, comedy, and mythology the deep Christian personalism that shaped so much of his own thought and spirit. And, of course, the Greek philosophers, too, because on the verge of overcoming the seemingly impossible Heraclitian/Parmenidean impasse, were finally able to anticipate the absolute value of the individual person. Socrates' "know thyself", Plato's Timaeus, Aristotle's Ethics, and the Stoics' "moving presentiment of the *caritas generis humani*" are all stunning examples of and monumen-

29 Cahill, Thomas, *How the Irish Saved Civilization*, New York: Doubleday, 1995, 39. Colleagues who specialize in Augustine have alerted me to scholarly debates revolving around whether the *Confessions* was an autobiography, and I am grateful to them for this, but my point is really about what seems to be a way of using the personal pronoun "I" in a way that was genuinely new to antiquity – something commensurate, perhaps, with the way it is used in the profession of faith in the *Apostles' Creed* of the first century: "I" believe in one God! I must qualify my remark here, however, by distancing myself from many contemporary accounts of Augustine's thought which imagine that "the self" is a central Augustinian category and a key to interpreting all his work. For more on this, see the excellent article by Cavadini, John C., "The Darkest Enigma: Reconsidering the Self in Augustine's Thought", *Augustinian Studies* 38, no. 1 (2007) 119–132.

30 Cahill, *How the Irish Saved Civilization*, 39.

31 Of all the important French personalities responsible for the personalist movement in modern times, perhaps no one was as important as Emmanuel Mounier (1905–1950). Considerable attention is given to his thought towards the end of this chapter.

tal achievements in the articulation of personhood. But in terms of penetrating and revealing the deepest mysteries of the personal which Christianity brings about, these all appear to be, as Mounier says, mere groping in the dark. Thus, I am inclined to agree with him when he writes:

> The Incarnation confirms the unity of earth and heaven, of the flesh and the spirit, as soon as the redemptive value of human work has been assumed by grace. The unity of the human race is for the first time both fully and doubly confirmed: every person is created in the image of God, every person is called to the formation of one immense Body, mystical and physical, in the Charity of Christ. This collective history of humanity, of which the Greeks had no idea, now makes sense and even has cosmic meaning. Even the conception of the Trinity, emerging from two centuries of controversy, produces the astounding idea of a Supreme Being which is an intimate dialogue between persons, and is of its very essence the negation of solitude.[32]

At any rate, by using a philosophically sophisticated and rich Greek linguistic apparatus, Christian theologians were able to agree upon some fairly solid solutions to major doctrinal problems, but other problems now emerged. Confusion and ambiguity persisted because, for one thing, not a few of the key Greek terms either did not appear in, or did not clearly correspond to, the Semitic terms and concepts in the Hebrew Bible. Moreover, the very first Greek translation of the Hebrew Bible, the *Septuagint*, often translated Hebrew terms into Greek terms that were not commensurate with, or rarely even used in, the technical language of the Councils.[33] As a result, subsequent Ecumenical Councils were convened to further refine and clarify problematic dogmatic quandaries that stubbornly refused to go away. For believers, at least this much was to be expected, given the innate limits of human language in attempting to give expression to unlimited eternal mysteries. Over time, therefore, another theological approach emerged alongside the rigorous task of doctrinal definition, which, in advocating an epistemology of mystery, insisted that the starting point in Christian theology must first be in determining what the divine reality is not rather than in what it is. This came to be the preferred theological process – not only for the mystics, but for a number of mainline theologians. Known as the *apophatic* approach in Greek and the *via negativa* in Latin, its origin was thoroughly Biblical, rooted in the very first word of the first commandment in the Hebrew Bible – itself a commandment: שמע (*sh'ma*): Hear or Listen or Silence, and in the event of the burning bush wherein Moses

32 Mounier, Emmanuel, *Personalism*, London: Routledge and Kegan Paul LTD, 1952, XIV.

33 This subject is far too vast and complex to enter into here; there are a plethora of excellent works (easily accessible) that deal with the many problems of translating the Bible from Hebrew into Greek and the related doctrinal problems that subsequently emerge.

could not see the divine presence directly. The Judaic tendency to emphasize the ineffable mystery of the divine was carried over into Judeo-Christianity and reached a high-point, perhaps, in the theological poetry of St. Ephrem the Syrian (d. 373). Distressed by the theological debates over Arianism, Ephrem stressed the need for humility and silence before the indescribable presence and workings of the divine reality. A silent and humble disposition was irreplaceable if any knowledge whatsoever of the divine was to be received. For Ephrem, even the Angelic persons, whose powers of investigation are far superior to that of human persons, fall short entirely when it comes to penetrating the divine mystery:

> A thousand thousands stood; ten thousands ten thousands ran. Thousands and ten thousands were not able to investigate the One. All of them in silence, therefore, stood to serve Him. He has no consort except the Child that is from Him. Seeking Him in silence. When Angelic Persons [Watchers] went to investigate they reached silence and are restrained.[34]

But as necessary as this is as a starting point for knowing God and for keeping the commandments (choosing life not death), radical receptive silence is only the beginning; any sustainable spirituality must lead to action – and action, as I believe Heidegger taught, depends on speech, and speech depends on understanding. I am not claiming that Ephrem was unaware of this; his deep mystical poetry reveals a profound understanding of divine mysteries. I am simply underlining what is a perennial problem for all the monotheistic religions: How is it possible using finite, creaturely speech, to speak about an uncreated infinite Creator that is totally other than, and in no way dependent on, creation, and which, strictly speaking,[35] was not compelled to create in the first place? How can such a mystery be understood, and in which way can it be understood? The answers to this fundamental question play a major role in the story I am trying to tell about the concept of person in Christianity, and there are certainly no dearth of them. I shall present some of these momentarily, not here, so as to adhere to the general chronological approach

34 Ephrem, "Hymn on the Nativity, No. 21", in: *Ephrem the Syrian: Hymns*, trans. and introduced by Kathleen McVey, New York: Paulist Press, 1989, 177–178. My emphasis in Italics; I have slightly altered McVey's translation in one place. She translates: "When Watchers [Angels] went..."

35 Whereas the mainline philosophers and theologians of the monotheistic religions agree on God's total otherness and radical independence from Creation, and likewise, on Creation's radical ontological dependence on God, there are differences among them regarding the *manner* in which God creates. Under the influence and inspiration of Plotinus and various Neo-Platonic works, Ibn Sīnā, for instance, will lean towards the doctrine of *emanation* wherein Creation proceeds necessarily and naturally through intermediaries from the very essence of God, something that Thomas will reject, preferring to stress the point that Creation proceeds directly from God via a free and fortuitous act of intellect and will.

I am taking; that is to say that some of the most formidable answers to such questions appear only after, and in many ways, because of, the rise of Islam, to which I now turn.

5 The Rise of Islam

Now within the official and strict, though not always clear, linguistic parameters marking the doctrinal redlines for Christian orthodoxy and heresy set by the first four Ecumenical Councils, linguistic and doctrinal development continued apace with further Christological refinement in subsequent Councils and theological treatises, drawing primarily upon Platonic and Neo-Platonic philosophical achievements for support. This trend would be seriously interrupted, but eventually deepened and complemented due to the rise of Islam. For beginning with the expansion of the *Umayyad Caliphate* into the West in the eighth century, many of Aristotle's writings (that had been translated into Arabic via Syriac during the *'Abbasid caliphate'*) were now translated into Latin and Hebrew, providing new opportunities for Jewish, Christian, and Muslim philosophers and theologians in the West to think and write more accurately about the inscrutable mysteries of their respective faiths. It is hard to overestimate the influence of these Syriac and Arabic translations of, and developmental commentaries on, the ancient "Greek"[36] intellectual heritage, since the scope was so wide and deep: mathematics, music, natural science, medicine, psychology, history, poetry[37], literature, linguistics, philosophy, and theology.

Most relevant for our purposes is the transmission and development of Aristotle's work via the incomparable intellectual efforts of four exceptional geniuses: Ibn Sīnā (ca. 980–1037), Ibn Rushd (1126–1198), Moses Maimonides (1135–1204) and Thomas Aquinas (1225–1274). It is not only impossible, but not necessary, to do justice here to the pivotal and irreplaceable role these thinkers played in the world's intellectual history via only their transmission and development of Aristotle's legacy, let alone all of their other contributions: their work in this one regard alone is

36 I have put "Greek" in quotation marks to draw attention to the fact that, although this rich intellectual heritage is written in Greek, it seems to be rooted in what might be called an original (both oral and written) *world human tradition* that stretches back to the very origins of human beings on earth. Such a bold statement is impossible to defend here, and may be impossible to convincingly defend anywhere, though there is some evidence available.

37 Strictly speaking, there were no translations of Greek poetry into Arabic poetry for various technical challenges; however, portions of the two most famous Greek epic poems, the *Iliad* and the *Odyssey*, do find their way into Arabic early on in varying contexts.

too vast, and their influence already solidly established. What I intend, rather, is only to reference, in a general and chronological way, a few key grains of influence[38] that these Muslim and Jewish thinkers had on the most important Christian thinkers (especially Thomas Aquinas) in terms of how these latter continued the work of cultivating newer and deeper meanings of the concept of person at both the divine and human level – a task inevitably associated with problems concerning language about the concepts of God, Creation, and their mutual relationship – and one which can never be understood properly unless we begin with the crucial contributions of Ibn Sīnā.

Other than the fact that Ibn Sīnā's breathtaking cosmological edifice was rooted ultimately in a Neo-Platonic/Islamic reading of Aristotle's Physics, Metaphysics and, especially, his Ethics with the concept of Eudaimonia thus taking center stage – a reading which would deeply influence Albert the Great and his greatest student, Thomas Aquinas, perhaps the most momentous fact regarding this influence is still one, even to this day, that has not received the attention it deserves: Aquinas' Avicennan doctrine of Creation.[39] One reason why Ibn Sīnā's Islamic synthesis and harmonization of all the ancient science and philosophy he inherited from the Greeks may have been so successful, is that he inherited it in Arabic; that is to say that the Syriac translations of the rich Greek legacy into Syriac and then from Syriac into Arabic were generally undertaken and overseen by Syriac speaking Christians of mostly Jewish descent who knew all three languages and traditions, and who were already privy to the most important translation project in history, though not from Greek into a Semitic language, but from a Semitic language into Greek: the *Septuagint*.

This fact, only now coming to light because of the growing interest in the hitherto much neglected dissemination of Christianity to the East, which began among the Jewish communities of the East, cannot be overemphasized.[40] What Aquinas receives when Ibn Sīnā's work is translated from Arabic into Latin, is an holistic self-consistent worldview that brings together all the various strands of an enormous Platonic, Aristotelian, Neo-Platonic intellectual legacy – unified via Shiite

38 Here and elsewhere in this essay, I do not mean by "influence" mere "borrowing". The latter is virtually never the case when it comes to the truly great and original thinkers throughout history. On the contrary, the influence I speak about is always a dynamic dialectic which presents the occasion for re-thinking and re-assessment.

39 See Pegis, Anton, "St. Thomas and the Origin of Creation", in: F. X. Canfield (ed.), *Philosophy and the Modern Mind*, Detroit: Sacred Heart Seminary, 1961, 49–65.

40 When in Chapter 11 of the *Acts of the Apostles* the author speaks about the early dissemination of Christianity to "none but Jews" this also includes the Jews of Mesopotamia – a fact somewhat overlooked in standard histories of early Christianity.

hermeneutics by a unique genius who deeply assents to, and rationally defends, Biblically commensurate notions of God and Creation present in the Qur'ān. Thus, that Aquinas accepted Ibn Sīnā's basic doctrine of Creation (with some qualification) should not be surprising to Christians; in fact, Ibn Sīnā gives him the tools to better explain the quandary which Augustine had already encountered and responded to in his City of God regarding the relation between the philosophical understanding of an eternal world and the monotheistic belief in Creation.[41]

This is an enormous topic which cannot be explored here. What is pertinent to this inquiry are implications of this highly complex discussion for the development of the concept of person at both the divine and human level, and the insights it provides for deeper and more intricate nuances regarding the *via negativa* and Aquinas' related doctrine of analogy, both of which are so central to the development of the concept of person and, indeed, all theological concepts in orthodox Christianity. One example (there are many) in this context comes from St. Thomas' *Summa Theologiae*[42] wherein he wants to show that, if understood according to the proper metaphysical principles, the eternity of the world in Aristotle's metaphysics does not necessarily contradict the revealed truth concerning Creation ex nihilo (out of nothing); for this reason he critically rejects all previous attempts on the part of Christian theologians (Bonaventure's for instance) to philosophically prove the revealed doctrine of Creation as a free and decisive act without intermediaries and "out of nothing" (*ex nihilo*). At the same time, Thomas does hold that through reason alone the philosophers did reach a basic idea of Creation, but were mistaken in the manner in which God creates since they suggested that God creates through intermediaries and that Creation was necessary. Thomas rejects the traditional phrase "that the world has being after non-being," as if non-being were an absolute substrate on par, as its opposite, with being, and makes a reference to the metaphysics of Ibn Sīnā's *The Healing* to better highlight the distinction between the temporal and ontological spheres. He then stresses that "out of nothing" does not refer primarily to the limits of the sequential or the temporal order, but to a radical ontological dependence; one implication, for the Christian concept of person, is that this ontological dependence is so radical that it allows, without compromising the absolute otherness of God, for an analogy of being (*analogia entis*)[43] be-

41 Thomas Aquinas, *Summa Theologiae:* Question 46, Article 2, see especially *Objection* 1 and the *Reply* to the *Obj.*

42 Ibid., *Objection* 2 and the *Reply* to the *Obj.*

43 I will say a bit more about the importance of this principle below, primarily in the context of the role St. Thomas' reading of Aristotle's *Categories* and *Metaphysics* plays in the evolution of the concept of person. In short, this Aristotelian/Thomistic principle seeks to forge an intelligible approach to the infinite Divine reality, which, strictly speaking, cannot be compared to, or even spo-

tween the Divine Persons of the Holy Trinity and human persons, since the very existence of these latter is held in being by the Divine Persons. To be sure, no such Trinitarian implications are to be found in Ibn Sīnā, but this does not mean that the personal implications (for both God and man) of this approach to the mystery of Creation were lost on him, nor does it mean that these could not have also influenced Aquinas at some level. In fact, according to one of the most important contemporary Western scholars of Islamic philosophy, Henry Corbin, Ibn Sīnā discloses the secret of his own personal mystical experience with the personal dimensions of the Divine or Holy Spirit in what Corbin describes as the "the trilogy of the Mystical Recitals or Romances."[44] Corbin insists that the recitals are not allegories about theoretical truths but real symbols or "figures which typify an intimate personal drama," contending that

> [t]he symbol is both key and silence; it speaks and it does not speak. It can never be explained once and for all. It expands to the degree that each consciousness is progressively summoned by it to unfold – that is to say, to the degree that each consciousness makes the symbol the key to its own transmutation – reminiscent at one level, perhaps, of the insights of Justin Martyr and Tertullian regarding the unfolding of the meaning of role or mask into face or person within the gradual progression of revelation in Sacred Scripture from the Old Testament to the New.[45]

---

ken about by, finite creatures. In many ways, this approach complements the *via negativa* in claiming that only negative statements about God are univocal statements. All positive or affirmative statements about God, such as, for instance, 'the Eternal Son of God *is* a *person*' is mere analogy. I say "mere" because St. Thomas will assert, as will the Fourth Lateran Ecumenical Council, that any similarity that exists in predicating the same term of God and creatures is always outweighed by a greater dissimilarity. In other words, analogy does not simply split the difference between univocal and equivocal terms, but leans towards equivocation. For what is perhaps the best modern philosophical account of this principle see Przywara, Erich, *Analogia Entis: Metaphysics, Original Structure and Universal Rhythm*, trans. John R. Betz/David Bentley Hart, Cambridge: William B. Eerdmans Publishing Company, 2014. Important modern Protestant theologians, especially Karl Barth and his school, strongly reject this Thomistic/Catholic principle and insist on the phrase 'analogy of faith' (*analogia fidei*) rather than 'analogy of being' (*analogia entis*) because of their conviction that all knowledge of God must proceed only from God's self-revelation, and not from God's creation. Some influential modern Greek Orthodox theologians, most notably, John Romanides, claim that both *analogia entis* and *analogia fidei* are Western Christian inventions and clearly alien to what the Fathers of the Church taught.

44 Corbin, Henry, *History of Islamic Philosophy*, London: Kegan Paul International, Institute of Ismaili Studies, 1970, 173. Available online at: http://www.fatuma.net/text/Corbin_-_The_History_of_Islamic_Philosophy.pdf

45 Ibid.

By considering next the precise role of another great Islamic philosopher, Ibn Rushd, on the evolution of the Christian concept of person, I am cognizant of just how one-sided my approach may appear since, as Henry Corbin has definitively proven, the standard Western narrative which sees the debate between al-Ghazālī and Ibn Rushd as the decisive one in the history of Islamic philosophy completely ignores the dynamic development of Islamic thought in the East, which continued apace completely unaffected by this so-called watershed debate.[46] Of course, because my intention is not to deal with the development of Islamic philosophy per se, but only with the very general development of the concept of person in Christianity, and, in particular, with the influence, again, in the most general terms, of Islamic and Jewish thinkers on (primarily) Thomas Aquinas, it is imperative to devote some time to the one whom Aquinas and others simply referred to as the commentator – due to his thorough and painstakingly critical systemic commentaries on almost all of Aristotle's works (nearly forty commentaries in total), the style and content of which clearly had an effect on Thomas's commentaries.

A first point concerns Ibn Rushd's well-known rejection of Ibn Sīnā's interpretation of Aristotle's doctrine of the *active and passive Intellect*; it has been examined extensively by scholars. But what is not as well-known and which deserves more attention, is the repercussion this had on the evolution of the concept of person. For whereas Ibn Sīnā had interpreted Aristotle's *active intellect* as separate from Creation, and universal in nature, making the *passive intellect* intrinsic to the individual created soul (person), Ibn Rushd thought that both the Active and the *passive intellect* were universally present and united in all human beings, and thus separate from any individual human soul (person). Clearly, St. Thomas was much closer to Ibn Sīnā's position and rigorously rejected Ibn Rushd's interpretation; one reason was that Aquinas' relational understanding of the human person – relational, that is to say, having been created in the image and likeness of the Divine Persons (Relations), could not be squared in any way with such a position. Aquinas rejected, in fact, many if not most Averroeian interpretations of Aristotle, which presents a new twist on the *via negativa:* Ibn Rushd, for Thomas, presents a clear and critical way of how not to interpret Aristotle! This did not lessen Thomas' respect for, and even gratitude to, this great Islamic thinker; on the

46 As Corbin rightly points out, the likes of brilliant thinkers in the East such as Naṣīr Ṭūsī, Mīr Dāmād, Mullā Ṣadrā, and Hādi Sabzavāri were totally unaware of what came to be considered the decisive turning point, for good or for ill, whichever side you took, on the fate of Islamic philosophy. Furthermore, even if they had been aware of the debate, it probably would not have mattered much since the problems and discourse they were consumed with were far more significant than the Averroes/al-Ghazālī polemic. See Corbin's masterful treatment of Ibn Rushd in his landmark work, *History of Islamic Philosophy*, 242–249.

contrary, it only increased it because it forced Thomas to sharpen his own arguments and to reinvestigate his own positions in terms of how revelation enlightens reason without contradicting it.

A final remark with respect to Ibn Rushd's influence on Aquinas concerns his commentary on Aristotle's *Categories*, and, in particular, his interpretation of the category of relation, which Aristotle treats in *Chapters Four* and *Seven* of that treatise. As far as we know, this fairly short Aristotelian treatise was one of the very few Greek philosophical texts accessible to the Latin West before the late tenth century and became the text upon which all theoretical speculation on the nature and role of relation(s), in both East and West, was based.[47] Boethius, for instance, in the sixth century, made it available to the Latin West by his accurate Latin translation accompanied by an elaborate and extensive commentary, which means Aquinas had access to both Ibn Rushd's and Boethius' interpretations. The importance of the *Categories* for the evolution of the concept of person in Christianity cannot be overemphasized since it is the only ancient text in the tradition that comprises a philosophical and systemic analysis of the concept of relation, and, as we have seen, it appears alongside the notion of person as helping to define it, since the time of Augustine. It is with Aquinas, however, that the concept of relation as not only associated with, but as profoundly identified as a synonym for, the concept of person, reaches a high point. While inheriting elements of the Platonic and Neo-Platonic tradition through Augustine and Pseudo-Dionysius, he also inherits the rich Neo-Platonic/Aristotelian legacy through the Muslims and the Jews, and is thus able to add substantially to the evolution of the term, person, in the context of the overall development of Christian doctrine. Beginning with his Trinitarian theology and then reverberating down to every other aspect of his work, including his theological anthropology, which we could even call, perhaps somewhat anachronistically, his anthropological personalism. And this new and deeper insight into the centrality of relationality, I claim, again, has as much to do with the Islamic and Jewish readings, translations, and commentaries that Aquinas fortuitously received, as it does with the Latin tradition passed down through Boethius – a tradition that transmitted only some of Aristotle's logical works.

Whatever the case may be, the Syriac/Arabic tradition that Ibn Rushd's receives and develops seems to have played an important role in the development of Aquinas' thought, despite the fact that of the three types of Averroeian commen-

47 For a thorough treatment of the impact of Aristotle's *Categories* on Medieval philosophy in general see Pasnau, Robert, "Latin Aristotle", in: Christopher Shields (ed.), *The Oxford Handbook of Aristotle*, Oxford: Oxford University Press, 2012, 665–689.

taries, in-depth comprehensive commentaries, brief general summaries, and a third kind which is somewhere in between, his commentary on the *Categories* falls into the latter category.[48]

Regarding this early Syriac/Arabic tradition, one of the earliest Arabic translations[49] of Aristotle's term relation, which in Greek literally means 'toward something' (*πρός τι, pros ti*),[50] we find the rich Arabic word, المضاف, *al-muḍāf,* coming from the verb أضاف, *aḍāfa*, which literally means 'to add' or 'to connect' or 'to bring in relation to', but also means 'to be in relation with someone', in fact, 'to receive someone as a guest into one's home'. Thus it conjures up all of the personal intimacy associated with ancient Semitic notions of hospitality as a sacred category, stretching all the way back to Abraham's hospitable welcome of his three mysterious guests.[51] As far as we know, the translator worked from a very early Greek manuscript, but with one of the very first Syriac translations at hand. The implications of this are significant, of course, and I shall return to these momentarily, but first it is necessary to address one final influence on Aquinas before attempting to summarize what all of this means for the development of the concept of person in Christianity. And this final influence comes from the most recognized Jewish scholar and sage of Medieval times, the great Rabbi, Moses Maimonides.

Maimonides' renowned magnum opus, *The Guide of the Perplexed,* is truly a masterpiece and one of the most authoritative works in Jewish intellectual history; in some ways, it is a continuation of the Islamic philosophical tradition initiated by al-Fārābī's attempt to reconcile a Platonic/Aristotelian synthesis of the divine (deeply dependent on Plotinus) with the God of Abraham: for if you extract from the *Guide* his direct references to, and indirect dependence on, al-Fārābī (872–950), the work loses some of its clout. In this regard, given the substantiated influence of Maimonides on Aquinas, al-Fārābī must be added to the list of the most important Islamic thinkers to have influenced Aquinas as well. But since this influence came indirectly, as it were, primarily via the influence of al-Fārābī on Ibn Sīnā, Ibn Rushd, and Maimonides, I cannot address al-Fārābī directly in such a short and general chapter.[52]

---

48 See Charles E. Butterworth's masterful translation and illuminating preface in *Averroes' Middle Commentaries on Aristotle's Categories and De Interpretatione*, Princeton: Princeton University Press, 1983.

49 See: http://folk.uio.no/amundbjo/grar/categoriae/Zenker_ar.pdf.

50 Just meaning the way an object may be related to another object. Examples: double, half, large, master, etc.

51 Gen 18.

52 Neither shall I address al-Ghazālī in this context, as I do not see any clear and direct influences on St. Thomas coming from his work, though the work of Amira Eran argues convincingly for

The points of agreement and disagreement between Maimonides and Aquinas are well established; the latter revolve primarily around the problem of the divine attributes, and the former around the proofs for the existence of God. What is most relevant for our purposes, however, is an area wherein they neither totally agree nor totally disagree, but in which they both were deeply interested and highly innovative: the problem of knowing an unknowable God, and the implications of this knowledge (or lack thereof) for knowing man, who has been made in God's image and likeness.[53] One fundamental conviction upon which both Maimonides and Aquinas fully agree in this regard is that the only chance and possibility of knowing anything at all about God is through the things that God has made, a point St. Paul similarly makes in his Letter to the Romans (1:20). Now, since God has made the human intellect, it is possible to get a glimpse of the nature of the One who made it by reflecting on its structure and mode of operation. Maimonides notices, following Aristotle, three distinct realities here: the intellect itself (*al-ʿaql*), the thinker (*al-ʿāqil*) and the intelligible/intelligized (*al-maʿqūl*). From here he is able to suggest that, since the Biblical text is referring to the incorporeal intellect of man (and not a physical form) when it speaks of man being made in God's image (*ẓelem*), God is also incorporeal. In fact, this is the very first point Maimonides makes in the opening chapter of the *Guide*,[54] which will then enable him to speak of three similar realities in God, but with this great difference: intellect, thinking, and the intelligible or intelligized object of thought, are all the same in the divine substance; they have the same meaning in the one indivisible essence of God. In this, Maimonides' basic understanding of the divine is clearly discernible: God is self-thinking thought (Aristotle) and radically indivisible, inscrutable, beauteous unity (Plotinus) at the same time, and cannot be spoken about using

al-Ghazālī's influence on Maimonides. See her 2001 article, "Al-Ghazālī and Maimonides on the World to Come and Spiritual Pleasures", *Jewish Studies Quarterly* 8:2 (2001), 137–166. Also see in this same regard, Davidson, Herbert, *Moses Maimonides: The Man and His Works*, Oxford: Oxford University Press, 2005.

53 For an excellent in-depth, text centered treatment of the common interest existing between Maimonides and Aquinas on the problem of the knowledge of God, see Rubio, Mercedes, *Aquinas and Maimonides on the Possibility of the Knowledge of God: An Examination of the 'Quaestio De Attributis'*, Dodrecht: Springer, 2006. Available online at: https://link.springer.com/content/pdf/bfm%3A978-1-4020-4747-3%2F1.pdf

54 "Some have been of the opinion that by the Hebrew term *ẓelem*, the shape and figure of a thing is to be understood, and this explanation led men to believe in the corporeality [of the Divine Being]: for they thought that the words 'Let us make man in our *ẓelem*' (Gen i. 26), implied that God had the form of a human being, i.e., that He had figure and shape, and that, consequently, He was corporeal." Maimonides, Moses, *The Guide for the Perplexed*, trans. M. Friedländer, New York: Dover Publications, 1956, 13.

human language, except the language of silence. The language of Biblical revelation (which, as we have seen above, includes a commandment to silence: the first word of the first commandment) moves in the direction of meaningful language about the divine, but only as long as allegory and homonymity are the unwavering, hermeneutical guiding lights.[55] Thomas does not disagree with any of this; in fact, he acknowledges his indebtedness to Maimonides' desire to be faithful to both Aristotle and Biblical revelation, but wants to go further – not based exclusively on his belief in the Incarnation per se, but based on his own desire to be faithful to The Philosopher.

6 The Category of Relation and the Unique Contribution of St. Thomas Aquinas

With this, it is now possible to return to the implications discussed above regarding the importance of the Aristotelian category of relation, and to summarize some of the general points to be gleaned from the brief discourse on the significance of Islamic and Jewish thought on the evolution of the Christian concept of person. Needless to say, there were other important Christian thinkers in this vibrant period, besides Aquinas, who played an important role in the development of our concept; Thomas's teacher, Albert the Great, to mention one, who may have been the first in history to ask so succinctly what it was precisely that the mind could know with certainty apart from revelation. And before him, the role of the Eastern (Greek and Syriac) Fathers of the Church was incredibly important as they continued to reflect upon the possible answers to Tertullian's provocative question: What has Athens to do with Jerusalem? To be sure, Eastern Christian theologians had reflected and written about the meaning of the category of relation in its connection to person long before Aquinas, since not a few of these Church Fathers were responsible for some of the first translations of the *Categories* into Syriac, but direct access to Aristotle in Thomas's own language, coupled with the insights he inherited from these Greek and Syriac Fathers, as well as from the commentaries on the *Categories* and other Aristotelian works by Muslim and Jewish philosophers and theologians, now also available in Latin, enabled Thomas to work out an elaborate and new metaphysical doctrine of analogy in which he could present the orthodox Trinitarian and Christological doctrines in novel and more intelligible ways.

---

55 At one level we could interpret the word "Guide" in the very title of Maimonides' *The Guide for the Perplexed*, as qualified by these two hermeneutical devices.

This was certainly an undertaking waiting to be accomplished because even after the authoritative theological clarifications of the fourth and fifth centuries, and even after the Ecumenical Council of the late seventh century which, in defining that Jesus had a human will,[56] authoritatively brought together and confirmed the two great Christological councils of the fifth century, a key problem of Christology remained in the question of how the Divine Person of the Logos could totally take on and identify with human nature without also becoming a human person, and how two natures, divine and human, infinite and finite, uncreated and created, could ever really be united in a Divine Person. A related difficulty in Trinitarian doctrine revolved around more intelligibly accounting for the real distinction among the Divine Persons, each of whom were said to totally and equally possess the one and same Divine Nature.

In Thomas's metaphysical application of the category of relation in the context of his principle of *analogia entis*, new light was shed on these mysteries of the Christian faith. With respect to the Trinity, by suggesting that the category of relation could help to explain how the real distinction among the Divine Persons resides in the relationship of each to the others and how the term person or *hypostasis* helps to describe the real rather than the merely virtual distinction among the Divine Persons, the mystery of the community of the Divine Persons was preserved. And with respect to Christology, Thomas's ontological interpretation of relation gave new theological impetus to the medieval theories of analogy and proportion, allowing for a more effective way to negotiate the perennial tension between Nestorianism and Monophysitism.[57]

There is much to sort out here. First, it is helpful to recall that Thomas was sympathetic to the *apophatic/via negativa* tradition in Christian theology and agreed with Pseudo-Dionysius and others who claimed that God cannot be named precisely because God's essence cannot be known[58] – a point that Maimonides stressed with convincing rigor, and with which Thomas whole-heartedly agreed. But, as alluded to above, Thomas was also committed to being faithful to

56 Confirming that Jesus had a human will confirms the earlier teaching that he had a human soul and thus a real human nature but raises again the questions concerning the meaning of personhood.

57 As important as these developments were for the proper development of Christian doctrine, other problems would remain and new problems would emerge; with the subsequent attempts to address the theological and related philosophical difficulties in later centuries, new insights emerge into the meaning of the key concept, person.

58 It is worth recalling here St. Thomas' statement: *Rerum essentiae sunt nobis ignotae* (the essence of anything remains unknown to us); if this is true of "anything" then how much more so when it comes to that Divine Being that is "beyond being" so to speak? See Josef Pieper's *In Defense of Philosophy*, San Francisco: Ignatius Press, 1992, 71.

Aristotle, and held fast to the Aristotelian maxim that only when the principle of a thing is known, can it then be said that that thing (whatever it may be) is also really known.

If God, then, is the principle of all things, which we know through both reason and revelation (which Maimonides also held), then the very possibility of knowing anything whatsoever must presuppose that we can know something about God. And if we can know something about God, then we must be able to say something about God since speech and knowledge are interdependent. Neither silence, nor employing a hermeneutics of allegory and homonymity while reading Sacred Scripture, as important as they are, are enough for Thomas: we must be able to speak intelligibly about God. To be sure, Maimonides was certainly moving in this same direction when he spoke about the indivisible unity of the intellect, thinking, and the two-fold object of thought in God, but there he stops and retreats back into a theology of Neo-Platonic silence and a scriptural hermeneutic that, for Thomas, is a mix between brilliant illumination and enigmatic vagueness.

The latter vagueness is to be expected, Thomas would say, because Maimonides does not read his own Jewish Scriptures as ante-types and precursors that point toward fulfillment and greater comprehension in the light of the life, passion, death, and resurrection of Jesus, the Messiah, as a Christian does. But, again, the solution Aquinas offers to the problem of knowledge and language about God, namely, analogy, is not an argument based on his Christian faith, in the Incarnation (though he makes this argument as well in another place) but one motivated by his commitment to the philosophy of Aristotle.

Another related Aristotelian principle that Aquinas wants to hold on to at all costs, and one that also plays a role in his expansion of the doctrine of analogy, is that the act of intellection is always in proportion to the thing known. Now since Creation is finite and God infinite, it would seem that God cannot have knowledge of Creation (nor his creatures) since there is absolutely no proportion between the infinite and finite. To present Thomas's full solution to this problem would necessitate a thorough presentation of his three modes of analogy, which is clearly beyond the scope of this essay. It is enough to point out here that Thomas attempts to overcome this problem in the context of his distinction (found primarily in his *Commentary* on the Sentences of Peter Lombard) between the analogy of proportionality and the analogy of attribution, opting for the latter as the proper mode of analogy when it comes to the question of God knowing Creation (and thus his creatures). That is to say that God's presence in Creation is everywhere and in everything in that he continuously holds all things in existence and therefore he knows Creation as a whole as well as in all its various parts. But wouldn't this imply (and this raised suspicions regarding Thomas' orthodoxy) that Creation is also somehow infinite and eternal? Strictly speaking, Thomas certainly applies the categories of infinity and eternity only to God, but he does stress, as we have seen above in his dependence on Ibn Sīnā, the philosophical difference between temporality and ontology in his doctrine of creation ex-nihilo, and, it will be shown below, that it is possible to speak about relative infinity in Creation.

Incidentally, the orthodoxy of another Dominican Friar, less than a century later, would also infamously be questioned for teachings regarding Creation (among other teachings) and, regrettably, unlike in the case of St. Thomas, these suspicions would remain for many centuries. I am referring to Meister Eckhart, whose profound and unquestionably orthodox writings shed light on another aspect of the answer Thomas gave to the question regarding God's knowledge of Creation, which occasioned, as already mentioned, a new dynamic doctrine of analogy – and one so crucial for the continued Christian cultivation of the philosophical notion of relation in the context of its ever-deepening comprehension of the concept of person.[59]

Once again, without bringing in the doctrine of the Incarnation/Hypostatic Union, which will eventually complement and complete his argument (and in his final Trinitarian doctrinal formulation in the most radical and strongest way possible[60]), Thomas's answer to the problem of God's knowledge of Creation draws upon Aristotle's doctrine of matter/potentiality – form/actuality. He claims that whereas nothing in Creation is absolutely infinite, there is a way to speak about different hierarchical kinds of relative infinities in Creation. He gives the example of wood which is "finite according to its own form, but still it is relatively infinite, inasmuch as it is in potentiality to an infinite number of shapes."[61] He also speaks about the relative infinity of created intellectual power as form united to matter (humans) and finally to created forms that are wholly separated from matter (angels).[62] Therefore, whereas there may not be an analogy of proportionality between an infinite God and a finite Creation, there very well could be an analogy of attribution since a relative infinity does exist in Creation – differently in the different things God has made – hierarchically, as it were. So not only can God know Creation, but the highest creatures on the chain of being, namely angels and humans, can also know God in return. Meister Eckhart will express this Tho-

59 I cannot do justice to this aspect of Eckhart's teachings here but will just point out that it will not be until our own day, and largely due to John Paul II's public pronouncements regarding the importance and orthodoxy of Eckhart's teachings, that his contributions to the personalist movement will be appreciated.

60 For Thomas, of course, any and all knowledge of the Trinitarian mystery is known only through the Incarnation.

61 Thomas Aquinas, *Summa Theologica*, Question 7, Article 1, Part 1: Second Article.

62 Ibid., Reply to Objection 2.

mistic teaching by speaking about an analogy between the "no-thing-ness of God" and the "no-thing-ness of the created intellect" – a real analogy of attribution whereby we can know and thus speak about the unknowable and unspeakable: the mystery of Divine Persons knowing and loving one another. Furthermore, it is precisely through this ability to know and speak of the Divine inner-life that created beings are eventually divinized by participation in it and come even to experience a mutual exchange (though of course not equal) of personal intimate love with the Divine Persons, which can then be communicated to all other created beings via their inter-personal relationships.

Equipped with new linguistic and philosophical tools and insights inherited from the rich metaphysical discourse in Islamic philosophy, which began some four hundred years before he was born (and was still going strong in his day), and supplied with the Jewish development of this rich legacy, especially with Maimonides' elucidation of Aristotle's *self-thinking thought* into a three-fold unity, Thomas was able to make, in conjunction with his Christian colleagues, invaluable contributions to the formulation of the Divine Persons as Divine Relations.

This final formulation, which still stands today in the Catholic Church as *De Fide dogma*, had an immeasurable effect on the Christian concept of person in all subsequent ages. The dogma specifies four divine relations: the relation of the Father to the Son, the Son to the Father, the Father and the Son to the Holy Spirit and the Holy Spirit to the Father and the Son. These two latter relations, according to the dogma, are only virtually distinct and therefore together constitute only one real relation. Thus, there are three *real relations* that are really distinct: the relation of the knower to the known or the speaker to the spoken word, defined as active generation or Fatherhood or the First Divine Person and first real Divine Relation; the relation of the known to the knower or the spoken word to the speaker, defined as receptive generation or Sonship or the Second Divine Person and second real Divine Relation; and finally, the relation of the Holy Spirit to the Father and the Son, defined as receptive spiration (receptive love) or the Third Divine Person and third real Divine Relation – with the relation of the Father and the Son to the Holy Spirit or active spiration (active love) being only virtually distinct from the real Divine Relation of receptive spiration.

The Third Divine Relation, which is a receptive relation, incorporates an active relation (spiration/love) into its constitution which is only virtually distinct from the receptive relation. This is analogous, in some ways, to the three-fold distinction of *self-thinking thought* in Maimonides: Intellect, Act of Intellection, and two-fold Object of Intellection (intelligible/intelligized) with the entire reality as radically one and united. Similarly, the divine relations/persons are one in essence: one *community* of three distinct Who-s – radically united in their infinite and eternal exchange of *personal knowledge* and *love*. One eternal speaker (Father) speaks one eternal word (Son), who goes out from the father in knowledge and love, and returns to the father in love (Holy Spirit) and knowledge. In this way, the elevation of the category of relation (in Aristotle's Categories) from one of nine other accidents qualifying substance to the level of substance itself (hypostasis) sheds new light on how the real distinction among the *divine persons* (hypostases) resides in the *real relation* of each to the others. I would venture to say here that the ancient insight of Tertullian regarding the persons of the Trinity as each having a distinct and permanent role as persons-in-dialogue was finally vindicated and its potential realized by St. Thomas' contributions. I say this because the very rationality of the dialogical principle of prosopographic exegesis was essentially established on the rational and coherent principles of logical Aristotelian debate which Aquinas perfected.[63]

This new attempt to address challenging problems in Trinitarian theology had significant repercussions on related Christological theological development, as was the case in the fifth century when theologians had to define Christological doctrines using the terms and concepts that had become accepted orthodoxy as a result of the Ecumenical Councils of the fourth century. As I stated above in my brief references to the early Ecumenical Councils, the theological and philosophical problems this caused were huge and not to be "solved" quickly. In fact, it is only after the new Thomistic insights into the concepts of person and relation, accompanied by a new doctrine of analogy, that some of these problems could be dealt with more satisfactorily. To be sure, the chronology of how these theological complications were dealt with in the early centuries, as compared to Thomas' age, was quite different; in the fourth century, the major terms and concepts were being presented for the first time, as an attempt to give expression to the fundamental Christian belief of the Trinity, again, for the first time, whereby by St. Thomas' time, these major terms and concepts had been reflected on in the light of Christian living and thought, for nearly a thousand years.

With St. Thomas' new ontological interpretation of relation,[64] anticipated by the early Syriac and Arabic translations and commentaries, the entire transmission process of which provides the ground for Thomas's predilection to bring out the metaphysical texture of the *Categories*, fresh life was given to the older me-

63 See Andresen, "Zur Entstehung und Geschichte des trinitarischen Personenbegriffs", 39.
64 Some contemporary experts specializing in Greek logic reject such interpretations and argue that this section of the *Categories* is clearly a technical treatment of the role of relational predicates in Aristotelian logic and nothing else. Such a view usually results from reading the *Categories* in isolation from the rest of Aristotle's corpus and apart from the tradition of how his overall thought was first received and transmitted and finally synthesized with the work of his master, Plato, by Plotinus.

dieval theories of analogy and proportion, which in turn allowed for a more coherent expression of the perennial Christological mysteries regarding how a divine person could totally take on and identify with human nature without also becoming a human person, and regarding how a divine (uncreated) and human (created) nature could even be compared, let alone united.

To what extent Thomism was successful in this regard is a matter of incredibly complex theological and historical debate, but there is general agreement in both Eastern and Western mainline Christianity, among theologians and historians, that the introduction of Aristotle's entire corpus into the Latin West via Arabic and the subsequent Jewish, Christian, and Islamic discourse that followed, raised philosophical and theological speculation to new heights and had a profound and lasting effect on the entire world's intellectual history and its key concepts, one of the most important of which, I am suggesting, is the concept of person.

7 Towards Modernity

Although the concept of person gradually and slowly began in Modernity to be distanced from its Christian theological origins, there can be no doubt that most of the ideas and thinking underlying it, as well as the concept itself, originally emerged within a dynamic back-and-forth between human thought (primarily Greek literature and philosophy) and early Christian faith. There can also be no doubt that the growth of this concept and the associated evolution of ideas and thinking accompanying it through history, were a result of attempts to give coherent expression to the ineffable Trinitarian and Christological mysteries of the Christian faith. Finally, it is also certain that a new stage of development occurred after the rise of Islam in the context of a dynamic Judeo-Christian-Islamic interplay in which the concept took on new meanings and greater significance. Thus, even though the concept began in Modernity to move away from the context of its origin and growth, it is still the case that it (nor any of the complex and rich ideas that lie behind and next to it) cannot be understood or appreciated properly (nor can it really live) completely apart from this context.

If this essay were a history of the concept of person in Christianity, it would be inexcusable to jump abruptly (as I will now) from the High Middle Ages to seventeenth century Mechanical Philosophy, thereby ignoring the Late Middle Ages in the West, the impact of the Reformation, and all the significant and related developments in Asia. But as it is not a history per se, and only a brief and partial reflection that draws upon the history of mainline Western Christianity as a general guideline, I shall now move to a key movement in the seventeenth century that marks the beginning of modern philosophy and contributes significantly to what is called Modernity and Post-Modernity.[65] Nonetheless, even though my essay is not strictly historical, it does follow a general chronology in terms of the development of the concept of person in Christianity and thus requires at least a word about Martin Luther. If our topic were the concept of freedom in Christianity, as in a previous KCID publication,[66] much more would have to be said about the significant and positive role of Martin Luther in this regard, but when it comes to the concept of person, things are a bit different and more nuanced.

8 Martin Luther and the Reformation

At one level, the concepts of freedom and person and their respective historical developments are intertwined and complementary. And given the enormous influence of Luther's famous and powerful 1520 treatise, *On Christian Liberty*,[67] one could argue that the Christian concept of person was deepened and developed in a significant way. His intense emphasis on how God's radical forgiveness sets his children free in such a way as to give them new births as Christian persons cannot be overlooked or downplayed. However, due to his severe attack on philosophy in general and Aristotelian philosophy in particular, which went a long way in alienating Christian philosophy from Christian theology, many qualifications are needed here.

First, because the very notion of Christian philosophy was rejected by Luther, he neglected much of the rich relational aspects of the concept of person (especially with respect to Trinitarian Theology) that had emerged in the Christian philosophical/theological tradition. One could argue that this led to an erosion of traditional Trinitarian theology and thus paved the way for a brand of Unitarianism. Prominent Unitarians today,[68] in fact, celebrate Luther's implicit rejection of the traditional Catholic definition of person in terms of relation, and only wish that he had been more explicit in this rejection since this would have shown that

65 The term is misleading. I prefer "late-modernity" since so many of the philosophical presuppositions of Modernity are still operative today.

66 Volume 3 (2019).

67 The work appeared in 1520 in both German, under the title of *Von der Freiheit eines Christenmenschen*, and in Latin, under the title of *De Libertate Christiana*. Though it is unclear which version was written first, there is agreement on its almost unprecedented influence in Christian Europe due to its power of expression, its content, and because of the newly invented printing press, which accounted for wide and timely dissemination.

68 See the work of Dale Tuggy here, a prominent American scholar who strongly argues, on the basis of the Bible, for Unitarianism against the doctrine of the Trinity.

the very idea of the Trinity is a Catholic invention, influenced by Greek philosophy, and cannot be found in the New Testament.

Since philosophy historically played a momentous role in the development of the concept of person, divine, angelic, and human, one could argue that Luther's contribution (given his rejection of Christian philosophy) to the development of the concept of person was minimal. Luther's thought certainly did contribute to the notion of the individual freedom of human persons, but less so to the concept of person per se and surely not to the movement of Christian philosophical personalism that has been so decisive for mainline Christianity in the twentieth and twenty-first centuries – a movement I will soon have much to say about.

9 The Mechanical Philosophy

The mechanical philosophy of the seventeenth century directly challenged the rich ontological/dialogical concept of person as being-in-relation to another, which, in the light of the dynamic analogy of being between divine, angelic, and human persons that St. Thomas introduced, had grown out of deeper and deeper reflection on the mystery of the communal inner-life of the Trinity. This challenge came by way of an attempt to mathematize reality resulting in that static and unfortunate dualistic notion of the human being as an atomistic independent thinking individual: *Cogito Ergo Sum.* This Cartesian experiment, garnering support along the way from British Empiricism, which incongruously both reacted against but also supported this experiment,[69] was the beginning, for all intents and purposes,[70] of the eventual emancipation of the concept of person from theological and metaphysical discourse and categories, resulting in a shift from the rich and hard-earned unearthing of personal individuality to the impoverished reductionist ideology of individual-ism. In many ways, this new ideology parasitically fed upon the discovery of personal uniqueness and partially eclipsed the comprehension of the essentially relational and dialogical qualities of the concept of person which had been in the making for thousands of years, beginning, perhaps, as I have already suggested, with the *Song of Moses*, the *Psalms of David* and the *Song of Solomon* (*Song of Songs*). And although individualism is still alive and well today, especially in its economic guise, otherwise known as unbridled consumer capitalism, it

69 In short, although Locke challenged Descartes' idea of innate ideas, he accepted the Cartesian epistemic suggestion that in the act of knowing extra-mental reality, it is the idea of a thing in the mind which is the direct object of knowledge, and not the extra-mental reality itself.
70 There are antecedents, of course, but they are not necessary to detail for the purposes of this essay.

did not take long before the seventeenth century mechanical philosophy upon which it was based[71] was so severely challenged in the very next century by Blake in England and Goethe in Germany, and then in the nineteenth and early twentieth century by existentialism and phenomenology, that the richer relational notion of person made a formidable comeback in what finally came to be known in the 1930s in Europe as a new Christian philosophical personal-ism.

But we should not be too hard on Descartes, since, although his dualistic philosophy gave birth in various ways to individualism and radical idealism, both of which undermine genuine individuality and a relational/dialogical understanding of the concept of person, simultaneously and paradoxically, his *Cogito* promotes a species of philosophical personal-ism, that sounds as if it could have been uttered just yesterday, although it has been almost four hundred years ago now. Just imagine how forceful his use of the personal pronoun, "I", really is in "I think, therefore I am," as the very starting point of his powerful meditation on personal existence. And any person is invited into this new philosophical meditation; this, of course, is the beginning of modern philosophy in the West. It is hard to appreciate just how radical this was then unless we also consider how overly impersonal and systemically arid much of scholastic philosophy had become by Descartes's time – a far cry from the vibrant and novel synthesis bequeathed to scholastic philosophy some four centuries earlier by Thomas's fresh synthesis (inspired by Islamic and Jewish thought) of the new Aristotelian ideas with Platonic, Patristic, Biblical, and Ecclesial doctrines and speculations.

At one level, then, Descartes re-introduces the dynamic notion of person which he had inherited from his own Catholic intellectual tradition, but at the same time, scatters the scientistic[72] seeds for what nearly becomes its ultimate demise. Blaise Pascal, too, could be mentioned here as a contemporary of Descartes in France, who, like him, simultaneously both promotes and, because of his Jansenist views of human nature, undermines the growing personal existentialist consciousness among many intellectuals in Europe at that time. And something similar could be said, perhaps, of the French Catholic theologian, priest, and philosopher of the same period, Nicolas Malebranche, whose Treatise on Ethics, as a fruit of

71 There is a sense in which British Empiricism also provides foundations for the destructive types of modern individualism and capitalism I am referring to here, even though it is at odds with much of the so-called Rationalistic Mechanical philosophy.

72 In my discussion below of John Henry Newman's *An Essay in Aid of a Grammar of Assent*, I will describe in some detail what I mean by 'scientism'.

his attempted synthesis of Descartes and St. Augustine, also paradoxically promoted and challenged the radically relational idea of the human person.[73]

10 Eighteenth and Early Nineteenth Century Developments

The story of the evolution of the concept of person in European Christianity becomes increasingly complex and even more convoluted as we move into the eighteenth and early nineteenth centuries, not only because of the paradoxical ideas in the previous century put forth by Descartes, Pascal, Malebranche, and Rousseau, but primarily due to the growing separation between Christian philosophy and Christian theology on the one hand (caused in part by the Reformation), and of both from all the other branches of knowledge (caused in part by modern science) on the other. Great philosophers, such as Leibniz and Kant, who, as believing Christians, still do metaphysics and thus dabble in Christian theology, each did their part in paving the way for what was quickly becoming not only a mere trend or movement in anthropology, but a full-blown philosophy of personalism in its own right. Just as with those key seventeenth-century thinkers, who paradoxically both promoted and challenged the radically relational idea of the human person, something similar can be detected in both Leibniz and Kant.[74]

The same cannot be said, however, about Blake and Goethe, both of whom promote the centrality of the person and the person's relational/dialogical character much more consistently and powerfully through their literature and poetry than any pure system of philosophy did at this time, though neither can be considered

---

73 I have already suggested how "modern" Augustine's use of the first-person singular pronoun, "I", is. In this regard, Malebranche's work is quite appealing. For a thorough treatment of whether and in which way Descartes was an Augustinian, see Menn, Stephen, *Descartes and Augustine*, Cambridge: Cambridge University Press, 1998.

74 Because Kant so convincingly stressed that human beings are not means, but ends in themselves, due to their inherent dignity, his thought may be seen as anticipating personalism. At the same time, however, as personalist thought develops in the nineteenth century, it strongly reacts against what could be defined as the Kantian-inspired rationalism of eighteenth century Enlightenment thought, which, in over-emphasizing the constitutive role of human rationality, promotes an individualistic, rationalistic, autonomous, self-enclosed notion of the human being (which could lead to a 'racist'-leaning anthropology) that devalues the *whole* person, who, above all else, according to personalist thought, is constituted *as a person* only in *loving intimate relation* to other persons.

a Christian personalist per se in that they veered too far away from the traditional Christian creed.

In the nineteenth century, Kierkegaard,[75] Marx, Nietzsche, Schelling, and Newman all deserve special mention for continuing, though in immensely dissimilar ways and for vastly different reasons, the process leading to Christian personalism par excellence in the twentieth century. What all these thinkers hold in common, however, is their passionate aversion to the many facets of dehumanizing impersonalization on the one hand and to the various individualistic strands moving in the opposite direction on the other. These two extremes are traced back, with varying points of emphasis, to Cartesianism, features of British Empiricism and eighteenth-century Enlightenment rationalism, and especially to Hegel's absolute idealism.[76] To be sure, hardly anyone at this time totally escapes certain aspects of the extremes they are trying to avoid; these four fundamental philosophical movements were simply too dominant and omnipresent to be completely tran-

75 From the perspective of what I shall call "normative Christian personalism" (though I am cognizant of the problems using such a phrase causes), Kierkegaard plays a particularly important role in its development in that he saw the inevitable danger in the grand Thomistic synthesis between Christian faith and Aristotelian reason. For him, being a Christian was based on a deeply personal, existential choice that one has to make all alone without the support of philosophy and reason, thus his famous "leap of faith". This insight alone anticipates and promotes Christian personalism in a singularly dynamic way, but the false dilemma he created by suggesting that Hegel's rationalism/absolute idealism was the inevitable consequence of the Thomistic synthesis and that one could find no support for faith in reason, or, more importantly in *other persons*, undermines normative Christian personalism because it promotes a radical individualism and introduces an unnecessary duality between faith and reason. It may be true that Hegel's work turns Christianity into something it is not, but it is also true that Hegel's system is not simply the necessary and only outcome of the attempt in the High Middle Ages to reconcile Aristotle and Christianity. For more on this, see MacIntyre, *A Short History of Ethics*, 211.

76 How and whether this idealism is connected to what has been described as Hegelian-inspired totalitarianism and/or racism, two related ideologies that all genuine personalists abhor, is much too complex to treat here. Politicians are forever taking the ideas of philosophers out of context to justify their own wicked ends, and there is ample evidence of Colonial masters using the philosophers to justify all kinds of injustices, including the African slave trade, but this is a topic far too complex to treat here. I will say, however, in cautious support of Hegel's idealism, that whereas absolute idealism can lead to impersonalization, it is also true that without it a different kind of impersonalism may also emerge. In other words, without a universal category of personhood that carries some ontological weight and sophistication, or without an idea/metaphysical concept that is both dynamic and immutable to ground the meaning of personhood, then other dubious categories or criteria enter to fill the void – criteria such as *autonomy*, for instance. The problem then is that we are tricked into believing that we have the autonomy to "draw the line between human beings who are persons and human beings who are not." See David Walsh's masterful work, *Politics of the Person 'as the' Politics of Being*, Notre Dame: University of Notre Dame Press, 2016, 20.

scended, but with respect to paving the way for Christian personalism, Schelling, and especially Newman, manage to partially transcend the dominant trends of their times in remarkable ways.

With regard to Schelling, perhaps no single work in the nineteenth century was as influential in overcoming radical idealism (a perennial enemy of personalism) as was his 1809 treatise, *Philosophical Investigations into the Essence of Human Freedom*, though its momentous importance was not duly recognized for at least a century. In fact, if Martin Heidegger's work plays a role in the story I am trying to tell, one contribution[77] comes by way of calling attention to the brilliance of Schelling's treatise, though I am not sure he really did it justice.[78] Regard-

77 In saying "one contribution" I do not mean to imply that there were many. Although Heidegger's early interest was in philosophical anthropology, he seems to have made a conscious decision to turn away from it, and thus was in no position to make any lasting contributions to the philosophy of personalism.

78 What is most valuable about Schelling's work, in my judgment, is the way he is able to reintroduce the subject of theodicy into the discussion of human freedom and personality in the context of a "mysticism" which echoes classical Abrahamic mystical themes. Ultimately, Schelling sees that to grapple adequately with the question of human freedom, it is first necessary to wrestle with the question of God's freedom – in particular to reconcile the notion of God's freedom with his necessary nature. To do this, he introduces two different ways of being: (*ground* – the principle of contraction) and (*ex-istence* – the principle of expansion); these principles can be found everywhere in nature and capture the ways in which things "are" in the world. The balance in nature emerges when these two "opposing" principles maintain their proper relation. When *ground* (or contraction) remains the "condition for" *existence* (or expansion) then the whole remains balanced and harmonious, but when *ground* becomes that for which the whole is conditioned, evil emerges. In God, according to Schelling, ground and existence, contraction and expansion, inwardness and outwardness, hiding and revelation, always maintain their proper relation, but not without divine struggle. This struggle is precisely where God's freedom is located, while his necessity lies in the fact that the result of this struggle is secure: *ground* never becomes absolute, but remains the condition for the self-revelation of the absolute. Although the two ways of being are in tension, they together form the unity of being where the true absolute (God) can be. Nature, too, and everything in it, including (and especially) human beings, enjoy these same two ways of being, but the outcome of the struggle is far from secure: evil often emerges because the contracting principle seeks to dominate the principle of expansion. In spite of Schopenhauer's scathing critique of Schelling, claiming, as he does, that Schelling is simply aping Kant while pretending to be original, I suggest that, on the contrary, Schelling goes much deeper than, and even reveals the inherent weaknesses in, Kant by identifying evil with a distortion of the *relation* between *ground* and *existence* whereby *ground* (or inwardness) becomes the perversely self-conscious, *rational* will of the *individual* that is no longer in real relation to anything but itself. In this, it is possible to read Schelling as not only not aping Kant but criticizing a particular form of Kantian rationalism. At any rate, if Schopenhauer's criticisms of Schelling are not accurate, there is still room for serious criticism of Schelling in that he never really tells us why the proper relation is maintained in God and not in nature or in human beings. In this, although his account of freedom and evil is weightier

less of whether Schelling slips into yet another species of the Hegelian idealism he is so bent on overcoming, and irrespective of how he seems to invent new and improved forms of both "Nestorianism" and "Monophysitism" simultaneously, it cannot be denied that he offers new and powerful insights into human freedom and personality by forcing all discussion of these themes to take seriously, once again, and as a starting point in the anthropological discussion, the nature and freedom of the divine persons.[79] Of course, Schelling's "personalism" if we can call it that, is not Christian personalism per se because, like Hegel before him, and so many German idealists after him, the traditional Christian doctrines were interpreted mythologically, not literally – not to mention that the hard and fast distinction between the Jesus of history and the Christ of faith was a fundamental and unquestioned assumption in these idealist systems.

11 John Henry Newman

Concerning Newman, his contributions to Christian personalism par excellence cannot be overstated. On the epistemological plane, his success at carving out a middle-way between the two major epistemological tendencies of the nineteenth century, namely, formalism and subjectivism, represented best in that century, perhaps, by Frege's 'logic' and Mill's 'contingent fact'. He creates the conditions necessary for a new Christian personalism not susceptible to relativism, and completely faithful to the traditional Christian creed while powerfully rejecting any idealist separation of the Jesus of history from the Christ of faith. His achievements in this regard come primarily by way of his 'real/notional' distinction and his 'cumulation of probability' theory which he presents in his *Essay in Aid of a Grammar of*

---

than virtually any other philosophical account in the nineteenth century, it is by no means the final word. Schelling's work reminds me of certain trends in the mystical traditions of the monotheistic religions. In particular, the Lurianic School of Kabbala with its emphasis on the teaching of *tsimtsum* (divine withdrawal) wherein God (in order to create out of nothing) becomes absent to himself in a kind of *contraction* so that "the void" or "nothingness" can come into existence, sounds a lot like Schelling's *ground/existence* distinction since this void (in the Lurianic School) then becomes the "place" where freedom originates. In Christian mysticism, too, one finds echoes of this in both the ancient and modern periods; one contemporary Christian mystic, Fernando Rielo, writes in terms strikingly close to what we find in the Lurianic School and is certainly commensurate with what Schelling proposes.

79 For a relatively new translation of, and excellent introduction to, Schelling's contributions in this regard see Schelling, F. W. J., *Philosophical Investigations into the Essence of Human Freedom*, trans. and intro. Jeff Love and Johannes Schmidt, New York: State University of New York Press, 2006, IX–XXIX.

Assent.[80] Newman resisted subjectivism because it called into question those objective truths that formalism held dear, but he also resisted formalism because of the way it limited truth and certainty to quantitative objective facts that could be mathematically demonstrated. By assigning such truths to the realm of the 'notional' and subjective or personal truths to the realm of the 'real', he was able to strike a balance by defining certainty as a notional assent to a real assent. This definition of certainty directly challenged Locke's entire theory of knowledge and his famed 'degrees of assent' theory, as well as the Cartesian epistemic structure upon which it was partially based. In this way he was also able to retain the personal dimensions of subjectivism without giving in to its relativistic tendencies. And by linking notional assent to 'theological' truth and real assent to 'religious' truth, he opened a new understanding of the long-held Christian conviction regarding the complementary nature of the relation between faith and reason, which, if not Thomistic per se, certainly complemented and continued Aquinas' synthesis of philosophy and theology in a way that laid an important part of the foundation upon which Christian personalism would eventually be constructed.

To understand the significance of Newman's contributions, it is necessary to examine in greater detail his Grammar of Assent, in which, as mentioned above, his 'real/notional' distinction and 'cumulation of probability' theory were presented. Significantly, the Grammar is the development of a letter written to a personal friend in response to that friend's (William Froude) formidable challenge of Newman's attempt to bridge the gap between probability and certainty in the realm of religious faith. Froude, a brilliant mathematician, inventor, and engineer had confided in Newman by expressing his serious doubts regarding the fundamental truths of the Christian faith – truths, which Newman claimed, could be known with certainty rather than with mere probability. Froude's substantive epistemological objection confronted Newman in a deeply personal way, compelling him to answer so as to dispel doubt and strengthen his friend's faith. When the opposite result ensued (Froude formally rejected the Christian faith and left the Church) Newman went back to his letter to strengthen and clarify his argument; the outcome, many years later, was the publication of the *Grammar.* The first thing Newman sought to do in this work was to expose the inadequacy that Cartesian-inspired Lockean epistemology which sought to map out the human mind and its human processes according to the principles of Newtonian physics entailed – one result of which would be the claim that certainty in formal assent could only be justified by mathematical proof. This would also limit certainty in general to,

80 Originally published in 1870; all references here come from the Image Books edition published in 1955.

and define all knowledge (science) as, only those truths that could be demonstrated by the proofs of mathematical physics or analogous proofs.

As a mathematician and scientist, Newman considered such an approach to be myopically scientistic, rather than genuinely scientific and tried to show the irreplaceable and vital role of the personal dimension in the act of knowing, suggesting that it was not only possible to be certain of things that could not be proven using the methods of mathematical demonstration, but that the most intimate and important truths, those upon which most people base their lives, were truths that could not be proven in this way. In some ways, this was commensurate with Pascal's "the heart has reasons which the mind knows not," but Newman went well beyond Pascal in that he provided an entirely new epistemic approach to support this claim. The real/notional distinction was central to this approach in that he applied it not only to assent, but to doubt and inference as well, thereby identifying six different kinds of apprehensions related to three different kinds of propositions: interrogative, conditional, and unconditional.[81]

Although he was primarily interested in the apprehension of real assent to real, categorical, unconditional propositions as related to the personal religious faith of a believer, he deals in detail with the other five apprehensions to clarify precisely what he means by real assent, as he attempts to "describe the structure of thought and to discover its mechanisms and movements by using thought itself as a starting point, in the same way as grammar derives the laws of language from current use."[82] The reference to "current use" in his analogy here is telling because he is emphasizing the category of the personal in both language and thought. And though his somewhat heady epistemic analysis and refined philosophical psychology is in part meant for the sophisticated challenges presented by the educated

81 Thus (1) real interrogative propositions (Was Newman a sage?) accompanied by an apprehension of real doubt; (2) notional interrogative propositions (Are most sages philosophers?) accompanied by an apprehension of notional doubt; (3) real conditional propositions (Newman, therefore, was a sage) accompanied by an apprehension of real inference; (4) notional conditional propositions (Most sages, therefore, are philosophers) accompanied by an apprehension of notional inference; (5) real, categorical, unconditional propositions (Newman was a sage) accompanied by an apprehension of real assent; and notional, categorical, unconditional propositions (Most sages are philosophers) accompanied by an apprehension of notional assent. Apprehension, for Newman, is not meant to cover all kinds of propositional attitudes; he is most interested in numbers (4) and (5) which he describes as "especially cognate" (*Grammar*, 31) that is to say, most naturally and most often found together. His interest in these distinctions, and particularly in number (4) is subordinate to his ultimate desire to write a complete "Grammar" of number (5) as it relates to the *personal* religious faith of a believer.

82 *Grammar*, 62.

Froude, Newman was perennially interested in the problems of certainty related to those with a lower level of education.

The seminal ideas regarding the problem of certainty, in fact, had been growing in Newman ever since his exposure as a young man at Oxford to Joseph Butler's *The Analogy of Religion*; in 1860, ten years before the publication of the Grammar, he wrote: "If I wrote a new work, it would deal with the popular, practical, and personal Proofs of Christianity, precisely inasmuch as they stand as antipodes of scientific demonstration."[83] These personal proofs, as he indicates here, are the exact opposite of the mathematical proofs his friends demanded from him as justification for joining the Catholic Church, but were based, nonetheless, on solid personal evidence, knowledge, and experience which, although subjective, could still produce, he claimed, concrete facts and objective certainty that could be cross-examined and held up to scrutiny. In this regard, Newman introduced the novel idea of "personal first principles" – analogous to Aristotle's first principles of thought that the intellect grasps intuitively and upon which all scientific demonstration, syllogistic and inductive, is then based.

He identified one of the first principles as the personal conscience, which, like Aristotle's first principles of thought (law of non-contradiction, etc.), was self-evident, certain, and logically impossible to prove through formal inference, but the truth of which guaranteed all subsequent truth, not only in the realm of formal inference, but also as related to morally good or bad choice (assent) and behavior. Moreover, this particular personal first principle was precisely what made rational and social human beings different in kind from the other animals, and, more importantly, for the purposes of this inquiry, what made them persons.

In addition to his new phenomenological description and analysis of assent, via his 'real/notional' distinction, Newman also introduced the novel and related idea of 'cumulation of probability', further deepening what I would describe as his profoundly personal philosophical psychology. Just as by defining certainty as a notional assent to a real assent, Newman sought to bring the two dominant and opposed epistemic tendencies of the nineteenth century to a common middle ground, so too with his 'cumulation of probability' theory he attempted to satisfy the requirement of proof and demonstration in reasoning demanded by formalism as well as the requirements of subjectivism, which insists on the importance of 'the personal' and 'the contingent'. To best appreciate this theory, it is necessary to examine it in the context of Newman's discussion of inference, which he sharply distinguishes from assent in that the former is conditional, while the latter (assent) is

---

83 Walgrave, J. H., *Newman the Theologian*, trans. A. V. Littledale, New York: Sheed and Ward, 1960, 61.

unconditional. What he wants to show is how a conditional act (inference) can lead to an unconditional act (assent). He acknowledges that while formal inference is a "sort of symbol of assent and even bears upon action, [it] neither determines our principles, nor our ultimate judgments – it is neither the test of truth, nor the adequate basis of assent."[84] Therefore, with respect to concrete, non-abstract, particular, primary existential truths, ultimate judgments, and personal facts, inference can only conclude probabilities.

In searching for 'real' personal first principles to guarantee certainty in the realm of religious truth, Newman was not calling into question the certainty of 'notional' first principles of thought as delineated by Aristotle, to which we assent because they are self-evident, intuitive truths immediately grasped with certainty by the intellect. What he wants, in fact, is something analogous, truths that cannot be logically demonstrated through formal inference, but upon which all logical inference then takes place: rock-bottom truths that anchor not only formal reasoning at the notional level, but certain truths that anchor all personal and existential reasoning. Once we possess certitude of these personal first principles, we can then reason (via the cumulation of probability) to the certainty of those truths that matter most – truths about God and his revelation, truths about the meaning of our concrete lives, truths about our personal vocations and missions. To be sure, Newman's cumulation of probability theory has nothing to do with adding probabilities together; he was fully aware of the fact that adding probabilities together in a quantitative way lessens probability rather than increases it.[85] What he means by cumulation here has to do with a deeply personal and intimate convergence of probabilities that is so strong and so convincing that we cannot help but see it: analogous to the force of the self-evident principles of thought that impose themselves on the mind intuitively when the mind is open, healthy, and properly receptive to what is experienced by the whole person, beginning with what we perceive through the physical senses.

In the light of Newman's pioneering epistemic work, new insights emerge into the mystery of what it means for a human person to think and speak about, and even to personally relate to, the Divine Persons of the Trinity – revealed in the Divine Person of Christ, who becomes a man through a woman. In this regard, and in the context of Newman's teaching on the 'development of Christian doctrine', he prophetically declares that one area of Catholic theology best positioned to develop substantially in the future is that of Mariology, a development which will engender new and greater insights into Christology and Eschatology – insights that will in-

84 *Grammar*, 229.

85 Two propositions of 90 % each when added together decreases their joint probability to 81 %.

evitably play a key role in the full-blown emergence of twentieth-century Catholic personalism.[86]

12 Normative Christian Personalism

Considering the incredibly complex and paradoxical nature of the nineteenth century intellectual scene, it is no wonder that although by the early part of the twentieth century there is a clearly recognizable philosophical personalism, there are also fairly diverse strands and almost contradictory expressions of the same. There are a number of core of thinkers who best embody, however, what I call normative Christian personalism, and without whom it could not have persisted as forcefully as it has, even up until the present day; Newman, in this regard, as I have tried to show, is foundational. I will only mention, of course, the influential (more or less orthodox) Christian thinkers[87] since this is an essay on the concept of person in Christianity, though the work of a Jewish philosopher, Martin Buber (1878–1965), warrants special mention as his foundational work lent incredible energy to the movement as a whole; but this raises the question regarding the relation between Christian personalism and personalist philosophy, which is also relevant to the reason I have had to straddle both philosophy and theology in my somewhat loose historical approach to our topic.

Roughly speaking, Buber's overall concern was 'theological' when we consider his interest in world religions, but what he actually did was more specifically 'philosophical/epistemological' in that he showed that scientism misses the deepest personal truth about knowledge: it is not our knowledge of the external universe that gives life its ultimate meaning but the inner life of personal relationships, an inner

86 I would like to suggest that this mature Catholic personalism, for which Newman paves the way, transcends even the dynamic personalism that resulted from the brilliant synthesis achieved in the High Middle Ages by St. Thomas Aquinas. But it goes almost without saying, at least in the light of Newman's own teaching about the principles governing the development and growth of doctrine, that these contemporary philosophical and theological achievements would not have been possible without the achievements in this regard during the High Middle Ages. The question of how Thomistic Newman's entire philosophical and theological approach was, is a complicated one, with arguments on both sides: one claiming he was thoroughly Thomistic, and others claiming he undermines Thomism. Both arguments, in my judgment, are flawed. See my revised doctoral dissertation: Alam, Edward J., *Out of the Shadows Into Reality*, Beirut: Notre Dame University Press, 2000, 133–186.

87 Given the context of the present project, the importance of the remarkably gifted and prophetic Muslim thinker, Mohammed Lahbabi (1922–1993) of Morocco, who embodies what could certainly be called an Islamic Personalism, should be mentioned here.

universe of meaning to which the reality of world religions has always testified. By specifying the difference between the I-it and the I-Thou relationship in his little 1923 masterpiece, *Ich und Du*, he offered a philosophical/epistemological reinterpretation not only of his own Jewish religion, but of all the world religions, including Christianity. Many Christian personalists were influenced by his thought and sought to develop it philosophically, but without always paying close attention to the precise relation between metaphysics and theology. Perhaps we could say that the most successful and influential Christian thinkers in this regard, Karol Wojtyla (1920–2005) and his preferred theologian, Hans Urs von Balthasar (1905–1988), were the ones who attempted to express what this precise relation consists of and who achieved what we might describe as a philosophical theology of Christian personalism, based on a dialectical and analogical relationship between philosophy and theology.[88]

At any rate, without the students of Edmund Husserl (1859–1938)[89] namely, Max Scheler (1874–1928), Edith Stein (1891–1942), Roman Ingarden (1893–1970),

---

88 This possibility is explored by John R. Betz, in his "After Heidegger and Marion: The Task of Metaphysics Today", *Modern Theology* 34, no. 4 (2018), 565–597. Betz summarizes what he attempted to do in this work in another article (forthcoming in the same journal) this way: "In keeping with the radical and ultimate dissimilarity proper to any genuine analogy, however, I also affirmed a dialectical moment proper to analogical metaphysics, specifically, regarding the analogy between philosophical and theological metaphysics. For Christ as the Word made flesh and a fortiori as the Word of the Cross, spells the end of philosophical metaphysics – the end, that is, of any metaphysics that presumes to get along without the light of revelation, once it is given, and so ends up positing itself, i. e., one or another construct, idolatrously in its place. There is therefore something to be said for the concerns of the Reformers, the dialectical theology of Barth, and every critique of onto-theology inspired by Heidegger. But this ending of philosophical metaphysics, I argued, is at the same time its real beginning. For if philosophy relinquishes its presumption to grasp the divine on its own terms (Gen 3:6–7) and submits to the passion of faith, in short, if it dies to itself, it is also born again as theological metaphysics. In other words, philosophical and theological metaphysics are bridged through a kind of death. Hence, I argued for a dialectical analogy as the proper form of the relationship between them, and therewith for the possibility of an ecumenical metaphysics that is able to do justice to the concerns of the Reformed and Lutheran traditions, as represented by theologians as different as the Reformed Barth and the Lutheran theologian Oswald Bayer, but also philosophical critics of metaphysics such as Heidegger and Marion."

89 Some legitimate questions, which I cannot answer here, with respect to Husserl's role in the evolution of the concept of person, and thus his influence on the philosophy of personalism, are the following: Is all Christian personalism ultimately rooted in Husserl's phenomenological move, given that his students are in many ways credited with being the 'creators' of the personalist philosophical movement? What is the precise relation between Husserl's phenomenology and personalism? It is interesting and relevant here to compare Husserl's phenomenological turn, announced in 1900, to Newman's achievements some forty years earlier. For if we are to characterize phenomenology as "an attempt to bring philosophy back from abstract metaphysical speculation

and Dietrich von Hildebrand (1889–1977); and without the French contribution by way of Jacque Maritain (1882–1973), Gabriel Marcel (1889–1973), and Emmanuel Mounier (1905–1950), in addition to what we might call a Russian personalism, best embodied perhaps in the work of Vladimir Solovyov (1853–1900) and Nikolai Berdyaev (1874–1948), there would not be, as it were, a philosophy (or philosophical theology) of Christian personalism. Of course, there are other highly significant twentieth century thinkers here; I have already mentioned Wojtyla and von Balthasar, but we could certainly add Joseph Ratzinger (b. 1927) and Raimon Panikkar (1918–2010) to the list as well.[90]

---

wrapped up in pseudo-problems, in order to come into contact with the matters themselves, with concrete living experience," as Dermot Moran does in his *Introduction to Phenomenology*, New York: Routledge, 2000, xiii, then we would have to credit Newman as an independent co-founder of phenomenology. In this regard, Ono Ekeh's very thoughtful piece: "The Phenomenological Context and Transcendentalism of John Henry Newman and Edmund Husserl", *Newman Studies Journal* 5, no. 1 (2008), 35–50, is very helpful. Going further, we might even say that not only is Newman's phenomenology earlier, but in some ways remains more faithful to this original impetus since he steers clear of any neo-Cartesian, neo-Kantian, idealist slippage into new forms of abstract metaphysical speculation on epistemological pseudo-problems divorced from the concrete facts of everyday experience – slippage into which Husserl's Hegelian-inspired emphasis on consciousness is forever prone. It could be argued that such an emphasis might be at the root of some racist-leaning blind-spots in the work of two of his most illustrious and brilliant students: Martin Heidegger and Hanna Arendt. The former's anti-Semitism, which is well-known, and the latter's alleged tendency towards what we might call anti-American Black-*ism*, go completely against the grain of Christian personalism, which proclaims the absolute dignity and unique value of each and every person.

90 This 'list' could easily be expanded to include not only great thinkers and scholars, but great personalities who allowed their personalist ideas to shape their lives in exemplary ways, and whose spheres of influence were wide and significant. I would hasten to mention in this regard, Dorothy Day (1897–1980) and Charles Malik (1906–1987). Needless to say, it is impossible to do justice here to the importance of all these extraordinary personalities (and there are others as well) on the development and articulation of Christian personalism, in which, we might say, our key concept reaches new heights and depths in the course of its evolution. I will allude here to a point I made at the beginning of this essay: that an actual concrete extra-mental reality corresponds to the mental concept (person) we are examining here and is forever (potentially at least) being deepened by the very reality, i.e., real persons, it attempts to name. In this sense, the idea or concept behind the original word which named the extra-mental reality, in this case, *prosopon*, is not only never lost, but is (or ought to be) continually refreshed by concrete interaction with the very thing it originally sought to name.

13 Conclusion

In closing, and in the light of my own Christian faith, I will now attempt to present a synopsis of the most central insights of Christian personalism, as I have been able to understand and internalize them after many years of not only reflecting on what it means to be a person, but on actually striving to be one. I approach the meaning of Christian faith here in the two dimensions of exclusivity and inclusivity while emphasizing both the complementary relation and ultimate unity of these two dimensions. With respect to inclusivity, my remarks are guided by two passages from the New Testament and by Gabriel Marcel's account of human knowledge founded on an opposition between believing and objectifying, which leads to the epistemic suggestion that faith is the act of renouncing abstraction.[91] The first passage, from the *Letter to the Hebrews*, describes faith or belief as "the assurance of things hoped for, the conviction of things not yet seen"; the second comes from the *Letter to the Galatians*, wherein Paul argues that because Abraham's faith was reckoned to him as righteousness, and that because in Abraham all the nations are blessed, any and all who believe are the legitimate children of Abraham. These passages, in addition to Marcel's epistemic suggestion regarding the essence of what it means to believe,[92] are applicable to any genuinely religious person, and even to someone who does not assent to a traditional religious creed, but who has an intuitive trust in the meaningfulness of life and death and who strives to cultivate intellectual and moral virtue.

---

91 For this and much that follows concerning the thought of Marcel, I rely upon M. J. Cosgriff's thesis, "The Spiritual growth of the person in the thought of Gabriel Marcel",.

92 Shedding light on Marcel's understanding of what it means to believe in the context of Marcel's conception of personal spiritual growth, Cosgriff states: "Man, [Marcel] says, has to believe in the intelligibility of the world so as not to give in to the temptation of thinking that it is absurd, and so as to acquire a real vision of it that is near to poetry. As well, man for Marcel has to believe in himself, so that he is not the captive of determinisms, to believe in the other in order to truly love him, and to believe in God, so that He is not an 'object' or an impersonal principle. Faith in all these senses shows that to reach 'being', for Marcel, the person cannot make do with speculation: Faith, in Marcel's sense here, is not first a mode of knowledge but of being. Marcel's faith demands the recognition of a new type of intelligibility which is essentially a mystery, as Marcel understands it. While objectifying thought cannot lead into the structure of reality, the faith which according to Marcel introduces man into truth is not able to be verified as science checks its hypotheses. Secondary reflection plays its part here by separating from the reality, to which the person adheres by faith, all that comes from objectifying, abstraction and the scientific spirit." From Cosgriff's thesis, "The Spiritual growth of the person in the thought of Gabriel Marcel", 27–28, available online; see reference above in footnote 84.

Christian personalism accepts these universal and inclusive descriptions of the meaning of faith, but would simply qualify the Biblical definition and say, "the assurance of things that every person, in so far as they are genuine persons, hopes for; the conviction held by every person, again, in so far as they are genuine persons, of those things not yet seen." But what are these things we may ask? And does it not beg the question to speak here of genuine persons? What is a genuine person? Well, we might begin by describing what these things are not, as a way of approaching the mystery of what genuine personhood is since the Christian personalist asserts, in keeping with clearly defined and consistent Christian doctrine, that Satan and the demons, whose names are legion for they are many in their convoluted divisions and perverse fragmentations, are also persons. But they are persons without personality, beings who have lost all being, and thus have nothing left to do but to feed parasitically on true being, genuine personhood and personality. The things hoped for by genuine persons, then, are diametrically opposed to the things lusted after by shadow persons: closed egocentric individualism as opposed to open individuality in loving communion; violent fragmentation as opposed to calm and peaceful unity; despairing fear as opposed to truthful pleasure and beauty; deceitful destructive violence and meaningless pain as opposed to loving joy and pleasant rest; crushing confusion and complexes as opposed to clarity and enlightening contemplation; endless darkness as opposed to infinite light; in a word, the isolated Self as opposed to the related Person.

On this account, then Socrates' know thyself had nothing to do with the quintessentially modern Cartesian obsession with a search for that thing called the self, as if the self were some sort of static core in the center of each human being just waiting to be discovered through the right scientific, psychological, moral, ontological, spiritual or technical, technique.[93] The fundamental impetus for the ancients and the overriding concern for the Christian or any other kind of personalist for that matter, is a kind of existential revival of the ancient impetus: knowing thyself means knowing what it means to be human, knowing how to live a good life, a life of virtue – not some sort of isolated and safe individualistic life of either deceptive self-righteous piety, or arrogant self-indulgence, but of an unpredictable, even dangerous life of flux and constant struggle to discover what it means to be a being essentially constituted towards the concrete, not abstract, other, what it means to be honest, to be courageous, to be chaste, to be faithful, to be prudent, to be daring, to be generous, to be grateful, to be magnanimous, to be humble, to be human, to be a person – ever aware that, tomorrow, this might mean something slightly

93 See, once again, John C. Cavadini's article, "The Darkest Enigma: Reconsidering the Self in Augustine's Thought", 119–132.

different than what it meant today precisely because we are and are being constituted each hour, each day as persons in relation to everything[94] and everyone around and next to us – beginning in the womb, continuing and intensifying as we grow more complex, at first totally receptive and then gradually becoming active. What we hear, smell, taste, touch, and finally and most powerfully, what we see when we emerge from the womb, what our brain perceives, what we suffer, everything we experience, is constantly constituting who and what we are. When we begin to grow and mature, this radical receptivity gradually turns into an activity. And then what we choose to do, to think about, to see, to hear, to touch, begins to mold our constitution in new dynamic ways. Our acts of virtue and vice, our being present or absent to the present moment, our thoughts, our desires, all constitute us as beings in relation, no, more than that, as relations by definition, persons par excellence, capable of uniting with the objects of our thought, our contemplation, our desires.

Now regarding the exclusive dimension of Christian faith, which, as I have said, I approach as complementing inclusivity, not contradicting it, I am likewise guided by the New Testament and insights from both Marcel, and especially, Emmanuel Mounier, who brilliantly stressed the need to protect individuality by sharply distinguishing collectivity from community. Of course, many others in the 1930s warned against the evils of impersonal totalitarianism, but the Christian Personalists had critiqued collectivism by juxtaposing it to a metaphysical community – to the greatest and central mystery of Christianity, the mystery of the loving communion enjoyed by the persons of the Holy Trinity, one of which was believed to reveal and communicate this divine presence to all of humanity by becoming a man through a woman. In his time, Mounier attempted to show how these two central mysteries of Christianity deepen the belief in the unique and personal individuality of every human being, without falling into the deadly pit of individualism.

Thus, in spite of how much Christian personalism has in common with other kinds of personalism, it is forever rooted in and distinguished by the central Christian mysteries of the Holy Trinity and the Incarnation, which inevitably entail a kind of exclusivity, but not one that necessarily excludes non-Christians, which it cannot, because it is grounded in the belief that there is only one God, Creator of all, who calls, through His Word, each and every person into intimate relationship. Paul's famous expression, "I have fought the good fight," is interpreted by Christian personalism as Paul responding to this concrete call to renounce abstract impersonalism and fight the fight of becoming a person, a personality, who participates in the battle of the angelic persons to pave the way for the divine persons to

94 All sentient beings including plants and animals.

divinize man, that is to say, to assist men in their struggle to become persons who will then enjoy intimate relations with the divine persons as sons of the Father, brothers of the Son, and brides of the Holy Spirit. The Incarnation, then, for the Christian personalist, is a fulfillment of the promise to Abraham to bless, through him and his nation, all the nations of the world. Paul's good fight is won in that he has allowed himself to be personalized by the personal victory of the divine person (*hypostasis*) Christ over all deadly tendencies to reduce a person to a mere object. In this the two ancient meanings of and words for person, *hypostasis* and *prósōpon*, are newly united and each and every person is invited to take his place in what the New Testament calls the Heavenly Jerusalem, at the Eternal Wedding Feast of God's Word – an incarnate divine Person – a sacrificial Lamb who through his death and resurrection has overcome all dehumanization and impersonal abstraction. The invitation to the Wedding Feast of the Lamb, then, according to the Christian personalist, is extended to all creatures, to all of creation, inviting human beings to become persons, to take on personality, so that they may enter the feast not as a mere guest, but as the bride herself, in all of the exclusive intimacy this naturally entails, and where the joyful wedding song (*Song of Songs*) is sung eternally, but not as *Cogito Ergo Sum.* I think, therefore I am, but rather as, I am loved, therefore I exist; I love, therefore I continue to exist.

Bibliography

Alam, Edward J., *Out of the Shadows Into Reality*, Beirut: Notre Dame University Press, 2000.

Andresen, Carl, "Zur Entstehung und Geschichte des trinitarischen Personenbegriffs", *ZNW* 52 (1961), 1–38.

Aquinas, Thomas, *Summa Theologica. First Complete American Edition in Three Volumes*, trans. Fathers of the English Dominican Province, New York: Benzinger Brothers, Inc., 1947.

Averroes, *Averroes' Middle Commentaries on Aristotle's Categories and De Interpretatione*, trans. and intro. Charles E. Butterworth, Princeton: Princeton University Press, 1983.

Balthasar, Hans Urs von, *Theo-Drama: Theological Dramatic Theory*, trans. Graham Harrison, San Francisco: Ignatius Press, 1992.

Betz, John R., "After Heidegger and Marion: The Task of Metaphysics Today," *Modern Theology* 34, no. 4 (2018), 565–597.

Cahill, Thomas, *How the Irish Saved Civilization*, New York: Doubleday, 1995.

Cavadini, John C., "The Darkest Enigma: Reconsidering the Self in Augustine's Thought", *Augustinian Studies* 38, no. 1 (2007) 119–132.

Corbin, Henry, *History of Islamic Philosophy*, London: Kegan Paul International, Institute of Ismaili Studies, 1970.

Cosgriff, M. J., "The Spiritual growth of the person in the thought of Gabriel Marcel", MA Thesis, University of Canterbury, 1977. https://ir.canterbury.ac.nz/bitstream/handle/10092/8629/cosgriff_thesis.pdf;sequence=1.

Davidson, Herbert, *Moses Maimonides: The Man and His Works*, Oxford: Oxford University Press, 2005.

Ekeh, Ono, “The Phenomenological Context and Transcendentalism of John Henry Newman and Edmund Husserl”, *Newman Studies Journal* 5, no. 1 (2008), 35–50.
Ephrem, “Hymn on the Nativity, No. 21”, in: Ephrem the Syrian, *Hymns*, trans. and introduced by Kathleen McVey, New York: Paulist Press, 1989, 177–178.
Eran, Amira, “Al-Ghazālī and Maimonides on the World to Come and Spiritual Pleasures”, *Jewish Studies Quarterly* 8, no. 2 (2001), 137–166.
Grillmeier, Aloys, *Christ in Christian Tradition*, London/Oxford: Moybrays, 1975.
Lossky, Vladimir, *The Mystical Theology of the Eastern Church*, New York, 1976.
Luther, Martin, On Christian Liberty (German: *Von der Freiheit eines Christenmenschen*; Latin: *De Libertate Christiana*), trans. W. A. Lambert, Ausburg: Fortress, 2003.
MacIntyre, Alasdair, *A Short History of Ethics*, New York: Routledge Classics, 2002.
Maimonides, Moses, *The Guide for the Perplexed*, trans. M. Friedländer, New York: Dover Publications, 1956.
Menn, Stephen, *Descartes and Augustine*, Cambridge: Cambridge University Press, 1998.
Meyendorff, John, *Le Christ dans la théologie byzantine*, Paris: Cerf, 1969.
Moran, Dermot, *Introduction to Phenomenology*, New York: Routledge, 2000.
Mounier, Emmanuel, *Personalism*, London: Routledge and Kegan Paul LTD, 1952.
Newman, John Henry, *An Essay in Aid of a Grammar of Assent*, 1870.
Newman, John Henry, *An Essay in Aid of a Grammar of Assent*, intro. Étienne Gilson, Garden City, N.Y.: Image Books, 1955.
Pasnau, Robert, “Latin Aristotle”, in: Christopher Shields (ed.), *The Oxford Handbook of Aristotle*, Oxford: Oxford University Press, 2012, 665–689.
Pegis, Anton, “St. Thomas and the Origin of Creation”, in: F. X. Canfield (ed.), *Philosophy and the Modern Mind*, Detroit: Sacred Heart Seminary, 1961, 49–65.
Pieper, Josef, *In Defense of Philosophy*, San Francisco: Ignatius Press, 1992.
Polkinghorne, J. (ed.), *The Trinity and an Entangled World: Relationality in Physical Science and Theology*, Grand Rapids: Eerdmans, 2010.
Powers, Richard, *The Overstory*, New York: W. W. Norton & Company, 2018.
Przywara, Erich, Analogia Entis: *Metaphysics, Original Structure and Universal Rhythm*, trans. John R. Betz, David Bentley Hart, Cambridge: William B. Eerdmans Publishing Company, 2014.
Ratzinger, Joseph, “Concerning the notion of person in theology”, *Communio* 17 (Fall, 1990), 439–454.
Ratzinger, Joseph, *Dogma and Preaching: Applying Christian Doctrine to Daily Life*, San Francisco: Ignatius Press, 2005.
Rubio, Mercedes, *Aquinas and Maimonides on the possibility of the Knowledge of God: An Examination of the ‘Quaestio De Attributis’*, Dodrecht: Springer, 2006.
Schelling, F. W. J., *Philosophical Investigations into the Essence of Human Freedom*, trans. and intro. Jeff Love/Johannes Schmidt, New York: State University of New York Press, 2006.
Walgrave, J. H., *Newman the Theologian*, trans. A. V. Littledale, New York: Sheed and Ward, 1960.
Walsh, David, *Politics of the Person ‘as the’ Politics of Being*, Notre Dame: University of Notre Dame Press, 2016.
Zubiri, Xavier, *On Essence*, Washington, D. C.: The Catholic University of America Press, 1980.

Suggestions For Further Reading

Alam, Edward J., *Out of the Shadows into Reality: A Philosophical Exposition of John H. Newman's Essay in Aid of a Grammar of Assent*, Beirut: Notre Dame University Press, 2000.

Balthasar, Hans Urs von, *Theo-Drama: Theological Dramatic Theory, Volume III*, trans. Graham Harrison, San Francisco: Ignatius Press, 1992.

Davidson, Herbert, *Moses Maimonides: The Man and His Works*, Oxford: Oxford University Press, 2005.

Grillmeier, Aloys, *Christ in Christian Tradition*, London/Oxford: Moybrays, 1975.

Meyendorff, John, *Le Christ dans la théologie byzantine*, Paris: Cerf, 1969.

Mounier, Emmanuel, *Personalism*, London: Routledge and Kegan Paul LTD, 1952.

Pegis, Anton, "St. Thomas and the Origin of Creation", in: F. X. Canfield (ed.), *Philosophy and the Modern Mind*, Detroit: Sacred Heart Seminary, 1961, 49–65.

Polkinghorne, John (ed.), *The Trinity and an Entangled World: Relationality in Physical Science and Theology*, Grand Rapids: Eerdmans, 2010.

Ratzinger, Joseph, *Dogma and Preaching: Applying Christian Doctrine to Daily Life*, trans. Michael J. Miller/Matthew J. O'Connell, San Francisco: Ignatius Press, 2005.

Thomas Aquinas, *Summa Theologica.* First Complete American Edition in Three Volumes, trans. Fathers of the English Dominican Province, New York: Benzinger Brothers, Inc., 1947.

Zubiri, Xavier, *On Essence*, trans. Robert Caponigri, Washington, D. C.: The Catholic University of America Press, 1980.

Peter G. Riddell

The Concept of Person in Islam

1 Introduction

Much ink has been spilt in preparing studies of various key Islamic actors and personalities: God, angels, various prophets (including Muḥammad and Jesus), and so forth. But less attention has been devoted to views of humanity in the Qur'ān and its associated literature. This chapter will begin with an overview of the key anthropological vocabulary of Qur'ān and *ḥadīth.* It will then explore diverse Islamic scholarly approaches to what it means to be human: creation and its purposes; humans and their nature; the debates surrounding free will; sin; the relationship between humans and God, and so forth. Also considered in this chapter will be various issues of contemporary debate: dignity of person, contraception, abortion, cloning and de-personalization.[1]

The core ritual duties for Muslims are expressed in the Five Pillars: pronouncing the creed; the compulsory daily prayers; giving in charity; fasting in the month of Ramadan; and performing the pilgrimage to the sacred sites in Arabia once in their life if they have the means to do so. Additionally, some Muslim thinkers and schools add *jihād* as a sixth pillar, with debates regarding the primary application of this term in the modern world. Most Muslims learn the pillars, and it is impressed upon them that performance of these pillars is a pre-requisite for a favorable outcome on the Day of Judgment.

In addition, Muslims are called to hold to core articles of faith: belief in God, angels, revealed books, prophets, the Day of Resurrection and Judgment, and God's decrees. The Qur'ān provides a concise listing of most of the pillars and beliefs:

> 2:177: Goodness does not consist in turning your face towards East or West. The truly good are those who believe in God and the Last Day, in the angels, the Scripture, and the prophets; who give away some of their wealth, however much they cherish it, to their relatives, to orphans, the needy, travellers and beggars, and to liberate those in bondage; those who keep up the prayer and pay the prescribed alms; who keep pledges whenever they make them; who

---

1 This chapter represents the culmination of a research project undertaken on and off in various contexts over a twenty-year period. Previous reports on research-in-progress appeared as articles by the author in the journals *Evangelical Quarterly* and the *South Asian Review of Religion and Philosophy,* both listed in the bibliography. The analytical framework used in this chapter has been trialed in various versions across the life of this research project.

https://doi.org/10.1515/9783110756715-004

> are steadfast in misfortune, adversity, and times of danger. These are the ones who are true, and it is they who are aware of God.[2]

However, it is noteworthy that although the pillars are set for Muslim people to carry out, and the articles of faith specify what Muslim people should believe about the nature of God, the angels, prophets, revealed books, Judgment Day and God's decrees, nowhere in these duties and beliefs is it spelt out what Muslims should believe about their own natures. The pillars and beliefs do not specify what it means to be human. It is to this question that this chapter devotes its attention.

2 Anthropological Vocabulary and the Sources of the Concept of Person in the Qur'ān and Ḥadīth

Before considering the history of thinking and debates about the concept of 'person' by Islamic scholars, it would be helpful to first identify what Arabic terms are used in the Qur'ān and *ḥadīth* to represent the notion of "person" within its full semantic range.

The primary texts employ several Arabic terms which are associated with the concept of 'person': *shakhṣ, insān/an-nās, nafs/anfus, rajul/rijāl,* and *wajh/wujūh.* Context often plays a role in determining which term is used in relevant verses.

2.1 *Shakhṣ*

The root *sh-kh-ṣ* appears on two occasions in the Qur'ān (14:42 as *tashkhaṣu*; 21:97 as *shākhiṣatun*),[3] where it signifies "that which is fixed in horror, as the sight of the eyes"[4]. It does not signify "an individual person" in Qur'anic usage.

The *ḥadīth* collection of Muslim b. al-Ḥajjāj (d. 875/261) includes the following: "*wa-lā shakhṣa aḥabbu ilayhi al-midḥatu min allāhi min ajli dhālika wa'ada Allāhu*

2 Unless otherwise specified, all renderings of Qur'anic text into English in this paper will be drawn from Abdel Haleem, M. A. S., *The Qur'ān: A New Translation*, Oxford: Oxford University Press, 2004.

3 Melbourne School of Theology, *Qur'an Tools*, https://qurantools.mst.edu.au/auth/login.php (accessed on 04.08.2022).

4 Penrice, J., *A Dictionary and Glossary of the Koran*, London: King & Co., 1873, 76.

al-jannata"[5] (and no one [*wa lā shakhṣ*] is more fond of praise than God on account of which God has promised Paradise). Lane's explanation is as follows: "*[shakhṣ]* being here metaphorically used for *[dhāt – essence]* or the meaning is, a person *[shakhṣ]* should not be more jealous than God."[6] This usage of *shakhṣ* to refer to God in the *ḥadīth* collection of Muslim is best understood metaphorically rather than as a physical being.

However, *shakhṣ* is commonly used in this sense in post-Qur'anic literary and modern Arabic variants. Lane records it as signifying "[t]he body, or bodily or corporeal form or figure or substance, (...) of a man", leading to it being a common form for "[a] man himself; a man's self, or person; (...) a being; an individual". As such, it is synonymous with *nafs*, according to Lane.[7]

2.2 *Insān/an-nās*

The root *'-n-s* appears in various forms on ninety-seven occasions in the Qur'ān.[8] For example, *an-nās* appears in 2:224: "[Believers], do not allow your oaths in God's name to hinder you from doing good, being mindful of God and making peace between people [*an-nās*]. God hears and knows everything."

Penrice's dictionary of the Qur'ān explains this term as signifying "[m]en, people; a collective noun regarded as the plural of (*insān*) A man, human being (...)". In this sense, it is cognate with Hebrew *īsh/anashīm* (man/people).[9]

Penrice continues: "It is said to embrace also the Genii and evil spirits, but I can recall no passage in the Koran where it is so employed."[10] This semantic extension of *an-nās* as a generic term to cover *jinn* as well as people is unlikely within a Qur'anic context, given the explicit differentiation drawn in 114:6, the chapter which is itself called *Sūrat an-nās:* "Say, 'I seek refuge with the Lord of people [*an-nās*], the Controller of people, the God of people, against the harm of the slink-

5 an-Naysābūrī, Muslim b. al-Ḥajjāj, "Ṣaḥīḥ Muslim, Book 19, *Ḥadīth* 22," published online: *Sunnah.com*, https://sunnah.com/muslim/19/22 (accessed on 04.08.2022). The Arabic text of *ḥadīth* references throughout this chapter are sourced from the sunnah.com website. English translations of these references at the same website have been substantially revised by the author.

6 Lane, Edward W., *An Arabic-English Lexicon*, vol. 4, London: Williams and Norgate, 1872, 1517.

7 Lane, *Lexicon*, vol. 4, 1517.

8 Melbourne School of Theology, *Qur'an Tools*, https://qurantools.mst.edu.au/auth/login.php (accessed on 04.08.2022).

9 Brown, F., *The New Brown-Driver-Briggs-Gesenius Hebrew and English Lexicon*, Massachusetts: Hendrickson Publishers, 1979, 35–36.

10 Penrice, *Dictionary*, 152.

ing whisperer – who whispers into the hearts of people – whether they be jinn [*al-jinnah*] or people [*an-nās*].'"

Yusuf Ali comments on this verse as follows: "This last clause amplifies the description of the sources from which the whisper of evil may emanate: they may be men whom you may see or invisible spirits of evil working within."[11]

Thus, we have a clear distinction: *an-nās* refers to visible created human beings, or mankind in a generic sense, while the *jinn* are invisible created beings. They share createdness but not personhood. Kassis' *Concordance* trawls through a copious set of verses where *an-nās* occurs and supports the above understanding when it concludes that *an-nās* means "mankind, men, people, others".[12]

As for the *ḥadīth* collections, the term *an-nās* also appears with a similar sense of "mankind, people" as seen in the following example taken from the collection of at-Tirmidhī (824–892/209–279): "Am I not the most deserving of it among the people (…)" [*a-lastu aḥaqqa an-nāsi bihā*].[13]

2.3 *Nafs/Anfus*

Nafs/anfus is the term most commonly rendered by "person/people" in the Qur'ān, appearing on 298 occasions.[14] The following verse emphasizes the distinction between *nafs* and *an-nās:*

> 5:32: On account of [his deed], We decreed to the Children of Israel that if anyone kills a person [*nafsan*] – unless in retribution for murder or spreading corruption in the land – it is as if he kills all mankind [*an-nās*], while if any saves a life it is as if he saves the lives of all mankind [*an-nās*]. Our messengers came to them with clear signs, but many of them continued to commit excesses in the land.

Nafs is defined in Penrice's *Dictionary of the Qur'ān* as "A soul, a living soul or person".[15] It is cognate with Hebrew *nefesh* ("soul, living being, life, self, person, desire, appetite, emotion, and passion").[16] Thus the two key terms, *an-nās* and *nafs*, are variously translated as "person"; the former is a generic term signifying

11 Ali, Yusuf, *The Meaning of the Holy Qur'ān*, Beltsville: Amana Publications, 1989, note 6310.
12 Kassis, H. E., *A Concordance of the Qur'ān*, Berkeley: University of California Press, 1983, 869.
13 at-Tirmidhī, Abū ʿĪsā Muḥammad, "Jāmiʿ at-Tirmidhī, Book 49, *Ḥadīth* 63," published online: *Sunnah.com*, https://sunnah.com/urn/635420 (accessed on 04.08.2022).
14 Melbourne School of Theology, *Qur'an Tools*, https://qurantools.mst.edu.au/auth/login.php (accessed on 04.08.2022).
15 Penrice, *Dictionary*, 149.
16 Brown, *Lexicon*, 35–36.

"mankind", while the latter is more specific, implying individual "self, soul". The latter is the most common use of *nafs*, as seen in 6:98: "It is He who first produced you from a single soul [*nafsin wāḥidatin*], then gave you a place to stay [in life] and a resting place [after death]. We have made Our revelations clear to those who understand."

Some verses use *nafs* to refer specifically to the physical person, such as 12:54: "The king said, 'Bring him to me: I will have him serve me personally' (*nafsī*) (...)."

While a more inner notion of "soul" is prominent within *nafs/anfus* in the following verse:

> 6:93 Who could be more wicked than someone who invents a lie against God (...) If you could only see the wicked in their death agonies, as the angels stretch out their hands [to them], saying, 'Give up your souls [*anfusakum*]. Today you will be repaid with a humiliating punishment for saying false things about God and for arrogantly rejecting His revelations.'

The term also occurs in the *ḥadīth* collections in a similar sense: "Do not lay the blame on one soul for another" (*lā tajnī nafsun ʿalā ukhrā*).[17]

Nafs signifying "self" is used on six occasions to refer to God in the Qur'ān, such as in 3:28: "The believers should not make the disbelievers their allies rather than other believers – anyone who does such a thing will isolate himself completely from God – except when you need to protect yourselves from them. God warns you to beware of Him (*nafsahu*): the Final Return is to God." This use of *nafs* for God is not found in later scholarly writings.[18]

This term also occurs once in the Qur'ān (6:130) to refer to both *jinn* (genies) and men: "Company of jinn and mankind! Did messengers not come from among you to recite My revelations to you and warn that you would meet this Day? They will say, 'We testify against ourselves.' The life of this world seduced them, but they will testify against themselves [*anfusihim*] that they rejected the truth."

The Qur'ān does not use *nafs* to refer to angels.

2.4 *Rajul/Rijāl*

The root *r-j-l* appears on seventy-three occasions in the Qur'ān, denoting a wide variety of meanings, but in its verbal noun form meaning "male human being,

---

17 Ibn Mājah, Muḥammad b. Yazīd, "Sunan Ibn Mājah, Vol. 3, Book 21, *Ḥadīth* 2672," published online: *Sunnah.com*, https://sunnah.com/urn/1269890 (accessed on 04.08.2022).

18 Calverley, E.E., "Nafs," in: EI^2, vol. VII, 880–883, Leiden: E.J. Brill, 1993, 880.

man, a person with heir."[19] However, 72:6 (*Surat al-jinn*) is worthy of note. Like 6:130 cited above, it uses one term (here *rijāl*) to refer to both men and *jinn:* "Men [*rijālun min al-ins*] have sought refuge with the jinn [*rijālin min al-jinn*] in the past, but they only misguided them further."

Penrice associates the root of *rijāl* with "feet" (*arjul*, sing. *rijl*), cognate with Hebrew *regel*,[20] and by association *rajul/ rijāl* means "man/men". The phrase from 72:6 *bi-rijālin min al-jinn* is translated by Penrice as "[w]ith certain of the jinn".[21] In *rajul/ rijāl* we have a common denominator covering humans and *jinn*, but it seems to be something like "legged creatures", some of which are visible, and some of which are invisible spirits.

An analysis of one hundred representative *ḥadīth* reports carrying a rendering into English of the term "person" drawn from across the *ḥadīth* collections revealed that *rajul/ rijāl* appears as the most common term in the two most authoritative Sunni *ḥadīth* collections of al-Bukhārī (810–870/194–256) and Muslim b. Ḥajjāj to represent an individual male person.[22] Examples include the following:

> Truly the most hated of men [*abghaḍa ar-rijāli*] in the sight of God is the argumentative [person].[23]
>
> A man formed his opinion [*arta'a rajulun*] according to what he wanted (...).[24]
>
> A man [*rajulun*] came to God's Apostle (...).[25]

But where the individual person appears in the same *ḥadīth* report as a collective group of people, both *rajulun* and *an-nās* can appear: "Indeed, a man [*rajulun*] may do the deeds of the inhabitants of Paradise in the eyes of the people [*an-nās*] yet he would be amongst the inhabitants of Hell (...)."[26]

---

19 Melbourne School of Theology, *Qur'an Tools*, https://qurantools.mst.edu.au/auth/login.php (accessed on 04.08.2022).

20 Brown, *Lexicon*, 919.

21 Penrice, *Dictionary*, 56.

22 Based on an analysis of 100 representative *ḥadīth* reports drawn from across the *ḥadīth* collections available at Sunnah.com. The analysis was carried out on June 25th 2019.

23 al-Bukhārī, "*Ṣaḥīḥ al-Bukhārī*, Book 46, *Ḥadīth* 18," published online: *Sunnah.com*, https://sunnah.com/bukhari/46/18 (accessed on 04.08.2022).

24 an-Naysābūrī, Muslim b. al-Ḥajjāj, "Ṣaḥīḥ Muslim, Book 15, *Ḥadīth* 182," published online: *Sunnah.com*, https://sunnah.com/muslim/15/182 (accessed on 04.08.2022).

25 al-Bukhārī, "*Ṣaḥīḥ al-Bukhārī*, Book 78, *Ḥadīth* 195," published online: *Sunnah.com*, https://sunnah.com/bukhari:6169 (accessed on 04.08.2022).

26 an-Naysābūrī, Muslim b. al-Ḥajjāj, "Ṣaḥīḥ Muslim, Book 46, *Ḥadīth* 19," published online: *Sunnah.com*, https://sunnah.com/muslim/46/19 (accessed on 04.08.2022).

2.5 *Wajh/Wujūh*

The root *w-j-h* appears in various forms seventy-eight times in seventy-one verses in the Qur'ān.[27] On occasion, the literal meaning of "face" is clear:

> 3:106 *yawma tabyaḍḍu wujūhun wa-taswaddu wujūhun fa-ammā l-ladhīna iswaddat wujūhu-hum akafartum ba'da īmānikum fa-dhūqū l-'adhāba bi-mā kuntum takfurūna.*
>
> On the Day when some faces brighten and others darken, it will be said to those with darkened faces, 'How could you reject your faith after believing? Taste the torment for doing so (…).'

However, on some occasions, the meaning of "person" is suggested, such as in 2:112: *balā man aslama wajhahu li-llāhi wa-huwa muḥsinun fa-lahu ajruhu 'inda rabbihi wa-lā khawfun 'alayhim wa-lā hum yaḥzanūna.* Yusuf Ali's translation captures the sense of "person, whole human being" for *w-j-h* in this context. This sense of *w-j-h* tends to occur mainly in eschatological contexts: "Nay, – whoever submits His whole self to Allah and is a doer of good, – He will get his reward with his Lord; on such shall be no fear, nor shall they grieve."

The surface meaning of some other verses relating to the direction of prayer specifies "face", but these verses seem to imply the entire body or, indeed, the whole human being: 2:177: *laysa l-birra an tuwallū wujūhakum qibala l-mashriqi wa-l-maghribi…* ("Goodness does not consist in turning your faces towards East or West (…)").

The various terms in Arabic used to render the concept of 'person' in the Qur'ān and *ḥadīth* as discussed above are summarized in the following table:

Table 1: Terms for "person" in the Qur'ān and *ḥadīth.*

Root	Form	Source	Semantic range
sh-kh-ṣ	*tashkhaṣu; shākhiṣatun*	Q14:42; Q21:97	"that which is fixed in horror, as the sight of the eyes." (Post-Qur'anic usage records *sh-kh-ṣ* referring to "person" synonymous with *n-f-s.*)
	shakhṣ	*Ṣaḥīḥ al-Bukhārī*, Book 93, Number 512	Metaphorical, not physical, reference to God's being.

27 Melbourne School of Theology, *Qur'an Tools*, https://qurantools.mst.edu.au/auth/login.php (accessed on 04.08.2022).

Table 1: Terms for "person" in the Qur'ān and *ḥadīth*. *(Continued)*

Root	Form	Source	Semantic range
'-n-s	*insān/an-nās;*	Q2:224; Q114:6 (97 occurrences in Qur'ān); *Jāmi' at-Tirmidhī* Vol. 1, Book 46, *Ḥadīth* 3667	"A man/human being, men/people"
n-f-s	*nafs/anfus*	Q5:32; Q6:98; Q6:93; (298 occurrences in Qur'ān); *Sunan Ibn Mājah*, Vol. 3, Book 21, *Ḥadīth* 2672	"A soul, a living soul or person"
		Q12:54 Q3:28 Q6:130	"a physical person" "self" (of God) "selves" (of jinn)
r-j-l	*rajul/rijāl*	Q72:6 (73 occurrences in Qur'ān); *Ṣaḥīḥ al-Bukhārī* Book 46, *Ḥadīth* 18 (most common term for "person" in the *ḥadīth*)	"man, person, legged creatures" (of men and jinn)
w-j-h	*wajh/wujūh*	Q3:106; Q2:112; Q2:177 (73 occurrences in Qur'ān)	"face, person"

As we proceed in our investigation, our primary focus will be on an understanding of person that is usually represented by *insān/an-nās*, *nafs/anfus*, and *rajul/rijāl*, as an individual physical person or individual soul, and how the relationship between that created person and his creator has been understood by different schools of thought.

3 Historical Developments Related to the Concept

With the death of Muḥammad, Messenger of Islam, in 632/11, the Muslim community entered a period of contestation, within and without. The reign of the first Caliph, Abū Bakr (r. 632–634/11–13) was characterized by military campaigns to hold together the Muslim community in the face of threatened fragmentation. His successor, the Caliph 'Umar (r. 634–644/13–23), oversaw a rapid expansion of the Muslim domains that continued for more than one century. The Islamic community gained control over many different nationalities, religious groups, and social systems. Military conquest resulted in the Muslim Arabs accessing wide-ranging fields of learning from the conquered peoples, which were subsequently disseminated and further developed throughout the Muslim territories.

An intensive process of translating Hellenistic works into Arabic, known as the Translation Movement, took place from the mid-eighth to the late tenth century, initiated under the patronage of the second Abbasid Caliph, Abū Ja'far 'Abd Allāh b. Muḥammad al-Manṣūr (r. 754–775/136–158) and directly encouraged and supported by certain later Abbasid caliphs.[28] The intellectual curiosity in the Islamic world was encapsulated in a statement by the father of the emerging Islamic philosophical tradition (*Falsafa*), Abū Yūsuf Ya'qūb b. Isḥāq al-Kindī (d. ca. 870/257), who wrote:

> Aristotle, the most distinguished of the Greeks in philosophy, said: "We ought to be grateful to the fathers of those who have contributed any truth, since they were the cause of their existence; let alone (being grateful) to the sons; for the fathers are their cause, while they are the cause of our attaining the truth." How beautiful is that which he said in this matter! We ought not to be ashamed of appreciating the truth and of acquiring it wherever it comes from, even if it comes from races distant and nations different from us. For the seeker of truth nothing takes precedence over the truth, and there is no disparagement of the truth, nor belittling either of him who speaks it or of him who conveys it. (The status of) no one is diminished by the truth; rather does the truth ennoble all.[29]

Greek philosophy was the trigger for both dialogue and debate between different schools of Islamic thought, especially between the growing *Falsafa* tradition and the emerging schools of scholastic theology (*Kalām*). According to the Greek philosophers Plato (d. 347 BCE) and his student Aristotle (d. 322 BCE), the faculty of reason distinguished humans from other living beings, with human reason overruling passions and the human spirit in the makeup of the human being. Aristotle developed Plato's teaching on reason, arguing that balance and well-being in human existence depended on the primacy of reason in shaping the human experience.

The above-mentioned al-Kindī was a crucial pioneer in adapting the thinking of Plato, Aristotle and the later Neo-Platonic School to the emerging Islamic context. In his classic treatise *On First Philosophy*, al-Kindī links the study of Greek-sourced metaphysics with the study of God:

> We do not find the truth we are seeking without finding a cause; the cause of the existence and continuance of everything is the True One, in that each thing which has being has truth. The True One exists necessarily, and therefore beings exist. The noblest part of philosophy and the highest in rank is the First Philosophy, i.e., knowledge of the First Truth Who is the cause of all truth.[30]

---

28 D'Ancona, Cristina, "Greek into Arabic: Neoplatonism in Translation," in: Peter Adamson/Richard C. Taylor (eds.), *The Cambridge Companion to Arabic Philosophy*, 10–31, Cambridge: Cambridge University Press, 2005.

29 al-Kindī, Ya'qūb b. Isḥāq/Ivry, Alfred L., *al-Kindī's Metaphysics: A Translation of Ya'qūb b. Isḥāq al-Kindī's Treatise "On First Philosophy" (Fī al-Falsafah al-Ūlā)*, Albany: State University of New York Press, 1974, 58.

30 al-Kindī/Ivry, *Al-Kindī's Metaphysics*, 58.

Subsequent Islamic philosophers, such as Abū Naṣr al-Fārābī (c. 870–950/256–339) who is considered in more detail later in this chapter, further developed the proposition that rational reflection could enable human beings to learn certain eternal truths. This view on the one hand recognized the overall sovereignty of God in the world and the universe while acknowledging that through reason humans could gain important insights into a number of basic theological notions: creation, the world, the nature of God, and the nature of the human being.

Arguably the greatest philosopher of the Islamic Golden Age, Abū ʿAlī al-Ḥusayn b. ʿAbd Allāh b. Sīnā (980–1037/370–428), developed sophisticated reason-based arguments regarding the existence of God and the separate existence of body and soul. While Aristotle had claimed that body and mind were not separate, Ibn Sīnā argued for an immaterial self (*nafs*) where the soul, born with the body, survives its death. He wrote:

> Each substance is either body or other than body. If (…) other than body, then it is either part of a body or it is not part of a body but is something altogether separable from bodies. If it is part of a body, then either it is its form or it is its matter. If it is separable [and] not a part of a body, then either it has some administrative relation to bodies in terms of moving [them] – and this is called "soul" [*nafs*] or it is free from material things in all respects and is called "intellect" [*ʿaql*].[31]

And further: "when divided, [the human] does not become multiple insofar as his nature – that is, insofar as he is a human – is concerned, but [the human] can become multiple in another respect: when divided into body and soul [*nafs*], he would have a body and a soul, neither of which [by itself] is a human."[32]

The *Muʿtazila* school of *kalām* embraced a reason-based approach to theology. They drew some influence from but were in less direct dialogue with the Greek philosophical heritage than was the case with the scholars of the *falsafa* tradition. Rippin and Knappert explain: "The Muʿtazilite position is that revelation is to be understood in the light of reason. God's actions which can be observed – that is, in the way in which the world operates – can be seen as rational; for God to be consistent, all His actions must be rational. Thus reason/rationality must interpret revelation."[33] The great medieval *Muʿtazilite* scholar ʻAbd al-Jabbār (d. 1025/415) wrote as follows, presenting conclusions about God's actions based on rational re-

31 Avicenna, *The Metaphysics of the Healing*, trans. ed. Michael E. Marmura, Provo, Utah: Brigham Young University Press, 2005, 48. See later discussion in this chapter for al-Fārābī's consideration of the Active Intellect.

32 Avicenna, *The Metaphysics of the Healing*, 76.

33 Rippin, Andrew/Knappert, Jan, *Textual Sources for the Study of Islam*, Chicago: University of Chicago Press, 1986, 19.

flection: " (...) we deny that God may commit evil actions (...) and we affirm of many actions that they – in so far as they belong to the category of the good – are His (...) Further, we affirm that it is incumbent upon God to act with grace *luṭf* towards the *mukallaf*."[34]

In opposition to the reason-based approaches of the *falsafa* and *kalām* traditions were conservative thinkers who took a more literalist approach to interpreting the Islamic sacred text. They came to be known as the *ahl al-ḥadīth*[35] and saw the rationalists as drifting away from divine command. They argued that divinely sourced Islamic scripture, in the form of the Qur'ān and the *ḥadīth*, offered answers to mankind's essential questions and represented the only legitimate source of law and morals. The *ahl al-ḥadīth* allocated priority to the *ḥadīth* in providing guidance for the detailed minutiae of human actions. They downplayed the role of personal discretion, or individual, personal opinion based on rational thinking (*ra'y*), in shaping human belief and behavior.

The debate was resolved in part by the great *kalām* thinker Abū al-Ḥasan al-Ash'arī (c. 874–936/ 260–324), a key name in tenth-century reform. He rejected rational metaphysics as the key to understanding the nature of God and the universe but accepted that reason could assist in drawing certain meanings from revelation and it also had a part to play in defending religious truth. Though criticized by followers of the literalist conservative jurist Aḥmad b. Ḥanbal (780–855/164–241) on the latter count,[36] al-Ash'arī's view gained widespread support, and in effect, al-Ash'arī had shaped a satisfactory compromise between the conflicting theological viewpoints. He affirmed the overwhelming centrality of the divine revelation, the ultimate yardstick against which reform could be measured, but allocated a significant place to reason.

The priority of revelation is encapsulated by many orthodox creeds, such as that of 'Aḍud ad-dīn 'Abd ar-Raḥmān al-Ījī (d. 1355), who had the following to say: "There is no judge over [God] (...) There is no judge except Him. Reason has no [power of] judging what things are good and what bad, and whether an action is an occasion for reward or for punishment. The good is what revelation declares good; the bad is what revelation declares bad."[37]

The debate concerning the respective priority of reason-based versus literalist approaches to understanding revelation continues up to the present day. The mod-

---

34 Calder, Norman, et al., *Classical Islam: A Sourcebook of Religious Literature*, London: Routledge, 2013.

35 Lapidus, Ira M., *History of Islamic Societies*, Cambridge: Cambridge University Press, 1988, 103. Lapidus referred to this group as *ḥadīth*-minded.

36 'Abduh, Muḥammad, *The Theology of Unity*, London: George Allan and Unwin, 1966, 36–37.

37 Watt, W. Montgomery, *Islamic Creeds: a Selection*, Edinburgh: Edinburgh U.P., 1994, 87.

ern Indian exegete Abu-l-Kalam Azad (d. 1958) distinguishes four stages of guidance for humanity: firstly by instinct, secondly by the senses, thirdly by reason, and finally by revelation and the prophets – "revelation 'perfects' the guidance, offered by reason".[38]

4 Different Islamic Perspectives on the Theological and Philosophical Principles

The rationalism-literalism tension described above has a direct bearing on our chosen topic of the concept of person in Islam. This tension has expressed itself in history in the form of two great internal divisions deriving from hermeneutical approaches to Islamic Scripture. The first derived from a literal reading of Revelation versus a reason-based reading of Revelation, and the second from a literal reading of Revelation versus a mystical reading of Revelation. These three streams correspond broadly with several great areas of Islamic learning: *fiqh* (jurisprudence), *kalām* (scholastic theology), *falsafa* (philosophy) and *taṣawwuf* (Sufism). Some of the differences of approach can be tabulated as follows:

Table 2: Competing Schools of Thought.

Championing Literalism	Championing Reason	Championing Mystical Thought
Applying a literalist hermeneutic in interpreting the revealed word	Applying a reason-based hermeneutic	Subjecting revelation to mystical speculation, seeing Scripture as multi-layered
Asserting that Scripture and legal texts are sufficient in themselves, supplemented by selected literalists' scholarly writings	Emphasizing Scripture plus scholarly writings by rationalist theologians and philosophers	Emphasizing Scripture plus saintly writings
Has led to radical revivalist movements periodically, calling for a return to scriptural basics. Also includes conservative traditionalist scholars (*'ulamā'*)	Was prominent among many theologians (e.g. the *Mu'tazila*) and philosophers from the eighth to the eleventh century	Enjoyed strong popular support throughout the ages, despite periodic persecutions by literalists

Theologians of the *kalām* schools, Sufis, and the scholars of the *falsafa* tradition engaged in vigorous debate on certain questions in the medieval period, with a

38 Baljon, J.M.S., *Modern Muslim Koran Interpretation (1880–1960)*, Leiden: Brill, 1968, 62.

scholar as prominent as Abū Ḥāmid al-Ghazālī (1058–1111/450–505), famous as both theologian and Sufi, charging al-Fārābī and Ibn Sīnā with innovation and heresy in their writings on the *nafs*. Questions in dispute related to whether 'personhood' was the soul per se, or the soul within an embodied corporeal existence, or that the soul was 'owned' by the human person. Furthermore, in the afterlife, would a soul constitute personhood or would there be also bodily resurrection?

Such fascinating questions could provide the primary focus of our attention in this chapter but they are more of historical than contemporary interest in relation to the concept of person as understood by the Muslim masses in the early twenty-first century. Rather, contemporary Islamic debates center more on the engagement between literalist and rationalist approaches to today's world, which at times touch upon but do not stay focused on these philosophical questions from the past. We will focus on these two approaches as they struggle for dominance on the world Islamic stage: those who champion literalist readings of revelation (Qur'ān and *ḥadīth*) and those who champion a reason-based approach to interpreting the primary Islamic texts.[39]

Those championing literalism fall into two groups in today's world. First come the scholarly *'ulamā'*, very often the products of formal religious schools, whose remit is to guide Muslim communities around the world through religious councils, legal committees, and diverse religious contexts. Second come the revivalist groups, modern-day radicals often lacking formal training in Islamic religious schools but who embrace a literalist reading of the Islamic sacred texts in engaging with the modern world.

Those championing reason, by contrast, are often graduates of Islamic educational institutions and embrace more liberal approaches to the interpretation of Islam's sacred texts. One notable example, the twentieth-century Palestinian-American philosopher Ismā'īl al-Fārūqī (1921–1986/1339–1406), wrote as follows:

> The Qur'anic revelation is a presentation to one's mind, to reason. There is no papal figure or ruling synod in Islam that can impose its views. [...] In Islam religious truth is a matter of

---

39 From an epistemological standpoint, even a "literalist" is exercising a rational form of argumentation in order to establish that a literal exegesis of scripture is more sound than an allegorical or metaphorical hermeneutics. The decision to base our analysis on a binary opposition between literalism and reason/rationalism was taken with some hesitation. No pair of terms would be entirely satisfactory; an analysis based on literalism versus allegory, or rhetorical versus demonstrative, would have generated similarly blurred and somewhat fluid boundaries. Our chosen analytical framework is widely used in the wider literature and should invite a broad base of readers in to the discussion.

> argument and conviction, a cause in which everybody is entitled to contend and everybody is entitled to convince and be convinced.[40]

Riffat Hassan (b. 1943/1362) similarly challenges more literalist approaches to scriptural interpretation in pointing out that the Qur'ān is not "an encyclopaedia which may be consulted to obtain specific information about how God views each problem, issue or situation".[41]

So instead of asking "What does Islam say about the concept of person?", it is better to ask "What various perspectives do different Muslims bring to bear in understanding the concept of person?"

Christianity has tended to focus on the person as an individual rational being, in contrast with emerging Islamic orthodoxy. The *Muʿtazila* and *ahlal-ḥadīth* debates of the eighth and ninth centuries and the ascendancy of the latter led to a demotion of the individual rational person empowered to shape one's own path in life and a promotion of the person whose primary function was service to the will of God.

4.1 Sources Consulted for Our Study

In the discussion which follows, we will refer to a wide range of Islamic scholars, thinkers, and activists, spread across different periods, centuries, and sectarian groups. The intention is to draw on a representative sample of Muslim writers to provide a helpful window into different Muslim perspectives down the ages on the concept of 'person' in Islam.

The list of scholars consulted below attempts to identify them according to whether they tended to embrace a more literalist or reason-based approach to the Islamic primary texts as they engage with the concept of 'person' in their scholarship. However, this differentiation must not be taken too rigidly. Any scholar may well develop in different ways in terms of a hermeneutical approach to scripture across a career, especially as they address different concepts. Indeed, some scholars may tend towards literalism on some concepts but towards more reason-based approaches on others.

The scholars are listed chronologically.

40 Iqbal, Mohammad, *Access to Assisted Human Reproductive Technologies in the Light of Islamic Ethics*, London, 2012 (PhD. Diss., University College London), 29.

41 Daniel C. Maguire, "Contraception and Abortion in Islam", *Patheos*, August, 6th, 2009, https://www.patheos.com/resources/additional-resources/2009/08/contraception-and-abortion-in-islam?p=2 (accessed on 07.08.2022).

Table 3: Sources consulted.

Name	Period	Biography	Literalist?	Reason-based?
al-Ḥasan al-Baṣrī	642–728/ 21–110	A prolific scholar theologian, exegete, judge and mystic of the third generation of Muslims (*tābiʿūn*). He is a key source on early reason-based thinking in Islam.		X
Muqātil b. Sulaymān	d. 767/150	An early Muslim thinker to whom has been attributed one of the earliest commentaries on the Qurʾān. A controversial figure, owing to heavy use of *ḥadīth* accounts prior to the codification of the *ḥadīth* collections, leaving his writings open to challenge regarding authenticity.	X	
Abū Yūsuf Yaʿqūb b. Isḥāq al-Kindī	c. 801–870/ 185–257	Regarded as the father of Islamic philosophy, he pioneered the study of the great Greek philosophers and adapted their thought to the emerging Islamic context.		X
Abū Jaʿfar Muḥammad b. Jarīr aṭ-Ṭabarī	839–923/ 224–310	Persian scholar, historian and Qurʾanic exegete, whose Commentary and History are both foundational in their respective Islamic disciplines.	X	
Abū Naṣr al-Fārābī	c. 870–950/ 256–339	Known as the 'Second Master' (*al-muʿallim ath-thānī*) following Aristotle, adapted and expanded Classical Greek philosophy to an Arabic audience.		X
Abū ʿAlī al-Ḥusayn b. ʿAbd Allāh b. Sīnā	980–1037/ 370–428	Arguably the greatest philosopher of the Islamic Golden Age, he developed a method for proving the existence of God. He also developed his "Floating Man Theory" to argue for the existence of the human soul.		X
Abū Muḥammad al-Ḥusayn b. Masʿūd b. Muḥammad al-Farrāʾ al-Baghawī	1041 (or 1044)–1122/ 433 (or 436)–516)	A famous medieval Persian Muslim scholar of Qurʾanic exegesis, traditions and jurisprudence.	X	

Table 3: Sources consulted. *(Continued)*

Name	**Period**	**Biography**	**Literalist?**	**Reason-based?**
Abū l-Qāsim Maḥmūd b. ʿUmar az-Zamakhsharī	1075–1144/ 468–538	A medieval Persian *Muʿtazilī* scholar, born in Khwarezmia, but spent most of his life in Bukhara, Samarkand, and Baghdad, whose greatest legacy is his commentary on the Qur'ān.		X
Ibn Taymiyya	1263–1328/ 661–728	Medieval Sunni Muslim theologian, Ḥanbalī jurist, and reformer, implacably opposed to certain Sufi practices such as tomb visitation. Prolific writer.	X	
Ibn Qayyim al-Jawziyya	1292–1350/ 691–751	Medieval Islamic Ḥanbalī jurist and theologian, a disciple of the abovementioned *Sunni* literalist reformer Ibn Taymiyya.	X	X
Abū ʿAbd Allāh Muḥammad as-Sanūsī	1435–1490/ 839–895	A product of the philosophical theology of Fakhr ad-Dīn ar-Rāzī. Wrote a commentary on the Divine Names.	X	X
Tafsīr al-Jalālayn	Late 15th/9th Century	A popular commentary upon the Qur'ān co-authored by Jalāl ad-Dīn al-Maḥallī (d. 1459/863) and Jalāl ad-Dīn as-Suyūṭī (d. 1505/911)	X	
Muḥammad b. ʿAbd al-Wahhāb	1703–1792/ 1115–1206	Conservative theologian, Ḥanbalī jurist, reformer, and ideologue from Najd in central Arabia who founded the *Wahhābī* movement. Advocated returning directly to the Qur'ān and *ḥadīth*, rather than depending on centuries of scholarly writings since the primary texts emerged. Hostile to shrine cults and saint worship and called for strict adherence to traditional Islamic law.	X	
Dāwūd b. ʿAbd Allāh b. Idrīs al-Faṭṭānī	d. 1847/1263	Famous scholar from Pattani, in southern Thailand, active in Mecca and Medina, writing prolifically on Islamic sciences and disseminating Islamic reformist ideas to Southeast Asia.	X	

Table 3: Sources consulted. *(Continued)*

Name	Period	Biography	Literalist?	Reason-based?
Sayyid Quṭb	1906–1966/ 1324–1386	Egyptian Islamist writer, exegete and poet. A key figure in the Muslim Brotherhood during the Egyptian presidency of Gamal Abdel Nasser, who had him executed for subversion.	X	
Syed Abū al-Aʿlā Maudūdī	1903–1979/ 1321–1399	Pakistani Muslim scholar, philosopher, jurist, political activist and imam. He was committed to political Islam and founded the Pakistan Jamaat-e-Islami political party.	X	X
Muḥammad Ḥusayn Ṭabāṭabāʾī	1903–1981/ 1321–1401	A leading exegete and philosopher of twentieth century *Shīʿa* Islam. His famous twenty-seven volume commentary, *Tafsīr al-Mizān*, was written over an eighteen-year period from 1954.		X
Ayatollah Madani (Mir Asadollah Madani Dehkharghani)	1914–1981/ 1332–1401	Born in East Azerbaijan, a prominent *Shīʿa* cleric and theologian, served after the Islamic Revolution in Iran as a politician and member of the Assembly of Experts until his assassination in 1981.	X	X
Ismāʿīl Rājī l-Fārūqī	1921–1986/ 1339–1406	A Palestinian-American theologian and philosopher. He was educated at Al-Azhar University in Cairo, then lectured at leading universities in the USA and Canada.		X
Fazlur Rahman	1919–1988/ 1337–1420	Pakistani scholar and philosopher of Islam, leaning towards liberal reform of Islam, committed to revival of independent reasoning. Encountered strong opposition from conservative Islamic scholars. Taught at several leading universities in the USA.		X
Mahmoud Abu-Saud	1911–1993/ 1329–1413	Economist, author, religious scholar and activist. A specialist in central banking, he had been instrumental		X

Table 3: Sources consulted. *(Continued)*

Name	Period	Biography	Literalist?	Reason-based?
		in establishing central banks and currency regulation in a number of countries including Kuwait and Afghanistan. He was a co-founder of the American Muslim Council.		
Jamāl al-Bannā	1920–2013/ 1338–1434	Egyptian author and activist, whose views were liberal-leaning and who opposed the notion of the Islamic political state.	X	X
Shahid Athar	1945–2018/ 1364–1439	Born in India and educated at the University of Karachi, Pakistan, Athar specialized in medicine in the USA, serving as Clinical Associate Professor at Indiana University School of Medicine. Author of seven books and many published articles on medical and Islamic topics.	X	X
ʿIkrima Saʿīd Ṣabrī	b. 1939/1358	Grand Mufti of Jerusalem and Palestine from October 1994 to July 2006. Removed from his post by Palestinian President Mahmoud Abbas, reportedly for his open expression of racially charged, one-sided political views.	X	
Abdulaziz Sachedina	b. 1942/1361	A Tanzanian-born American citizen who has published widely on various aspects of the Islamic sciences and has been on faculty at the University of Virginia and George Mason University in Fairfax, Virginia.		X
Riffat Hassan	b. 1943/1362	A Pakistani-American progressive Muslim theologian. She was educated in Pakistan and at Durham University, and taught at leading universities in the USA.		X
Mohammad Hashim Kamali	b. 1944/1363	Originally from Afghanistan, Kamali studied Islam and Law at the University of London. He was a long-serving Professor of Law at the In-		X

Table 3: Sources consulted. *(Continued)*

Name	Period	Biography	Literalist?	Reason-based?
		ternational Islamic University of Malaysia.		
Jalaluddin Rakhmat	b. 1949/1368	Long-serving faculty member at Pajajaran University in Indonesia. Active member modernist Muhammadiyah movement, and one of Indonesia's most prominent *Shi'ite* theologians. Entered politics as member of parliament in 2014.		X
Muḥammad al-ʿĀṣī	b. 1951/1370	Imam at the Islamic Center of Washington. He is preparing a work on Quranic exegesis in English.	X	
Muhammad Ṭahir-ul-Qadri	b. 1951/1370	A Pakistani-Canadian Islamic scholar and former politician. Prolific author who has taught international constitutional law at the University of the Punjab.		X
Shaykh Muḥammad Ṣāliḥ al-Munajjid	b. 1960	A scholar in the modern *Salafi* movement. He established the *IslamQA.info* website, one of the most popular *Salafi* websites online.	X	
Ismail b. Musa Menk	b. 1975/1395	Scholar, author and jurist, serving as Grand Mufti of Zimbabwe and head of the *fatwā* department of The Council of Islamic Scholars of Zimbabwe. Named one of the 500 Most Influential Muslims in the world by the Royal Aal al-Bayt Institute for Islamic Thought in Jordan in 2013, 2014 and 2017.	X	
International Islamic Fiqh Academy	Est. 1983/1403	Academy for advanced study of Islam based in Jeddah, Saudi Arabia, established in June 1983. Based in traditional Islamic sciences, seeks to apply principles of Islamic law and ethics to current societal issues.	X	

Table 3: Sources consulted. *(Continued)*

Name	Period	Biography	Literalist?	Reason-based?
Marwan Hadidi bin Musa	b. 1985/1405	Indonesian theologian, educated in Indonesia, a prolific author on the Islamic sciences.	X	
Indonesian Ministry of Religious Affairs commentary	Late 20th C	The Ministry of Religious Affairs was established when Indonesia attained independence. It has oversight for all of Indonesia's official religions, and published relevant works, including its commentary upon the Qur'ān.		X
Abu Fadl Mohsin Ebrahim		Originating from the Seychelles, he studied in Karachi and at Al-Azhar University in Cairo before doing his PhD under Ismaʿīl al-Fārūqī at Temple University. He served on faculty at the University of KwaZulu-Natal in South Africa.	X	
Nooraini Othman		A specialist in Education and Psychology, she did her PhD at the International Islamic University Malaysia. She is on faculty member at the Universiti Teknologi Malaysia, Kuala Lumpur.		X
Mufti Faraz Adam		Specialized in Islamic law at Darul Iftaa Mahmudiyyah, Durban, also completing a Master's Degree in Islamic Finance, Banking and Management at Newman University in 2017. Mufti Faraz is the director of Amanah Finance Consultancy Ltd, a platform for specialist global Shariah advisory services.	X	
Munawar Anees		Pakistani-born, a biologist by training, prolific author with several books and over 300 articles on religion and science, bioethics, and Islamic studies. Founding editor of *Periodica Islamica* and *International Journal of Islamic and Arabic Studies.*		X

Table 3: Sources consulted. *(Continued)*

Name	Period	Biography	Literalist?	Reason-based?
		Founding Member and former Trustee of the International Society for Science and Religion, Cambridge University. Nobel Peace Prize nominee in 2002.		
ʿAbd al-Malik b. Aḥmad al-Ramaḍānī l-Jazāʾirī		*Salafist* supporter of the *Khilafa* movement.	X	

Having considered the rich vocabulary available within the Arabic sources to express the various concepts related to person, as well as the reflections of early philosophers and theologians on humans as constituting body and soul, we now turn our attention to related questions that have arisen down the centuries and that trigger debates between those inclined to more literalist readings of revelation and those leaning toward more rationalist interpretations. A first question arises: "For what purposes did God create humans?"

4.2 The Purpose of the Creation of Human Beings

4.2.1 Championing Literalism

Q23:115 states clearly that humans were created for a purpose by God: "Did you think We had created you in vain, and that you would not be brought back to Us?"

This overriding sense of God's sovereignty is also captured in many reports from the prophetic Traditions, such as the following:

> Narrated ʿAbdullah: God's Messenger (...) the truthful and credible, said, "Each one of you is gathered in his mother's womb for forty days and then becomes a clot for an equal period and then becomes a piece of flesh for a similar period. Then God sends an angel and four things are commanded; i.e., his provision, his age, and whether he will be of the wretched or the blessed. And by God, one among you – or the person [*ar-rajul*] – may do deeds of the people of the Fire till there is only an arm-length distance between him and [the Fire], but then that which is written takes precedence, and he does the deeds of the people of Paradise and enters therein; and the person [*ar-rajul*] may do the deeds of the people of Paradise

> until there is nothing between him and it but an arm-length or two, and then that writing takes precedence and he does the deeds of the people of the Fire and enters therein."[42]

Sura 51 includes statements helping to clarify the purpose of creation of humans by the sovereign God:

> 51:56. I created jinn and humans [*ins*] only to worship Me:
> 51:57. I want no provision from them, nor do I want them to feed Me–
> 51:58. God is the Provider, the Lord of Power, the Ever Mighty.

The eleventh century commentator Abū Muḥammad al-Ḥusayn b. Masʿūd b. Muḥammad al-Farrāʾ al-Baghawī (1041 [or 1044]–1122/433 [or 436]–516) offers the following comment on the key verse 56, pointing again clearly to the overall sovereignty of God. He identifies his favorite sources in the process and presents an interesting variant reading as well: "(*I created jinn and humans only to worship.*) Kalbī, Ḍaḥḥak, and Sufyān said: This is especially for those obedient to Him from both groups, as the reading of Ibn ʿAbbās indicates: (I created jinn and humans) among the believers (only to worship). Then he added: We have hurried unto hell many jinn and humans [*ins*]."[43]

Egyptian thinker Jamāl al-Bannā (1920–2013/1338–1434), drawing on these verses from Q 51, stresses that the principal purpose for humans is connected with their role as *khalīfa* (vice-gerent), "who has to relate to this earth on behalf of God, and in accordance with his guidance and values, not just by pursuing personal interest"[44].

The contemporary Indonesian exegete Marwan Hadidi bin Musa (b. 1985/1405) writes as follows about Q 51:56:

> This was the purpose of Almighty God in creating jinn and humans [*manusia*][45], and He delegated the prophets to summon them, in order that they worship Him, involving coming to know Him and love Him, to return to Him, and to approach Him and turn away from

---

42 al-Bukhārī, "*Ṣaḥīḥ al-Bukhārī*, Book 82, *Ḥadīth* 1," published online: *Sunnah.com*, https://sunnah.com/bukhari/82/1 (accessed on 04.08.2022).

43 Abū Muḥammad al-Baghawī, "*Maʿālim at-Tanzīl*", published online: Aal al-Bayt Institute for Islamic Thought (ed.), *altafsir.com*, https://www.altafsir.com/Tafasir.asp?tMadhNo=0&tTafsirNo=13&tSoraNo=51&tAyahNo=56&tDisplay=yes&UserProfile=0&LanguageId=1 (accessed on 04.08.2022). Unless otherwise indicated, all translations into English of Arabic text from al-Baghawī's commentary are undertaken by the author.

44 Baraka, M., "Islam and Development from the Perspective of an Islamic Thinker and a Labour Unionist: Gamal al-Banna," *Islamic Quarterly* XXVIII (1984), 208. Al-Bannā was liberal in his theology and is one theologian who could appear to be literalist and reason-based according to issue.

45 Indonesian language derivation of *ins*.

> other than Him. This depends on knowledge of Him (...) each time a servant increases in his knowledge, his worship is also perfected. This is why Allah created humans and jinn, not because he was in need of them (...).[46]

The notion of relating is mentioned by both al-Bannā and Bin Musa. But human relating to God is one of unquestioning subservience.

4.2.2 Championing Reason

What about those championing reason? How would they answer the question: "What is the purpose of the creation of humans?"

An early proponent of a reason-based approach to Scripture, al-Ḥasan al-Baṣrī (642–728/21–110), affirms the above determinist view in stating "[God] ordered them to worship Him which is why He created them." Nevertheless, he still strongly supported human free will, rejecting the notion that God would create people to worship Him, guide them away from that purpose, and then punish them: "God would not have created them for a purpose and then come between them and (the purpose) because He does not do harm to His servants."[47]

Al-Ḥasan al-Baṣrī 's approach is borne out by the famous Muʿtazilite exegete Abū l-Qāsim Maḥmūd b. ʿUmar az-Zamakhsharī (1075–1144/468–538), who comments as follows on the above-mentioned Q 51:56:

> (*I created jinn and humans only to worship Me*) i.e. I created the jinn and humans only for the sake of worship, and I did not wish anything from them except that. And I said if it was a wish that worship would come from them, then would[n't] they all be worshippers? I said truly I wanted them to worship by choice, not by obligation, because they were created with possibilities: some of them chose to leave worship as was their wish. And if I wished for coercion and eviction, it would have been found in them all.[48]

The boundaries between scholars championing literalism and those championing reason are not always clear-cut. On certain topics, the same scholar may cross the boundary line. One such scholar is the twentieth century Pakistani Islamist Abū al-

---

46 Ibn Musa, Marwan Hadidi, *Tafsir Al Qur'an Hidayatul Insan*, vol. 4, fn. 1264, cf. www.tafsir.-web.id (accessed on 04.08.2022). Translated from the Indonesian text by the author.

47 Cited in Rippin/Knappert, *Textual sources*, 116.

48 az-Zamakhsharī, Abū l-Qāsim Maḥmūd, *al-Kashshāf*, published online: Aal al-Bayt Institute for Islamic Thought (ed.), *altafsir.com*, https://www.altafsir.com/Tafasir.asp?tMadhNo=0&tTafsirNo=2&tSoraNo=51&tAyahNo=56&tDisplay=yes&UserProfile=0&LanguageId=1 (accessed on 04.08.2022). Translated from the Arabic text by the author.

Aʿlā Maudūdī (1903–1979/1321–1399), who, at times, appears to champion literalism but on this topic articulated a somewhat reason-based understanding of human free will rather than simply quoting sacred writ, in commenting as follows on Q 51:53:

> That is, I have not created them for the service of others but for My own service. They should serve Me, for I am their Creator. When no one else has created them, no one else has the right that they should serve him; and how can it be admissible for them that they should serve others instead of Me, their Creator? (…) Only the jinn and men have been granted the freedom that they may serve God within their sphere of choice if they so like; otherwise they can turn away from God's service as well as serve others beside Him. The rest of the creatures in the world do not have this kind of freedom…[49]

So, for both streams of thought, the human person is created primarily to worship God, but for the literalists, the fact that some err reflects God's sovereign plan, whereas for those inclined more towards reason, those who err choose to do so and will suffer the consequences.

Having addressed the question of the purposes of God's creation of humans, a further question appears in the Islamic scholarly literature: What is the nature of the human being?

4.3 The Nature of Humans

4.3.1 Championing Literalism

We saw earlier how the great Islamic philosopher Ibn Sīnā developed his floating man theory to present a proof for the existence of the human soul (*nafs*). According to those championing literalism, in order for a person to satisfy the God-given purpose of service, guidance is needed, given the nature of the *nafs*. Abū Jaʿfar Muḥammad b. Jarīr aṭ-Ṭabarī (839–923/224–310), who tended towards literalism,[50] pro-

49 Maudūdī, Abū al-Aʿlā, *Tafhīm al-Qur'ān – The Meaning of the Qur'an*, cf. http://www.englishtafsir.com/Quran/51/index.html (accessed on 10.02.2019), modified.

50 Although Ṭabarī supported pluralistic meanings of the Qur'anic text by reporting varying interpretations from scholars of the first three Islamic centuries, nevertheless, he was heavily dependent on traditions in his method of interpretation and, as such, can be considered among the literalists.

poses three states of *nafs* in commenting on *Sūra* 12 verse 53, which states "man's very soul [*nafs*] incites him to evil".[51]

The first state is the *nafs al-ammāra bi-s-sū'*, "the soul which commands towards evil", namely that which inclines to do evil. The above-mentioned exegete al-Baghawī described this soul in the following terms: "The *nafs al-ammāra bi-s-sū'* has Satan as its ally. He promises it great rewards and gains, but casts falsehood into it. He invites it and entices the soul to do evil. He leads it on with hope after hope and presents falsehood to the soul in a form that it will accept and admire"[52].

Secondly, the *nafs al-lawwāma*, "the soul that blames," is conscious of its own imperfections, and is described by the conservative Ḥanbalī theologian Ibn Qayyim al-Jawziyya (1292–1350/691–751), one of the greatest scholarly writers on *nafs*, in the following terms:

> It has been said that the *nafs al-lawwāma* is the one which cannot rest in any one state. It often changes, remembers and forgets, submits and evades, loves and hates, rejoices and becomes sad, accepts and rejects, obeys and rebels.
>
> The soul that always blames is also the soul of the believer... It has also been mentioned that the soul blames itself on the Day of Resurrection – for every one blames himself for his actions, either his bad deeds, if he was one who had many wrong actions, or for his shortcomings, if he was one who did good deeds. All of this is accurate.[53]

Thirdly, the *nafs al-muṭma'inna* is the soul at peace, described by aṭ-Ṭabarī, citing the Follower Qatāda b. Di'āma (680–735/60–117) from Baṣra, as follows:

> It is the soul of the believer, made calm by what God has promised. Its owner is at rest and content with his knowledge of God's Names and Attributes, and with what He has said about Himself and His Messenger ..., and with what He has said about what awaits the soul after death: about the departure of the soul, the life in the *Barzakh*, and the events of the Day of Resurrection which will follow. So much so that a believer such as this can almost see them with his own eyes. So, he submits to the will of God and surrenders to Him contentedly, never dissatisfied or complaining, and with his faith never wavering. He does not rejoice at

---

51 Note the comment on this verse in the famous Jalālayn commentary: "Yet (I do not exculpate my own soul), of slipping into error; (verily the soul, as such, is ever inciting to evil, except that whereon), meaning the person [upon whom], (my Lord has mercy), and so protects [from sin]. (Truly my Lord is Forgiving, Merciful'). al-Maḥallī, Jalāl al-Dīn/ as-Suyūṭī, Jalāl al-Dīn, *Tafsīr al-Jalālayn*, trans. Feras Hamza, Amman: Royal Aal al-Bayt Institute for Islamic Thought, 2007, 248.

52 *Ma'ālim at-Tanzīl*, 8 vols., Cairo, 1308. Cf. al-'Akiti, A. 'Afifi, "The Meaning of Nafs," published online: BICNews, *Living Islam*, May 4, 1997, https://www.livingislam.org/nafs.html (accessed on 20.07.2019), copied 20 July 2019, modified. 'Afifi al-'Akiti, a Fellow in Islamic Studies at the Oxford Centre for Islamic Studies, is a specialist in the philosophical writings of al-Ghazālī.

53 al-Jawziyya, Ibn Qayyim, *Madārij al-sālikīn fī manāzil iyyāka na'budu wa iyyāka nasta'īn*, ed. 'Imād 'Amir. Cairo : *Dār al-Ḥadīth*, 1416/ 1996, vol. 1, 308, cf. al-'Akiti, "Meaning," modified.

> his gains, nor do his afflictions make him despair – for he knows that they were decreed long before they happened to him, even before he was created (...).[54]

Al-Baghawī described this soul as follows:

> The peaceful soul has an angel to help it, who assists and guides it. The angel casts good into the soul so that it desires what is good and is aware of the excellence of good actions. The angel also keeps the self away from wrong action and shows it the ugliness of bad deeds. All in all, whatever is for God and by him, always comes from the soul which is at peace.[55]

Ibn Qayyim al-Jawziyya did not regard the above as three independent entities but rather as states that could interchange, aiming for *nafs al-muṭma'inna* (the soul at peace) as a final "aim of perfection (...)".[56] For such to occur, a believer must follow the scriptures revealed through the prophets in service to God. Ibn Qayyim al-Jawziyya's teachings on the *nafs*, which he used interchangeably with *rūḥ*, came to represent orthodoxy and was based on a three-fold view:

> The *nafs* was itself a body, different from the physical body, of the nature of light;
> It was created but everlasting;
> It remains in the grave awaiting the Resurrection.[57]

4.3.2 Championing Reason

For a significant variation on the theme of the nature of humans, we can consider the thinking of another early Islamic philosopher, Abū Naṣr al-Fārābī (c. 870–950/ 256–339), one of the great names of the *falsafa*-Tradition of the Islamic Golden Age, along with Ibn Sīnā. If there is a sense of a straight-jacket in the portrayals of the nature of humans by those who championed literalism, this is far from the case with al-Fārābī. He considers the 'Active Intellect', explaining as follows:

> (...) neither the rational faculty nor what is provided in man by nature has the wherewithal to become of itself intellect in actuality (...) it needs something else which transfers it from potentiality to actuality, and it becomes actually intellect only when the intelligibles arise in it (...) something like the light which the sun provides to the sight of the eye (...) In the

54 aṭ-Ṭabarī, *Jāmi' al-bayān 'an ta'wīl āy al-Qur'ān*, vol. 13, Būlāq 1323/1905, cited in al-'Akiti, "Meaning," modified.
55 Cited in al-'Akiti, "Meaning," modified.
56 *Madārij*, cited in al-'Akiti, "Meaning,".
57 Calverley, "Nafs," 882.

> same way the 'material intellect' becomes aware of that very thing which corresponds to the light in the case of sight (...) It is therefore called 'Active Intellect' (...)[58]

This Active Intellect is one of the stages of emanation of the First Cause, namely God. The Active Intellect, al-Fārābī argues, "gives the human being a faculty and a principle by which to strive, or by which the human being is able to strive on his own for the rest of the perfections that remain for him. That principle is the primary sciences and the primary intelligibles attained in the rational part of the soul".

From this statement, we already have a sense of the greater freedom accorded to the human individual, as well as al-Fārābī's interest in approaching the question from the angle of reason. He sees human will as a multi-stage process. The first stage is "only a longing from sensation", while the second will is "a longing from imagination".

It is in describing the third will that al-Fārābī's thought demonstrates an openness absent in the writings of those championing literalism, who were preoccupied with emphasizing the overriding sovereignty of God at every turn.

For al-Fārābī, the third will is

> the longing from reason. This is what is characterized by the name 'choice'(...) Through this, a human being is able to do what is praiseworthy or blameworthy, noble or base. And because of this, there is reward and punishment (...) Voluntary good and voluntary evil – namely, the noble and the base – are both generated by the human being in particular.[59]

Majid Fakhry writes of al- Fārābī's view that the "chief characteristic of a virtuous person is moderation (*tawassuṭ*), defined as the ability to determine 'the time, the place, the agent, the patient, the origin and the instrument of the action as well as the reason for which the action is done'".[60]

In her examination of al-Fārābī's thought, Nadja Germann fittingly concludes that "[e]very human being, thus, can attain the individual felicity of the here-

---

58 al-Fārābī, Abū Naṣr, *al-Fārābī on the Perfect State: Abū Naṣr al-Fārābī's Mabādi' ārā' ahl al-madīna al-fāḍila: a Revised Text with Introduction, Translation, and Commentary*, trans. Richard Walzer, Oxford: Clarendon Press, 1985, 199–203.

59 al-Fārābī, Abū Naṣr, *The Political Writings*, vol. II, trans. C.E. Butterworth. Ithaca: Cornell University Press, 2015, 62–63.

60 Fakhry, Majid, *Al-Farabi, Founder of Neoplatonism. His Life, Works and Influence*, Oxford: One-World, 2002, 94.

after".[61] A comparison of al-Fārābī's thinking and that of the champions of literalism provides an insight into the great debates that have surrounded an understanding of the nature of person among Muslim theologians and philosophers down the ages.

4.4 The Individual's Relationship with God and Society

A further question which arises is how human beings, constituting body and *nafs* (according to Ibn Sīnā), benefiting from an *'aql* mobilized by the Active Intellect (according to al-Fārābī), relate to both their Creator, the First Truth (al-Kindī), and to each other.

4.4.1 Championing Literalism: Guidance is Provided

Given the hadith report from al-Bukhārī encountered earlier that everything Muslims do and say is pre-written, that their purpose is to worship God, and that their nature may well lean towards evil, what are Muslim people to do to set themselves up for a positive outcome on the Day of Judgment, according to those who champion literalism?

The answer provided by this stream of thinking is that the path is mapped out ahead, with guidance provided in terms of the divine Law, incorporating key beliefs and pillars, leaving the individual no justification to stray from the prescribed path. Muslims themselves do not know ahead of time how their deeds will be weighed on Judgment Day, though God has foreknowledge of this. So, they do well to follow the guided path.

Sura 114, the final *sūra* of the Qur'ān according to its standard arrangement, reminds Muslims of their refuge in God against the temptations of Satan:

> 1Say, "I seek refuge with the Lord of people [*an-nās*],
> 2the Controller of people,
> 3the God of people,
> 4against the harm of the slinking whisperer—
> 5who whispers into the hearts of people—
> 6whether they be jinn or people."

---

61 Germann, Nadja, "Al-Farabi's Philosophy of Society and Religion," published online: Edward N. Zalta (ed.), *The Stanford Encyclopedia of Philosophy* (Summer 2018 Edition), https://plato.stanford.edu/archives/sum2018/entries/al-farabi-soc-rel/ (04.08.2022).

Al-Baghawī highlights the devious ways of Satan in his commentary on this sūra: "The one who whispers in the breasts of the people, with hidden words that penetrate the understanding of the heart without being heard."[62]

In his comment upon Chapter 114 of the Qur'ān, the twentieth-century Islamist Sayyid Quṭb (1906–1966/1324–1396) underscores individual responsibility to follow the guidance given and the dire consequences of failing to do so. An individual can shun temptations in the most challenging circumstances, simply by turning to the Creator: "This concept of the battle and the source of evil in it, whether provoked by Satan himself or by his human agent, inspires man [*insān*] to feel that he is not helpless in it; since God, his Lord and Sovereign of the universe controls all creations and events."[63]

Some modern scholars, such as al-Bannā and Quṭb, were inspired by the prominent medieval literalist Ibn Taymiyya (1263–1328/661–728), who held that "man's purpose is not to know [God], but to obey Him."[64] Ibn Taymiyya disdained the view of Islamic philosophers such as al-Kindī, al-Fārābī, and Ibn Sīnā that rational thinking could reveal eternal truths about God. Also targets of his ire were the Sufi mystics, who devoted their attention to knowing God and, in the more extreme mystical speculative approaches, realizing union with God. He was especially critical of al-Ghazālī, according to Fazlur Rahman who quotes Ibn Taymiyya:

> [The Philosophers] hold that the happiness of the soul consists in the knowledge of eternal things (...) [al-Ghazālī] also suggests this (...) he has made the goal of human life (...) the knowledge of God, His attributes, His actions, and angels (...) [this] is worse than the beliefs of the idolatrous Arabs, let alone of Jews and Christians.[65]

Thus Ibn Taymiyya, consistent with the champions of literalism, affirms the doctrine of *bi-lā kayfa* (without asking why), whereby Muslims should not use limited human powers of reason to attempt to prove the truths of God-given Revelation but should accept them without question. This view is endorsed by the twentieth-century Pakistani scholar Abū al-A'lā Maudūdī: "the sphere of human percep-

---

62 Al-Baghawī, "*Ma'ālim at-Tanzīl*," published online: Royal Aal al-Bayt Institute for Islamic Thought (ed.), *altafsir.com*, Amman, Jordan, https://www.altafsir.com/Tafasir.asp?tMadhNo=0&tTafsirNo=13&tSoraNo=114&tAyahNo=1&tDisplay=yes&UserProfile=0&LanguageId=1 (accessed on 21.07.2019).

63 Quṭb, Sayyid, *In the Shade of the Qur'ān*, vol. 30, London: Islamic Foundation, 1979, 300.

64 Williams, John, *Islam*, London: Prentice-Hall International, 1961, 206.

65 Williams, *Islam*, 209–210.

tions as against the vastness of this great universe is not even comparable to a drop of water as against the ocean."[66]

Some questions should therefore not be asked, according to those championing literalism, such as whether God's attributes were integral to His essence (*dhāt*) or additional to it. Dāwūd b. ʿAbdallāh b. Idrīs al-Faṭṭānī (d. 1847/1263), a scholar from the Malay Patani region resident in Arabia, drew on the Egyptian Shāfiʿī scholar Muḥammad as-Suhaymī (d. 1764/1177) in commenting:

> It is not required (...) to discuss the attributes [of God] and their relations, whether they are the *Dhāt* or not. In fact, the Companions of the Prophet and their followers themselves abstained from addressing such issues. [Indeed they] forbade discussion of them. It is better and much safer for us not to discuss something which is beyond our intellectual ability.[67]

Also unacceptable were such questions as "Is God powerful enough to have a son?" or "Is God powerful enough to squeeze the world into an egg shell?", according to Dawud al-Faṭani in his *ad-Durr ath-Thamīn* ("The Precious Pearls"), where he branded them as *bidʿa* ("unacceptable innovation").[68]

4.4.2 Championing Reason: Relating to God

Another dimension is added to the rationalist quest by the modern Indonesian *Shiʿite* theologian Jalaluddin Rakhmat (1949–2021/1368–1442), in commenting:

> All Muslims feel that Islam is not just about regulating the relationship between mankind and God. All groups agree, both fundamentalists and liberals, that in our religion there must be a relationship between the individual and God, but one must still be cognizant that one is part of a society. What then becomes a challenge is to formulate our position in the midst of that society.[69]

---

66 Maudūdī, Abū al-Aʿlā, *Meaning, Commentary on Sura 72*, cf. http://www.englishtafsir.com/Quran/72/index.html (accessed on 04.08.2022).

67 *Ad-Durr ath-Thamīn*, cf. Mukti, M. F. Bin Abdul, *The Development of Kalam in the Malay World: The Teaching of Shaykh Dawud al-Faṭani on the Attributes of God*, PhD diss., Univ. of Birmingham, 2001, 148.

68 Mukti, *Development*, 158.

69 Rakhmat, Jalaluddin, "Tentang Syariat, Islam Fundamentalis dan Liberal," published online: *Tempo Interaktif*, 11 December 2000, http://media.isnet.org/kmi/islam/gapai/Syariah.html (accessed on 15.08.2022). Translated from the Indonesian by the author.

Rakhmat thus considers that individuals should devote attention and effort to their relationship with both God and their social context, taking care not to allow attention to the former to marginalize necessary focus on the latter.

4.5 The Source of Sin

In their relationship to God and each other, human beings do not always follow their God-given guidance but are guilty of sin. How is this accounted for by the different streams of Islamic scholarly thinking?

4.5.1 Championing Literalism

Tony Lane points to the need to consider sin in seeking to understand the concept of person in the religions. In surveying Augustine's doctrine, he constructs a statement that is helpful in delineating Christian and Islamic doctrines. His survey statement follows, in which I insert in *italics* a likely literalist Muslim response to key statements:

> Adam was created good (*Indeed he was*). Before the fall, Adam did not need to sin (*wa-l-Lāhu a'lam – God knows best*) – he was able not to sin (…) (*according to God's decrees*) but he also had the capacity to sin (…) (*according to God's decrees*). He was created with free choice of the will (*not so. God's preordained plan is at the helm*) and was able to exercise this for or against God (*only if God so willed it*), though as he was good the former came more naturally to him (*according to God's decrees*). In the garden he was on trial or probation (*as God willed it to be so*) and he fell (*no, he was cast out*) of his own free choice (*not so*). In this event not only Adam fell but also, in him, every human being (*not so. All are born good, as was Adam*).[70]

Hence, the Islamic thesis holds that as Adam did not fall through an act of free choice and there is no original sin leaving a legacy for succeeding generations of a broken relationship between God and humans, there is no need for a savior to provide a bridge between God and the human sinner. Rather, a mechanism is needed in the form of Scripture and Law, serving as a blueprint of divine instructions for humans to follow in order to earn God's favor on the Day of Judgment.

The medieval commentary by the *Jalālayn* on Q 53:31 underscores how God's overriding sovereignty is reflected in the act of doing good or committing sins by people:

---

70 Lane, Anthony N. S., "Lust: the Human Person as Affected by Disordered Desires," *Evangelical Quarterly* 78 (2006), 24.

> And to God belongs whatever is in the heavens and whatever is in the earth; that is, He owns all of that, among which also are the misguided one and the rightly guided one, leading astray whomever He will and guiding whomever He will, that He may requite those who do evil for what they have done by way of idolatry and otherwise and reward those who are virtuous, by their affirmation of God's Oneness and other acts of obedience with the best reward namely Paradise (...).[71]

We are reminded of this divine sovereignty even more clearly by a statement in al-Baghawī's commentary on the same verse where he writes: "Truly He is able to reward the doer of good and the evil doer as He is the Great Ruler, as He states: 'God is the owner of what is in heaven and what is in the earth.'"[72].

This theme of supreme sovereignty and the giving of guidance comes through clearly in some *Shī'ah* exegesis as well, as seen in the following commentary on Q 53:31:

> The main cause for the creation of the world of being is that man, the superior being in the world of existence, be guided toward the path of perfection through existential, legislative, and didactic schedules applied by Prophets. Thus, the blessed Verse in question closes with the consequence of such Possession by saying that the creation of the world aims at requiting those who do evil with that which they have done and reward those who do good with what is best.[73]

4.5.2 Championing Reason

Like the literalist theologians, rationalist-minded Muslim scholars have rejected the Christian doctrine of original sin. That said, there is nevertheless some space between the views of literalists and those of rationalists on the question of the sources of sin. A different, more open view is found in the work of Qur'anic exegesis issued by the Indonesian Ministry of Religion. Its comment on the discussion of sin in Q 53:31 is as follows:

> [God] created all beings and governs them according to His will. He could have made all humanity believe, but he did not wish to because he had equipped them with reason, guidance and freedom of choice. Thus, He will reward and punish those who do evil according to what

71 al-Maḥallī/as-Suyūṭī, *Tafsīr al-Jalālayn*, 625. Punctuation added by the author for clarity.
72 Al-Baghawī, *Ma'ālim at-tanzīl*, published online: Royal Aal al-Bayt Institute for Islamic Thought (ed.), *altafsir.com*, Amman, Jordan, https://www.altafsir.com/Tafasir.asp?tMadhNo=0&tTafsirNo=13&tSoraNo=53&tAyahNo=31&tDisplay=yes&UserProfile=0&LanguageId=1 (accessed on 22.07.2019).
73 Imam Ali Foundation (ed.), *An Enlightening Commentary into the Light of the Holy Qur'an*, vol. 17, https://www.al-islam.org/printpdf/book/export/html/29731 (accessed on 22.07.2019).

they have done and He will give reward and grace to those who do good with a better reward, namely heaven with all its pleasures and beauty.[74]

4.6 The Person of God?

We saw earlier in this chapter how the terms *shakhs* and *nafs* appear occasionally in the Islamic primary texts to refer to God. Can the concept of 'person' be applied to God Himself?

4.6.1 Championing Literalism: God is not a Person

The Christian doctrine of God as "three persons" is alien to and rejected by those Muslim scholars championing literalism.

The fifteenth century North African scholar Abū 'Abd Allāh Muḥammad as-Sanūsī (1435–1490/839–895) summarizes God's attributes as follows:

> It is necessary for Our Lord the Exalted to have twenty attributes; they are Existence, Eternity, Permanence, Difference from all the created, Self-Subsistence as He has no need of any place or any specifier (*mukhaṣṣaṣ*), Oneness meaning He has no need of any partner in His Being nor in His attributes, nor in His acts. The first of these six attributes is *nafsiyya* (personal), which is Existence (*al-wujūd*), while the five others are *salbiyya* (negative). Then it is necessary for God to have seven attributes which are known as *al-maʿānī* (the attributes of Ideal Realities); they are Power and Will which are associated with possibilities (*al-mumkināt*), Knowledge which is associated with all necessary, possible and impossible things, Life which is not associated with anything, Hearing and Sight which are associated with all things existent (*al-mawjūdāt*), and Speech, which is associated with whatever is connected with Knowledge (*mutaʿllaqātuhu*). Then there are seven attributes known as *ṣifāt maʿnawiyya* (the attributes of Ideal Modalities) which are necessary (*mulāzima*); these are that He is Powerful, Willing, Knowing, Living, Hearing, Seeing and Speaking. The twenty attributes which are opposite to these are impossible for God.[75]

74 "Tafsir an-Najm (53) Aya 31," published online: *Kementerian Agama*, 2017, https://quran.kemenag.go.id/surah/53 (accessed on 04.08.2022). Translated from the Indonesian by the author.
75 From as-Sanūsī's *Umm al-Barāhīn*, transl. in Barny, F. J., "The Creed of al-Sanusi," *The Muslim World* 23 (1933), 48–51; and Awang, O., "The *Umm al-Barāhīn* of al-Sanūsī," *Nusantara* 2 (1972), 159–161, modified.

The contemporary writer Abu Fadl Mohsin Ebrahim emphasizes the separation between God and the human person by stressing that "[m]an was created to know and serve God (...)."[76]

To suggest that God came to earth in the form of a person is a bridge too far for those championing literalism. God's attributes and those of people are seen as quite different. God is eternal, without beginning or end, whereas the soul of the created person is not eternal. As enunciated by the early thinkers of the *falsafa*-tradition, souls were created, so they have a beginning but no end, as they wait patiently for Judgement Day, which will result in either eternal reward or eternal torment.

God's attributes are without limit whereas those of people are limited. People can hear and speak, but only within limits. On the other hand, God can hear all and say all. People can act but require instrumental assistance, writes Dawud al-Faṭani: "[T]here is no writing without a pen as well as no cutting without a saw (...), knife (...), or axe (...)."[77] In contrast, God can act without need of any assistance.

God is self-subsistent, neither being begotten nor begetting (*sūra 112*). God's power is without limit; the power of humans is miniscule compared with that of the Creator. A human being is made of the four elements (soil, water, air and fire) and his life therefore needs a specific environment to survive; God, however, is living in a way which is not dependent. In short, God has no physical connection with created beings, and to suggest there is a connection with a human person is to commit the great sin of *shirk* (association).

So, those who champion literalism view a person as a created human being, distinguishable from God on every score, created not to wonder why but rather to serve and follow God's guidance according to the sacred Scripture and revealed Law.

Hence, the literalist objection (also commonly held beyond literalists) to the Trinitarian use of the word "person", seen as implying the humanization of God. In the literalist Islamic view, God did not become what he was not: a human person.

---

76 Ebrahim, Abu Fadl Mohsin, *Abortion, Birth Control and Surrogate Parenting: An Islamic Perspective*, Indianapolis: American Trust Publications, 1989, 102.
77 *Ad-Durr ath-Thamīn*, cf. Mukti, *Kalām*, 153–3.

4.6.2 Championing Reason: God is Transcendent

We saw earlier how Muslim scholars with more rationalist than literalist leanings considered the concept of relationship between God and the human person. How is such an Islamic approach to ensure that emphasizing relationship between the individual and God does not reduce God in his majestic transcendence?

The twentieth century Muslim academic Mahmoud Abu-Saud (1911–1993/1329–1413) explains transcendence in rational terms as follows:

> (a) God, the sole Creator of all beings, the Lord and the Owner of everything, the Absolute and the Ultimate; (b) the human community as an entity integrated in the cosmos; (c) the human individual who is ordained to be responsible for himself, his collectivity and his environment; (d) Man is made of matter and spirit. He attains cognition by means of the logistics of his meditative faculty and the awareness of his spirituality; (e) the revealed standard of values, commandments and basic criteria which regulate, govern and guide human behavior.[78]

According to Abu-Saud, God's purpose in creating humans is threefold: Firstly, that they worship God; secondly, that they act on God's behalf in overseeing the creation, a role for which humans are selected as only they among the creatures have the required faculties. Thirdly, humans are created "to cause growth on earth and make it more resourceful for [their] own benefit, welfare and prosperity"[79].

There are clearly certain different perspectives between those championing reason and those championing literalism. Nevertheless, key foundational principles are shared: God is transcendent and ultimately 'other', and humans are created to serve God. Learning about God through powers of reasoning does not compromise the principal objective of serving God; a servant may know a great deal about his master without there being intimacy. 'Person', for those championing reason, is somewhat released from the shackles of the literalist doctrine of *bi-lā kayf* but not to the extent of being able to challenge God's majestic otherness.

How would those championing reason answer the question: "What makes a person whole?" In this group, we hear the closest echo of a Christian view which might identify key elements of personhood as rationality, morality/will, relationality, and physicality. But it should be stressed that for those championing reason, such a view is still clearly enclosed within the confines of subservience to a transcendent God.

The different perspectives between our two streams of thought encountered in our discussion thus far can be summarized as follows:

---

78 Abu-Saud, Mahmoud, "Economics Within Transcendence," *Islamica* 1 (1993), 4–9, 6.

79 Abu-Saud, "Economics," 6.

Table 4: Summary of Issues of Debate Regarding the Concept of Person in Islam.

	Champions of Literalism	Champions of Reason
The purpose of the creation of humans	To worship God	To worship God as an act of choice; to serve God as an act of choice; represent God in guardianship over creation; to make the earth abundant and prosperous
The nature of humans	Inclined to evil so guidance is needed	Empowered to achieve by the "active intellect"; possesses the capacity of will in stages (al-Fārābī)
Relationship with God and society	Balanced relationship depends on following the divine Law to avoid the temptations of Satan	Balanced relationship between both individual and God and individual and society is encouraged and discussed
Questioning and reflecting	Discouraged; risking *bid'a*; promote doctrine of *bi-lā kayf*	Encouraged
The source of sin	No original sin; everything is sourced in God; guidance is provided to overcome tendency to do wrong	No original sin; humans have reason and free choice; sin represents abuse of that freedom
Is God a person?	No, such a suggestion is blasphemy; God and person are separate in every way	No, God is transcendent. Humans can seek to know aspects of God's nature and will, but the transcendent distance is maintained

4.7 Person versus Personality in Islam

This topic cannot be easily divided into the views of champions of literalism and reason, as different perspectives such as they occur are nuanced and specific to individual scholars. The discussion of this topic therefore takes a more generic approach.

The prominent Pakistani Sufi scholar Muḥammad Ṭahir-ul-Qadri (b. 1951/1370) argues that just as there is a celestial balance in the universe, God has shaped the individual person to have an internal balance. He argues: "Almighty God, according to Islam, has created a balance between all faculties of human personality (…). God has commanded us three kinds of rights: the rights of God and his Prophet, the rights of self or our own life and the rights of people. So, for a good Islamic life, God wants a balance between all kinds of rights."

He argues that there are seven aspects to human personality: biological, social, cultural, economic, psychological, psychical, spiritual and transcendental aspects.

"Islam never allows any aspect of human personality to create any sort of clash or conflict with the rest of the personality", Ṭahir-ul-Qadri argues.

> The same balance, the desirable beauty of poise and equilibrium and the finery of tolerance and peaceful togetherness have been given to the celestial order of the universe... The whole creation prostrates before the Sovereign Lord and nothing can depart or deviate from the path of obedience. And the balance keeps going. God Almighty has created the whole universe on the basis of the same formula.[80]

Nooraini Othman considers how to attain meaning in life, observing that "[...] faith and action join together to integrate the personality of the individual and make his life meaningful". Again, balance, or her term 'integration', is key. For her, personality is connected with action and behavior. Quoting L. A. Abdul, she observes that "[h]uman personality in the Islamic tradition is understood through the total make up of body, mind and soul". Without drawing an overt connection, Othman is affirming the tripartite combination of the early philosophers of body, intellect and soul.

She is careful to distinguish between Islamic and non-Islamic personality, again underscoring the importance of behavior: "The Islamic personality is a clear and distinct personality. Its fabric is the Book of God, and its thread is the Sunnah, and these two are inseparable from it. It is a sincere and determined personality educated and refined upon a precise methodology which does not contain even the slightest deficiency (...)."[81]

While Ṭahir-ul-Qadri is a charismatic Sufi leader and Othman is a scholar, Mufti Ismail bin Musa Menk (b. 1975/1395) of Zimbabwe provides a populist voice to this discussion. But his message is essentially the same, though expressed in more accessible terms. In a public lecture on 'Developing an Islamic Personality' on a lecture tour in Colombo, Sri Lanka in 2011, Menk argued that personality is about goodness or the absence of goodness and is shaped by behavior. Devout Muslims, he argued, who practice the Five Pillars[82] without distraction will gain a positive personality; those who allow their minds to wander, such as during communal prayers, and do not "lower their gaze" away from distractions and temptations with consumer goods, lustful thoughts, and so forth will have a poor personality: "Our personality is not being developed because we have not understood the es-

---

80 Ṭahir-ul-Qadri, Muḥammad, "Islam on Human Personality," published online: *The Nation*, 28 August 2007, https://www.minhaj.org/english/tid/667/Islam-on-human-personality.html (accessed on 23.07.2019), modified.

81 Othman, Nooraini, "A Preface to the Islamic Personality Psychology," *International Journal of Psychological Studies* 8 (2016), 20–27, modified.

82 The creed, prayer, charity, fasting, pilgrimage.

sence of our prayer." His summary argument was that personality is about achieving goodness, and the way to do so is to follow the five pillars faithfully and with commitment.[83]

So, digesting the above comments, it would appear that for the scholars quoted, personality is related to ethical or unethical behavior. In contrast, personhood is an aspect of the inner self, understood according to scriptural teaching and theological and philosophical interpretation.

5 Islamic Responses to Contemporary Issues

So far, we have considered a range of issues by reference to scholars from both the distant past and more recent times. It would be useful to further ground our discussion in current events, considering certain topics of contemporary debate relating to the issue of personhood.

5.1 The Dignity of Person

In late 2017, an issue related to human dignity arose in the Muslim-majority country of Malaysia. The owner of a public launderette restricted access to its facilities to Muslims only, arguing that Islamic regulations regarding ritual cleanliness meant that non-Muslims should not be using the same facilities for cleaning their clothes as Muslims. This incident prompted a barrage of media debate, but there was also scholarly discussion as to whether such an exclusivist approach as was taken by the launderette owner was in accordance with Islamic notions of human dignity.

Mohammad Hashim Kamali (b. 1944/1363) is a leading scholar on the question of the Islamic position on human dignity. In responding to the launderette incident, Kamali wrote against the launderette owner's position and pointed to Q 17:70, declaring "This verse is self-evident in its recognition of inherent dignity for all human beings without qualification of any kind".[84]

---

83 Menk, Ismail b. Musa, "Developing an Islamic Personality (Part 1)," published online: *Youtube*, December 2011, https://www.youtube.com/watch?v=nlZn1ltJ4sI (accessed on 04.08.2022); also December 2011, "Developing an Islamic Personality (Part 2)," published online: *Youtube*, https://www.youtube.com/watch?v=xhI9ubr8B24 (accessed on 04.08.2022).

84 Kamali, Mohammad Hashim, "Human Dignity in Islam and its Impact on Society," published online: *New Straits Times*, October 25, 2017, https://www.nst.com.my/opinion/columnists/2017/10/294803/human-dignity-islam-and-its-impact-society (accessed on 04.08.2022).

Some researchers argue that Qur'ān verses addressing the issue of human dignity do so either explicitly or implicitly. Those that are explicit are especially Q 17:70, supported by Q 6:69, Q 27:62, and Q 35:39. The twentieth century *Shi'ite* exegete Muḥammad Ḥusayn Ṭabāṭabā'ī (1903–1981/1321–1401) sees human dignity as the product of a particular wisdom which enables humans to distinguish between good and evil, and useful and harmful, setting them apart from other creatures. Further, Ṭabāṭabā'ī argues that all descendants of Adam, not just Muslims, enjoy the honor of being vicegerents of God, thereby reinforcing the notion of human dignity for all.[85]

As for verses where the concept of human dignity is implicit, Q 45:13 is key: "And He has subjected to you whatever is in the heavens and whatever is on the earth – all from Him. Indeed in that are signs for a people who give thought." This verse was considered by the early seventeenth century Shi'ite philosopher Mullā Ṣadrā to point clearly to human dignity, as it pointed to "man's superiority; for God created whatever is in earth and sky for the interest of man".[86]

Lavasani and Kalantarkousheh also refer to the Christian doctrine of original sin as distinguishing Christianity from Islam on the question of human dignity, writing "in a comparison between the Quran and the Bible, according to the Quran verse, the view of children regarding their father, Adam [...], was a position of dignity whereas the Bible views humans as condemned to be sinners, having to endure punishment as a result of Adams's actions."[87]

In a study on the subject of human dignity, Kamali wrote of two schools of thought which debated whether dignity applied to all humans or was reserved especially for Muslims. One school, termed the "universalists" by Kamali, was led by *Ḥanafī* legal scholars, who argued that the inviolability of human dignity (*'iṣma*) encompassed all people regardless of creed, race, and so forth. Kamali argued that Qur'ān verses relating to fighting unbelievers were time-bound, relevant to the particular context of early seventh century Muslim struggles against the Meccans but not of relevance today.

Standing against this position is what Kamali terms a "communalist" position which reserved dignity for Muslims and which saw struggle against unbelievers in the early seventh century as a model for today.[88] These two groups, universalists

85 Lavasani, Sayyid Mohammad Hasan/Seyed Mohammad Kalantarkousheh, "The Roots of Human Dignity according to Quranic Verses," *Australian Journal of Basic and Applied Sciences* 7 (2013), 394.

86 Ibid., 395.

87 Ibid., 394.

88 Kamali, Mohammad Hashim, "Human Dignity in Islam," published online: International Institute of Advanced Islamic Studies (IAIS) Malaysia (ed.), 2007, https://iais.org.my/publications-sp-

and communalists, broadly cohere respectively with the distinction presented in this chapter between reason-based and literalist approaches to interpretation of scripture.

Kamali cites a range of scholars who support the universalist perspective: Abū Ḥāmid al-Ghazālī (Shāfiʿī), Ibn Rushd al-Qurṭubī (Mālikī), Ibn Qayyim al-Jawziyyah, Shihāb ad-Dīn al-Ālūsī, Muṣṭafā as-Sibāʿī, Aḥmad Yusrī, and Sayyid Quṭb. Developing the idea of twentieth-century scholarly support for a universalist position on the question of human dignity, Kamali notes that "dignity is not earned by meritorious conduct; it is established as an expression of God's grace as a natural and absolute right of every human person as of the moment of birth. It is God-given, hence, no individual or state may take it away from anyone."[89]

Certain *ḥadīth* reports can also be seen to support a universalist position on the question of human dignity according to Kamali. The following is an example:

> I heard ʿAbd al-Raḥmān ibn Abī Layla say: Sahl ibn Ḥunayf and Qays bin Saʿd were sitting in Qadisiyah, A funeral procession passed by so they stood up. They were told that [the deceased] was one of the local community, i. e. from the dhimmi communities. They said that a funeral procession passed by the Prophet PBUH, so he stood up. He was told that it was the funeral of a Jew. He said, 'Is it not a soul [*nafs*]?' [90]

Some scholars argue that the level of dignity enjoyed by a person increases and decreases according to behavior. Schroeder and Bani-Sadr assert that human dignity increases as one honours another person or non-human creature. Furthermore, intake of matter to the body will affect the level of human dignity according to the quality of the matter consumed. Moreover, "[t]o exercise and defend rights increases human dignity. To reconsider truth and to speak it, even if we suffer for it (Koran 4:135), also increases dignity."[91]

A final point to consider relates to the approach to human dignity taken by Islamic Human Rights documentation. *The Cairo Declaration on Human Rights in Islam* (1990) affirms the universalist position regarding dignity presented by Kamali, in stating in Article 1a: "All men are equal in terms of basic human dignity and basic obligations and responsibilities, without any discrimination on the basis of

---

1447159098/dirasat-sp-1862130118/media-articles/item/36-human-dignity-in-islam (accessed on 29.05. 2022).

89 Kamali, "Human", p. 2.

90 al-Bukhārī, "*Ṣaḥīḥ al-Bukhārī*, Book 23, Ḥadīth 70," published online: *Sunnah.com*, https://sunnah.com/bukhari/23/70 (accessed on 04.08.2022).

91 Schroeder, D./Bani-Sadr, A., "Dignity in the Middle East," in: D. Schroeder/A. Bani-Sadr, *Dignity in the 21st Century*, New York: Springer, 2017, 83.

race, colour, language, belief, sex, religion, political affiliation, social status or other considerations."[92]

5.2 Contraception: Prevention of a Person

While early Islamic theologians and philosophers debated a diverse range of issue such as the soul, sovereignty of God, human free will, and so forth, today's Muslims and Christians face increasing ethical challenges relating to human intervention via new medical techniques in what have always been seen as the arena of God. Muslim scholars and thinkers are increasingly posing questions such as "should human beings interfere via contraception with the God-given process which creates life?"

Certain conservative Muslim theologians inclined towards literalism point to Qur'anic verses in debating contraception, such as Q 11:6 "There is no moving creature on earth but its sustenance depends on God."[93]

Their concerns are, firstly, that uncontrolled contraception can be seen as derogating the role of God. In more conspiratorial terms, the Islamist group Al-Muhajiroun warns that:

> The idea of birth control propagated nowadays stretches far back to a historical and an ideological conspiracy which the disbelievers concocted against the Muslims for fear of the rapid demographic growth of the Islamic Ummah, which was threatening their objectives, their areas of influence and their interests […]. Indeed the growing birthrate of the Muslims does not only concern the Jews, but the whole world, for their proliferation would make them a major force.[94]

Some other conservative scholars inclined to literalism do allow for some nuance in shaping views on contraception. Shaykh Muḥammad Ṣāliḥ al-Munajjid (b. 1960/1379) established the popular *fatwā* website *IslamQA.info*, which provides answers to questions in line with *Salafi* thinking. In answer to online Question 587 received,

---

92 Mozaffari, Mohammad Hossein, "Human Dignity: An Islamic Perspective," published online: *Hekmat Quarterly Journal* 4 (2011), https://www.researchgate.net/publication/327237458_Human_Dignity_An_Islamic_Perspective (accessed on 04.08.2022).

93 Cf. the Islamist group Shariah4Mauritius statement "Islamic Verdict on Contraception," https://www.facebook.com/Shariah4Mauritius/posts/islamic-verdict-on-contraceptionintroductionthe-issue-of-birth-control-and-famil/2002265896722278/ (accessed on 04.08.2022).

94 Cf. Al-Muhajiroun's statement "Islamic Verdict on Contraception", http://www.almuhajiroun.com/Islamic%20Topics/Islamic%20Fiqh/Contraception.htm, copied January 2003. Reproduced at https://www.facebook.com/Shariah4Mauritius/posts/2002265896722278 (accessed 11.05.2023).

asking whether contraception was allowed, Shaykh al-Munajjid ruled that contraception is permitted under certain conditions:[95]

- There is mutual agreement of both husband and wife.
- It does not cause harm.
- It is not to be practiced on a permanent basis, but rather for a temporary period (such as two years until the breastfeeding of the current baby is completed, for example).

Abu Fadl Mohsin Ebrahim shows flexibility regarding contraceptive use: "[...] where pregnancy may injure the health of the woman or may even threaten her life, the higher purpose of protecting life [...] would prevail, requiring a woman to make use of contraceptive devices to protect her health or life."

Nevertheless, his flexibility is not without limits, with his next statement pointing clearly to his primary points of reference on this question: "The use of contraceptive devices for other reasons by mutual consent between the husband and wife is *makrūh* (undesirable, improper) [...] but not necessarily *ḥarām* (forbidden) under the *sharīʿa.*"[96] In other words, his views on contraception are shaped by a literal reading of Islamic legal stipulations rather than a reasoned consideration of the issue in the context of the realities of modern-day society. He arrives at his viewpoint by looking back to the *Sharīʿa* (Islamic Law).

Questions about contraception are increasingly visible in online *fatwā* sites. As one example, the *fatwā* site of Darul Ifta, Darul Uloom Deoband, was asked as follows (edited for improved English style):

"I am a medical student. I am planning to nikah next year with a girl who is completing her education. At the time of nikah [...] two years will be left [for her studies] & after that she will come to live with me [...] my question is can we meet & do sex during these 2 years?" The response was quite curt: "(1) Yes, you can meet and have sexual relation after nikah. (2) It is against the will of Shariah to use contraceptive method without exigent need."[97]

Another online site leaning towards literalism is the *Darul Fiqh* online platform, launched in 2011 by British-trained scholar Mufti Faraz Adam. Mufti Adam assesses the acceptability of two macro-types of contraception: irreversible

---

95 Al-Munajjid, Sheikh Muhammed Salih, "Permissibility of Contraception," published online: *Islam Question & Answer*, http://islamqa.info/en/answers/587/permissibility-of-contraception (accessed on 04.08.2022).

96 Ebrahim, Abu Fadl Mohsin, *Abortion, Birth Control and Surrogate Parenting. An Islamic Perspective*, Indianapolis: American Trust Publications, 1989, 102.

97 "Fatwā: 1695/1387/D=1430," published online: *Darul Ifta*, http://www.darulifta-deoband.com/home/en/qa/16023 (accessed on 17.08.2019).

contraception (vasectomy and tubectomy) and reversible contraception (barrier methods and hormonal methods). In his view, irreversible contraception is almost always unacceptable under *sharīʿa* Law, whereas he presents reversible contraception as acceptable according to circumstance, such as health issues, while travelling, impending divorce, and so forth.[98]

Reason-based scholars show greater openness to contraceptive use. Fazlur Rahman (1919–1988/1337–1420) considers a literal interpretation of Qur'anic references to God's power and promise such as Q 11:6 above to be "infantile": "The Qur'ān certainly does not mean to say that God provides every living creature with sustenance whether that creature is capable of procuring sustenance for itself or not."[99] Abdulaziz Sachedina (b. 1942/1361) reports widespread liberal attitudes among jurists among whom "there is no objection if the woman decides to use any method of birth control to avoid becoming pregnant without her husband's approval as long as that method does not cause any harm to her health."[100]

Literalists and reason-based scholars both accept some contraceptive use, though the former set stricter limits. Neither group sees contraceptive use as a matter of personal choice determined simply by pleasure and sexual fulfilment, especially outside wedlock, as is widespread in modern secular lifestyles.

5.3 Abortion: Termination of a Person

In addressing the contentious issue of terminating life, especially abortion, several reports in the *ḥadīth* collections provide many Muslims with some guidance. The following report from *Ṣaḥīḥ al-Bukhārī* was cited earlier; here we provide a relevant excerpt:

> Narrated ʿAbdullah: God's Messenger (…) the truthful and credible, said, 'Each one of you is gathered in his mother's womb for forty days and then becomes a clot for an equal period and then becomes a piece of flesh for a similar period. Then God sends an angel and four

98 Adam, Mufti Faraz, "Is contraception permissible in Islam?," published online: *Darul Fiqh*, 2012, http://darulfiqh.com/is-contraception-permissible-in-islam/ (accessed on 17.08.2019).

99 Maguire, Daniel C., "Contraception and Abortion in Islam", August, 6th, 2009, published online: *Patheos*, https://www.patheos.com/resources/additional-resources/2009/08/contraception-and-abortion-in-islam?p=2 (accessed on 07.08.2022).

100 Sachedina, Abdulaziz, *Islamic Biomedical Ethics: Principles and Application*, Oxford: Oxford University Press, 2009, 127.

> things are commanded; i.e., his provision, his age, and whether he will be of the wretched or the blessed (...)'[101]

Those inclined to literalism find direction in such scriptural references. An online *fatwā*[102] from the site of Shaykh Muḥammad Ṣāliḥ al-Munajjid helps us on this question, making clear reference to the above-mentioned *ḥadīth* report:

> Question 42321 (Publication: 11–03–2003): What is the ruling on aborting a pregnancy in the early months (1–3) before the soul is breathed into the foetus?
>
> [Ruling:] 1 – It is not permissible to abort a pregnancy at any stage unless there is a legitimate reason, and within very precise limits.
>
> 2 – If the pregnancy is in the first stage, which is a period of forty days, and aborting it serves a legitimate purpose or will ward off harm, then it is permissible to abort it. But aborting it at this stage for fear of the difficulty of raising children or of being unable to bear the costs of maintaining and educating them, or for fear for their future or because the couple feel that they have enough children – this is not permissible.
>
> 3 – It is not permissible to abort a pregnancy when it is an *'alaqah* (clot) or *mudghah* (chewed lump of flesh) (which are the second and third periods of forty days each) until a trustworthy medical committee has decided that continuing the pregnancy poses a threat to the mother's wellbeing, in that there is the fear that she will die if the pregnancy continues. It is permissible to abort it once all means of warding off that danger have been exhausted.
>
> 4 – After the third stage, and after four months have passed, it is not permissible to abort the pregnancy unless a group of trustworthy medical specialists decide that keeping the foetus in his mother's womb will cause her death, and that should only be done after all means of keeping the foetus alive have been exhausted. A concession is made allowing abortion in this case so as to ward off the greater of two evils and to serve the greater of two interests.

Both the above *ḥadīth* report and the online *fatwā* and, indeed, those Islamic writers inclined toward literalism, are challenged by the complex issue of ensoulment discussed by the early philosophers of the *falsafa* tradition. The above references do not address the paradox of whether there can be a soul that exists independently of the body, given that it is breathed into it. For the literalists, a surface reading of revelation takes priority over rational reflection on such complex issues.

Medical specialist Shahid Athar considers a seeming prohibition on abortion in verses such as:

---

101 al-Bukhārī, "*Ṣaḥīḥ al-Bukhārī*, Book 82, *Ḥadīth* 1," published online: *Sunnah.com*, https://sunnah.com/bukhari/82/1 (accessed on 04.08.2022).

102 Al-Munajjid, Shaykh Muḥammad Ṣāliḥ, "Ruling on Aborting a Pregnancy in the Early Stages," published online: *Islam Question & Answer*, https://islamqa.info/en/answers/42321/ruling-on-aborting-a-pregnancy-in-the-early-stages.

> Q 17:31 Kill not your children for fear of want: We shall provide sustenance for them as well as for you. Verily the killing of them is a great sin.

Nevertheless, on reflection, Athar allows for abortion as acceptable as a last resort where the mother's life is in danger. Apart from that case, Athar argues that abortion of a viable fetus is equivalent to infanticide.[103]

Abu Fadl Mohsin Ebrahim reminds his audience that "[a]nalysis of the ethical issues in bio-medical technology should be derived from the guidance of God, Who alone has absolute knowledge of good and bad"[104]. So in his view, the texts – and a literal reading of them – are the final arbiter in this discussion. He cites the *Ṣaḥīḥ Muslim ḥadīth* collection which carries the following report:

> Each of you is constituted in your mother's womb for forty days as a *nutfah*, then it becomes an *ʿalaqah* for an equal period, then a *mudghah*, then an angel is sent, and he breathes the soul into it.[105]

Scholarly debates rage around the issue of abortion, with Islamic Law schools arguing differently. Most liberal is the *Ḥanafī* school, which allows the woman the right to abort without her husband's consent under certain circumstances. By contrast, the *Mālikī* school of law sets a blanket prohibition on abortion. The *Shīʿī Jaʿfarī* school has waxed and waned in a changing political context. Abortion was initially made illegal after the Iranian Revolution of 1979; after a decade it was permitted under strict conditions, where the fetus was abnormal or where the mother's life was in danger.[106]

The debate among Muslim scholars is clearly due in part to uncertainty about the ensoulment process. The conservative *Shīʿī* jurist Ayatollah Madani (1914–1981/1332–1401) issued a *fatwā* as follows: "It is impossible to determine the exact time for ensoulment. Only God Almighty knows the exact time (...) the exact time of allocation of the soul cannot be discerned even from (...) *ḥadīth.*"[107]

In the United Arab Emirates, the General Authority for Islamic Affairs and Endowments (*awqāf*) has offered call-in *fatwā* advice in both Arabic[108] and English[109]

---

103 Athar, Shahid, "The Islamic Perspective in Medical Ethics," in: Shahid Athar (ed.), *Islamic Perspectives in Medicine*, Indianapolis: American Trust Publications, 1993, 190.

104 Ebrahim, *Abortion*, 101, modified.

105 Ebrahim, *Abortion*, 75.

106 Mir-Hosseini, Ziba, *Islam and Gender: The Religious Debate in Contemporary Iran*, London: Tauris, 1999, 39, 41.

107 Ibid., 41.

108 https://www.awqaf.gov.ae/ar/Pages/default.aspx (accessed on 18.08.2019).

109 https://www.awqaf.gov.ae/en/Pages/Default.aspx (accessed on 18.08.2019).

since the first decade of the twenty-first century[110] Demand was such that the service employed fifty religious scholars to issue *fatāwā* to callers in late 2016, including three women. In one example, a woman had previously had two stillborn babies prior to falling pregnant again. Advice from her doctor suggested that the foetus had little chance of survival. The caller asked whether an abortion in such circumstances was permissible under Islam. Moroccan scholar Sheikha Naeema, a female religious scholar employed by the *Awqāf* service, gave the following advice: "If the foetus is severely ill and will not survive, you may have an abortion [...] You must take advice from your physician, he will guide you. Religion does not conflict with medicine."[111]

Abdulaziz Sachedina provides a rationalist perspective on the issue of ensoulment. He writes of:

> a possible distinction between a biological and moral person because of the silence of the Qur'ān over when the ensoulment occurs in this process. [A] majority of the Sunni and some Shi'i scholars, make a distinction between two stages in pregnancy divided by the end of the fourth month (120 days) when, according to some traditions ascribed to the Prophet, ensoulment takes place. On the other hand, majority of the Shi'i and some Sunni legists have exercised caution in making such a distinction because they regard the embryo in the pre-ensoulment stages as alive and its eradication a sin.[112]

In seeking to offer clear advice, Sachedina comments further as follows:

> Abortion is permitted in some circumstances and is required in others, especially when the mother's life is in grave danger. Islamic sources have recognized a threat to mother's life as grounds for abortion; but they have not given the same consideration to the condition of the fetus because until recently it was not possible to know anything about the genetic or medical makeup of the fetus before birth. Any consideration regarding the fetus's health raises serious questions as to what constitutes a sufficient defect to warrant abortion.[113]

---

110 Ahmad, Anwar, "*Awqaf's* Online *Fatwā* Service also on its English Website," published online: *Khaleej Times*, January 11, 2011, https://www.khaleejtimes.com/article/awqafs-online-fatwa-service-also-on-its-english-website (accessed on 04.08.2022).

111 Ghafour, Hamida, "The *Fatwā* Hotline: 'We have Heard Everything'," published online: *The Guardian*, August 20, 2016, https://www.theguardian.com/world/2016/aug/20/heard-everything-women-fatwa-hotline-abu-dhabi (accessed on 18.08.2019).

112 Sachedina, Abdulaziz, "Islamic Perspectives on Cloning," published online: https://www.ummah.com/forum/forum/general/the-lounge/13596-islamic-perspectives-on-cloning (accessed on 08.08.2022).

113 Sachedina, Abdulaziz, *Islamic Biomedical Ethics: Principles and Application*, Oxford: Oxford University Press, 2009, 141.

Sachedina's comments point to the greater willingness of scholars championing reason to tackle the difficult issue of ensoulment, suggesting that personhood commences from the moment of ensoulment. Muslim scholars continue to reflect on the issue of abortion, though the momentum leans towards restricting its practice. What is absent is a critical mass of Islamic thinkers arguing for abortion on demand. Both literalists and rationalist theologians would consider such a policy to be hijacking what rightfully belongs to God; i.e. the creation and sustaining of human life.

5.4 Cloning: Artificial Creation of a Person

Cloning has increasingly attracted the scholarly attention of Muslim thinkers in the late twentieth and early twenty-first centuries. For example, the Islamic *Fiqh* (Jurisprudence) Academy met in Mecca from June 28th to July 3rd, 1997 to discuss the Islamic position on cloning (*istinsākh*), concluding:

> (...) the majority of the Academy members after discussion reached the conclusion that cloning is permissible in case of plants as well as in case of animals except human beings. The extension of cloning to human beings would create extremely complex and intractable social and moral problems. Therefore, cloning of human beings cannot be permitted.[114]

The meeting in Mecca was followed in subsequent years by meetings about cloning in other locations. At a 1998 meeting in Dubai, Pakistani-born Munawar Anees, an internationally recognized writer and social critic, reiterated the view of the Mecca meeting the previous year as follows:

> The Quranic paradigm of human creation, it would appear, preempts any move towards cloning. From the moment of birth to the point of death, the entire cycle is a Divine act. The humankind is simply an agent, a trustee of God and the body a trust from God. As such, any replication is simply a redundant act. In the absence of a Quranic axiom on body as property, genetic policing would appear to be quite unethical.[115]

114 Usmani, Mufti Taqi (Deputy Chairman, Islamic Fiqh Academy), *Islamic Fiqh Academy: Deliberations of the 97 Meeting*, 28 June – 3 July, Mecca, https://islamqa.org/?p=22327 (accessed on 09.08.2022).

115 Anees, Munawar A., "Re-defining the Human: Triumphs and Tribulations of Homo Xeroxiens," *Intellectual Discourse* 7 (1999), 185–195. See Anees' CV at http://islamicresourcebank.org/bios/aneesmuna.pdf (accessed on 29.05.2022).

Since these statements, the issue of cloning has increasingly appeared in Islamic public discourse, especially in the context of requests for *fatāwā*. The previously mentioned Shaykh Muḥammad Ṣāliḥ al-Munajjid has been approached with requests for a ruling. One of his responses is as follows:[116]

> Question 21582 (Publication: 26–05–2001): What is the ruling on cloning of human beings? How does it affect lineage, marriage, inheritance and other rulings on family matters?
>
> [Ruling:] (1) That human cloning (...) that leads to reproduction of human beings is *haraam* [forbidden].
>
> (2) If there is any transgression of the *Sharīʿa* [religious] ruling mentioned above, then the consequences of that should be discussed to explain the *Sharīʿa* rulings concerning such cases.
>
> (3) All scenarios in which a third party may be added to the marital relationship are forbidden, whether that involves a womb (surrogacy), eggs, sperm or cells for cloning.
>
> (4) It is permissible in Islam to use the technology of cloning and genetic engineering in cases of germs and microscopic creatures, plants and animals, within the limits and guidelines of *Sharīʿa*, for the purpose of serving interests and warding off harm.

Discussion of this issue has reached across the Muslim world. Another group of conservative literalists, the Council of *ʿUlamāʾ* of Dagestan, Russia, issued a *fatwā* arguing that Islam prohibits cloning, pointing to the following *ḥadīth:* "Who is more wrong than he who tries to create, like Allah creates."[117]

A similar approach was recommended by the Malaysian Union of Islamic Scholars, the *Persatuan Ulama' Malaysia*, which issued a *fatwā* banning human cloning, saying the procedure was "unnatural and totally against Islam"[118].

The prominent champion of reason Abdulaziz Sachedina begs to differ, however, suggesting that the jury is still out on this issue and arguing that the science of cloning is an emerging field, so Islamic scholars should proceed slowly on the issue. Nevertheless, Sachedina insists that cloning, if practiced, should adhere to the framework of God's overall plan, not at the whim of mankind:

> A tenable conclusion, derived by rationally inclined interpreters of (...) Qurʾān [23:12–14], suggests that as participants in the act of creating with God, (God being the Best of the creators) human beings can actively engage in furthering the overall well estate of humanity by inter-

---

116 "Ruling on Cloning of Human Beings," published online: *Islam Question & Answer*, https://islamqa.info/en/answers/21582/ruling-on-cloning-of-human-beings (accessed on 04.08.2022).

117 al-Bukhārī, "*Ṣaḥīḥ al-Bukhārī*, Book 97, *Ḥadīth* 184," published online: *Sunnah.com*, https://sunnah.com/bukhari:7559 (accessed on 04.08.2022).

118 Singh, Jasbant, "Malaysia's Islamic Decision-Making Body Bans Human Cloning," *Associated Press*, March 13, 2002, http://cairunmasked.org/wp-content/uploads/2009/12/CAIR_Alerts_501-600ed.htm (accessed 15.08.2022).

> vening in the works of nature, including the early stages of embryonic development, to improve human health.[119]

He demonstrates his creative thinking by adding:

> […] since the therapeutic uses of cloning in IVF appears as an aid to fertility strictly within the bounds of marriage, both monogamous and polygamous, Muslims have little problem in endorsing the technology. The opinions from the Sunni and Shi'i scholars […] indicate that there would be almost a unanimity in Islamic rulings on therapeutic uses of cloning, as long as the lineage of the child remains religiously unblemished.[120]

The human cloning debate erupted into public discourse following the December 2002 announcement by a research group connected with the Raëlian religious sect that it had produced a human clone. There was wide condemnation by Muslim groups of this development.[121]

In a survey of over 1000 Muslims around the same time by the Council on American-Islamic Relations, 81% strongly opposed human cloning. Abdulaziz Sachedina repeated his cautionary note: "[I]n light of the limited knowledge that we have about who would be harmed by cloning or whose rights would be violated."[122] The Organization of the Islamic Conference through its press committee issued a statement[123] pointing to "underlying fears that the [human cloning] technique could fall into the hands of some unscrupulous elements who could abuse it for their nefarious purposes." At the same time, it approved cloning experiments on plants and animals.

---

119 Sachedina, Abdulaziz, "Human Clones: An Islamic View", *The Fountain*, 1999, n. 26. https://fountainmagazine.com/1999/issue-26-april-june-1999/human-clones-an-islamic-view (accessed 09.05.2023).

120 Ibid.

121 The somewhat eccentric Raëlians believe that human civilization was created by extra-terrestrials.

122 Council on American-Islamic Relations, "Resources: Islam and Human Cloning," Newsletter, December 27, 2002, reproduced: https://www.islam101.com/science/cloning.htm (accessed on 11.05.2023).

123 This was originally issued on 28 October 2002, but widely re-distributed following the *Raelian* announcement.

5.5 Transformation: De-Personalization

Can a person cease to be a person? If so, what does this mean for the human soul? Scholars inclined to literalism argue from a surface reading of Islamic sacred text that humans can cease to be persons under certain circumstances.

Some Qur'anic verses suggest that God has punished some people by transforming them into monkeys and pigs: Q 5:60 "Those who incurred the curse of God and His wrath, those of whom some He transformed into apes and swine (...)."

Further reference to this occurs in the Prophetic Traditions:

> Narrated Abū 'Āmir or Abū Mālik al-Ash'arī (...) that he heard the Prophet saying, 'There will be people from among my ummah who will accept licentiousness, silk, wine, and musicians as lawful (...) God will [crush them] and He will turn others into apes and pigs until the Day of Resurrection.'[124]

Muqātil b. Sulaymān specifies Jews as the particular recipients of this punishment in his commentary upon verses 6–7 of chapter 1 of the Qur'ān:

> (The Way of those on whom You have bestowed Your Grace) means show us the path of those on whom You have bestowed blessing, meaning the prophets who have been blessed with prophethood (not of those who earned Your Anger) meaning, he showed us the religion other than that of the Jews with whom God was angry, so He made of them monkeys and pigs, (nor of those who went astray) He says: Nor the religion of the polytheists, meaning the Christians.[125]

Muḥammad b. 'Abd al-Wahhāb, founder of the revolutionary *Wahhābī* movement, stated the following in his *Kitāb at-Tawḥīd:* "God transformed some of the Jews into apes because the ape outwardly resembles the human being, although they are separate and distinct from them. Likewise, the Jews used to commit transgressions which, in some ways, outwardly appeared to be good deeds, while in fact they were false."[126]

This theme recurs in today's world in statements by radical Muslims when discussing the state of Israel. The contemporary Algerian Salafist 'Abd al-Malik b.

---

124 al-Bukhārī, "*Ṣaḥīḥ al-Bukhārī*, Book 74, *Ḥadīth* 16," published online: *Sunnah.com*, https://sunnah.com/bukhari/74/16 (accessed on 05.08.2022).

125 Muqātil b. Sulaymān, "Tafsīr Muqātil b. Sulaymān," published online: Royal Aal al-Bayt Institute for Islamic Thought (ed.), *altafsir.com*, Amman, Jordan, https://www.altafsir.com/Tafasir.asp?tMadhNo=0&tTafsirNo=67&tSoraNo=1&tAyahNo=7&tDisplay=yes&UserProfile=0&LanguageId=1 (accessed on 05.08.2022), translated from the Arabic by the author.

126 'Abd al-Wahhāb, Muḥammad b., *Kitāb at-Tawḥīd*, cf. http://islamicweb.com/beliefs/creed/abdulwahab/KT1-chap-21.htm (accessed on 05.08.2022).

Aḥmad ar-Ramaḍānī al-Jazāʾirī, author of the widely-distributed *Madārik an-naẓar fī s-siyāsa bayna at-taṭbīqat ash-sharʿiyya wa-l-infiʿālāt al-ḥamāsiyya* ("Perceptions of politics between legitimate applications and enthusiastic emotions"), laments what he considers as the two great calamities of the twentieth century, the abolition of the Caliphate by Kemal Attaturk in 1924 and the establishment of Israel in 1948. On the latter, he states that it was founded by "the brothers of apes and swine in the core of the Islamic lands from where the Prophet [...] had ascended to the Heavens (i.e. Jerusalem)"[127]. In a similar vein, the Mufti of Jerusalem and Palestine, Sheikh ʿIkrima Saʿīd Ṣabrī (b. 1939/1358), foresaw the fate awaiting Jews in a sermon at the Aqṣā Mosque on the Temple Mount in Jerusalem on July 11, 1997: "Allah will take revenge on the colonialist settlers who are sons of monkeys and pigs. [...] forgive us, Muhammad, for the acts of these sons of monkeys and pigs who sought to harm your sanctity."[128]

Similarly, leaflets produced by the Palestinian revivalist group *Ḥamās* often carry this metaphor. The very first *Ḥamās* leaflet, dated January 1988, began: "O all our people, men and women. O our children: the Jews – brothers of the apes, assassins of the prophets, bloodsuckers, warmongers – are murdering you [...]. Only Islam can break the Jews and destroy their dream."[129] In a similar vein, textbooks prescribed as part of the formal curriculum in Saudi Arabian schools have long carried the theme of Jews transformed into apes and pigs, although efforts were underway at the time of writing by Saudi education authorities to reduce this theme in textbooks.[130]

With the dissemination of such statements, inevitably questions find their way into requests for *fatāwā* on the topic. We return again to Salafist scholar Shaykh Muḥammad Ṣāliḥ al-Munajjid who issued an online *fatwā* on the issue:

---

127 Al-Jazāʾirī, ʿAbd al-Malik b. Aḥmad ar-Ramaḍānī, *Madārik an-naẓar fī s-siyāsa bayna at-taṭbīqat ash-sharʿiyya wa-l-infiʿālāt al-ḥamāsiyya* (Perceptions of Politics between Legitimate Applications and Enthusiastic Emotions), al-Qāhira: Dār al-Furqān, 2008/1429, accessible under https://archive.org/details/MadareekNadharSiyasahShar3eyah (accessed on 05.08.2022).

128 Rosenthal, A.M., "Management by Arafat," published online: *The New York Times*, August 5, 1997, https://www.nytimes.com/1997/08/05/opinion/management-by-arafat.html (accessed on 10.08.2022).

129 Johnson, Alan, "Hamas and Antisemitism", *The Guardian*, May 15, 2008, https://www.theguardian.com/commentisfree/2008/may/15/hamasandantisemitism (accessed on 10.08.2022).

130 Dadouch, Sarah, "Saudi Arabia has been Scrubbing its Textbooks of Anti-Semitic and Misogynistic Passages," published online: *The Washington Post*, January 30, 2021, https://www.washingtonpost.com/world/middle_east/saudi-arabia-textbooks-education-curriculum/2021/01/30/28ebe632-5a54-11eb-a849-6f9423a75ffd_story.html (accessed on 10.08.2022).

> Question 14085 (Publication: 10.01.2002): Could you please tell me about monkeys. Are they humans who were turned into monkeys for disobeying God's commandments? if so which people were they and what did they do?
>
> Ruling: these monkeys and pigs that exist nowadays are not the people from the earlier nations who were transformed, because God does not enable those who have been transformed to have offspring, rather He causes them to die after being transformed, so they have no offspring.
>
> Muslim (2663) narrated that ʿAbd Allāh ibn Masʿūd said: 'A man said, 'O Messenger of God, are the monkeys and pigs those who have been transformed?' The Prophet (peace and blessings of God be upon him) said: 'God does not enable those who have been transformed to have offspring or children. The monkeys and pigs existed before that.' Al-Nawawī (...) said: 'The Prophet's words 'The monkeys and pigs existed before that' means that they existed before the Children of Israel were transformed, which indicates that they are not from among those who were transformed.'[131]

While the matter of Jews being transformed into monkeys and pigs is arguably the most prolific example of depersonalization in the Islamic literary corpus, there are other instances in Islamic folklore where God transformed people into other creatures out of anger. Jan Knappert records an Algerian legend that relates that King David was deceived by certain people he had engaged to invent weapons. David prayed to God that the inventors be punished and, in response, God transformed them into porcupines. Knappert also provides another example from Algerian folklore:

> The Kabyles of Algeria also narrate that the monkeys of the mountains are the descendants of holy men who became immoral hypocrites and deceivers of the people. The jackals, they say, were once cobblers who cheated their customers by selling bad shoes made of worthless leather. The tortoises, according to those people, were in better days tailors, but they too deceived their clients by substituting bad cloth for the good materials that their patrons had paid for. It is believed that one day God will forgive these souls in animal bodies and restore them to their human appearances, when they have learnt that deception does not pay.[132]

Thus, Islamic scripture and associated literature record the transformation of some humans from 'person' to 'non-person'. The reason is that they have shunned the guidance God has given them and corrupted His word. The American Muslim

---

131 Al-Munajjid, Sheikh Muḥammad Ṣāliḥ, "Are the Monkeys and Pigs that Exist Nowadays Humans who have been Transformed?," published online: *Islam Question & Answer*, https://islamqa.info/en/answers/14085/are-the-monkeys-and-pigs-that-exist-nowadays-humans-who-have-been-transformed (accessed on 05.08.2022).

132 Knappert, Jan, *Islamic Legend. Histories of the Heroes, Saints and Prophets of Islam*, vol. 1, Leiden: Brill, 1985, 124.

writer Mohammed al-Asi (b. 1951/1370) explains why Jews are the principal targets of such a process of de-personalization:

> Whether during, before, or after Moses, these Israelis display a consistency of misbehavior, disobedience, defiance, and malfeasance [...] the Qur'ān is speaking to these Israelis about an affair of their own deviation [...] it was God who succored and supported them and made it possible for them to move into the appointed land [...] But, as usual, the children of Israel flouted and frustrated the divine design [...] they misquoted what was in effect a divine address to all the children of Israel and not only to those who took it upon themselves to misdirect the words or the meaning of the divine communiqué. 'And We sent down on them a calamity from the sky because of their iniquity.'[133]

Islamic radicals, champions of literalism, embrace such scriptural hermeneutics to dehumanize Jewish persons in order to justify continual warfare/*jihād* against them and thereby to serve God according to their reading of God's wishes.

Modern-day champions of reason within Islamic communities do not embrace this hermeneutic of de-personalization. At the same time, such scholars have largely remained silent on this issue, with a notable absence of authoritative *fatwā*, challenging those who promote this ideology in the modern day. Moreover, so far no Islamic scholars of either stream have addressed the question of potential dis-ensoulment implied by the process of de-personalization.

6 Conclusion

In this chapter we have grappled with various angles of approach to the complex concept of personhood in Islam. We have encountered a rich vocabulary used to refer to the concept in the Islamic primary texts. The chapter also laid the groundwork for the main discussion by considering the relevant historical background, which is material to the discussion and debate between early Islamic theologians and philosophers. This background discussion established a fundamental, if at times blurred, distinction between scholars who approach the concept of personhood in Islam by applying a literalist hermeneutic in interpreting the Islamic primary texts and scholars for whom a reason-based hermeneutic has greater appeal.

The chapter then proceeded to consider diverse scholarly perspectives on a range of questions that emerge naturally from the topic of personhood in Islam: the purposes of human beings; their nature; the individual's relationship with God and society; human sin and its source; God as a person. In approaching

---

133 al-Asi, Mohammed, "Qur'ān's Exposure of Distortions by the Children of Israel," *Crescent International* 27, 7 (16–30 June, 1998), 7.

these questions, different perspectives were sought according to the varying hermeneutical principles mentioned above.

The chapter concluded by relating the discussion to pressing issues in today's world: human dignity; contraception; abortion; cloning; transformation from person to non-person. Each of these issues represents an arena of significant and passionate, at times bitter, debate, as seen in the scholars consulted and materials presented.

Our approach has hopefully achieved a number of objectives. First, it has opened a window into an area of Islamic thought that is often neglected, due to the necessary primary attention of the Muslim masses falling upon the Five Pillars and core articles of faith. Second, whereas much scholarly study tends to place focus upon classical or modern scholarship, our chapter has included a broad sweep of both classical and modern Islamic scholarly writings. Third, this chapter has hopefully helped to undermine stereotyping of Islamic viewpoints, by presenting diverse Islamic scholarly perspectives on wide-ranging questions and issues, reflecting and engaging with scholarly debate at the heart of early twenty-first century Islam.

Bibliography

Abdel Haleem, M. A. S., *The Qur'ān: A New Translation*, Oxford: Oxford University Press, 2004.

ʿAbduh, Muḥammad, *The Theology of Unity*, London: George Allan and Unwin, 1966.

Abu-Saud, Mahmoud, "Economics Within Transcendence," *Islamica* 1 (1993), 4–9.

Adamson, Peter, "Al-Kindi and the Reception of Greek Philosophy," in: Peter Adamson/Richard C. Taylor (eds.), *The Cambridge Companion to Arabic Philosophy*, 32–51, Cambridge: Cambridge University Press, 2005.

Ali, Yusuf, *The Meaning of the Holy Qur'ān*, Beltsville: Amana Publications, 1989.

Anees, Munawar A., "Re-Defining the Human: Triumphs and Tribulations of Homo Xeroxiens," *Intellectual Discourse* 7 (1999), 185–195.

Al-Asi, Mohammed, "Qur'ān's Exposure of Distortions by the Children of Israel," *Crescent International* 27, 7 (16–30 June, 1998), 7.

Athar, Shahid, "The Islamic Perspective in Medical Ethics," in: Shahid Athar (ed.), *Islamic Perspectives in Medicine*, Indianapolis: American Trust Publications, 1993, 187–194.

Avicenna, *The Metaphysics of the Healing*, trans. ed. Michael E. Marmura, Utah: Brigham Young University Press, 2005.

Awang, O., "The Umm al-Barāhīn of al-Sanūsī," *Nusantara* 2 (1972), 159–161.

Baljon, J.M.S., *Modern Muslim Koran Interpretation (1880–1960)*, Leiden: Brill, 1968.

Baraka, M., "Islam and Development from the Perspective of an Islamic Thinker and a Labour Unionist: Gamal al-Banna," *Islamic Quarterly* XXVIII (1984), 201–216.

Barny, F. J., "The Creed of al-Sanusi," *The Muslim World* 23 (1933), 48–51.

Brown, F., *The New Brown-Driver-Briggs-Gesenius Hebrew and English Lexicon*, Massachusetts: Hendrickson Publishers, 1979.

Al-Bukhārī, "*Ṣaḥīḥ al-Bukhārī*, Book 46, *Ḥadīth* 18," published online: *Sunnah.com*, https://sunnah.com/bukhari/46/18

Calder, Norman, et al. *Classical Islam: A Sourcebook of Religious Literature*, London: Routledge, 2013.

Calverley, E.E., "Nafs," in: EI², vol. VII, 880–883, Leiden: E.J. Brill, 1993.

D'Ancona, Cristina, "Greek into Arabic: Neoplatonism in Translation," in: Peter Adamson/Richard C. Taylor (eds.), *The Cambridge Companion to Arabic Philosophy*, 10–31, Cambridge: Cambridge University Press, 2005.

Ebrahim, Abu Fadl Mohsin, *Abortion, Birth Control and Surrogate Parenting. An Islamic Perspective*, Indianapolis: American Trust Publications, 1989.

Ebrahim, Abu Fadl Mohsin, *Organ Transplantation, Euthanasia, Cloning and Animal Experimentation: An Islamic View*, Markfield: The Islamic Foundation, 2001.

Fakhry, Majid, *Al-Farabi, Founder of Neoplatonism. His Life, Works and Influence*, Oxford: OneWorld, 2002.

Al-Fārābī, *The Political Writings*, vol. II, trans. C.E. Butterworth, Ithaca: Cornell University Press, 2015.

Al-Fārābī, Abū Naṣr, *Al-Fārābī on the Perfect State*, trans. Richard Walzer, Oxford: Clarendon Press, 1985.

Hourani, Albert, *A History of the Arab Peoples*, Cambridge: Harvard University Press, 2002.

Iqbal, Mohammad, "Access to Assisted Human Reproductive Technologies in the Light of Islamic Ethics," London, 2012 (PhD. Diss., University College London).

Jacka, Keith/Caroline Cox/John Marks, *Rape of Reason. The Corruption of the Polytechnic of North London*, London: Churchill Press, 1975.

Al-Jawziyya, Ibn Qayyim, *Madārij al-sālikīn fī manāzil iyyāka na'budu wa iyyāka nasta'īn*, ed. 'Imād 'Amir. Cairo : Dār al-Ḥadīth, 1416/ 1996.

Al-Jazā'irī, 'Abd al-Malik bin Aḥmad ar-Ramaḍānī. *Madārik an-naẓar fī s-siyāsa bayna at-taṭbīqat ash-shar'iyya wa-l-infi'ālāt al-ḥamāsiyya* (Perceptions of politics between legitimate applications and enthusiastic emotions), al-Qāhira: Dār al-Furqān, 2008/1429.

Kassis, H. E., *A Concordance of the Qur'ān*, Berkeley: University of California Press, 1983.

Khan, Muhammad Muhsin, *The Translation of the Meanings of Ṣaḥīḥ al-Bukhārī*, 9 vols., Medina: Dar Ahya Us-Sunnah Al Nabawiya, n.d.

Al-Kindī, Ya'qūb b. Isḥāq/Ivry, Alfred L., *Al-Kindī's Metaphysics: A Translation of Ya'qūb b. Isḥāq Al-Kindī's Treatise "On First Philosophy" (fī Al-Falsafah Al-Ūlā)*, Albany: State University of New York Press, 1974.

Knappert, Jan, *Islamic Legends. Histories of the Heroes, Saints and Prophets of Islam*, vol. 1, Leiden: Brill, 1985.

Lane, Anthony N. S., "Lust: The Human Person as Affected by Disordered Desires," *Evangelical Quarterly* 78 (2006), 21–36.

Lane, Edward W., *An Arabic-English Lexicon*, vol. 4, London: Williams and Norgate, 1872.

Lapidus, Ira M., *History of Islamic Societies*, Cambridge: Cambridge University Press, 1988.

Lavasani, Sayyid Mohammad Hasan/ Kalantarkousheh, Seyed Mohammad, "The Roots of Human Dignity according to Quranic Verses," *Australian Journal of Basic and Applied Sciences* 7 (2013), 393–397.

Al-Maḥallī, Jalāl ad-Dīn/ as-Suyūṭī, Jalāl ad-Dīn, *Tafsīr al-Jalālayn*, trans. Feras Hamza, Amman: Royal Aal al-Bayt Institute for Islamic Thought, 2007.

Mir-Hosseini, Ziba, *Islam and Gender: The Religious Debate in Contemporary Iran*, London: Tauris, 1999.

Menk, Ismail b. Musa, "Developing an Islamic Personality (Part 1)," published online: *Youtube*, December 2011, https://www.youtube.com/watch?v=nlZn1ltJ4sI (accessed on 04.08.2022).

Menk, Ismail b. Musa, "Developing an Islamic Personality (Part 2)," December 2011, published online: *Youtube*, https://www.youtube.com/watch?v=xhI9ubr8B24 (accessed on 04.08.2022).
Mukti, M. F. Bin Abdul, *The Development of Kalam in the Malay World: The Teaching of Shaykh Dawud al-Faṭani on the Attributes of God*, Birmingham, 2001 (PhD diss., Univ. of. Birmingham).
Muqātil b. Sulaymān, "Tafsīr Muqātil b. Sulaymān," published online: Royal Aal al-Bayt Institute for Islamic Thought (ed.), *altafsir.com*, Amman, Jordan,
Othman, Nooraini, "A Preface to the Islamic Personality Psychology," *International Journal of Psychological Studies* 8 (2016), 20–27.
Penrice, J., *A Dictionary and Glossary of the Koran*, London: King & Co., 1873.
Quṭb, Sayyid, *In the Shade of the Qur'ān*, vol. 30, London: Islamic Foundation, 1979.
Riddell, Peter G., "Islam, Personhood And ... Where Is God in All This?" *Evangelical Quarterly* 71 (2005), 47–63.
Riddell, Peter G., "Islam and the Person: Historical and Contemporary Debates," *South Asian Review of Religion and Philosophy* 1 (2019), 38–51.
Rippin, Andrew/Knappert, Jan, *Textual sources for the Study of Islam*, Chicago: University of Chicago Press, 1986.
Rubin, Uri, *Between Bible and Qur'ān. The Children of Israel and the Islamic Self-Image*, Princeton: The Darwin Press, 1999.
Sachedina, Abdulaziz, *Islamic Biomedical Ethics: Principles and Application*, Oxford: Oxford University Press, 2009.
Schroeder, D./Bani-Sadr, A., "Dignity in the Middle East," in: D. Schroeder/A. Bani-Sadr, *Dignity in the 21st Century*, 66–88, New York: Springer, 2017.
Watt, W. Montgomery, *Islamic Creeds: A Selection*, Edinburgh: Edinburgh U.P., 1994.
Williams, John, *Islam*, London: Prentice-Hall International, 1961.

Websites

Adam, Mufti Faraz, "Is contraception permissible in Islam?," published online: *Darul Fiqh*, 2012, http://darulfiqh.com/is-contraception-permissible-in-islam/ (accessed on 17.08.2019).
Ahmad, Anwar, "*Awqaf's* Online *Fatwā* Service Also on its English Website," published online: *Khaleej Times*, January 11, 2011, https://www.khaleejtimes.com/article/awqafs-online-fatwa-service-also-on-its-english-website (accessed 04.08.2022).
Al-ʿAkiti, Muhammad ʿAfifi. "The Meaning of *Nafs*," published online: *BICNews*, 4 May 1997, *Living Islam*, https://www.livingislam.org/nafs.html (accessed 20.07.2019).
Al-Baghawī, Abū Muḥammad, "*Maʿālim at-Tanzīl*," published online: Aal al-Bayt Institute for Islamic Thought, https://www.altafsir.com/Tafasir.asp?tMadhNo=0&tTafsirNo=13&tSoraNo=51&tAyahNo=56&tDisplay=yes&UserProfile=0&LanguageId=1 (accessed on 04.08.2022).
Al-Bukhārī, "Ṣaḥīḥ al-Bukhārī, Book 97, *Ḥadīth* 184," published online: *Sunnah.com*, https://sunnah.com/bukhari:7559 (accessed 15.08.2022).
Council on American-Islamic Relations, "Resources: Islam and Human Cloning," Newsletter, December 27, 2002, reproduced at: https://www.islam101.com/science/cloning.htm (accessed on 11.05.2023).
Dadouch, Sarah, "Saudi Arabia has been Scrubbing its Textbooks of Anti-Semitic and Misogynistic Passages," published online: *The Washington Post*, January 30, 2021, https://www.washington

post.com/world/middle_east/saudi-arabia-textbooks-education-curriculum/2021/01/30/28ebe632-5a54-11eb-a849-6f9423a75ffd_story.html (accessed on 10.08.2022).

Darul Ifta, "Fatwā: 1695/1387/D=1430", http://www.darulifta-deoband.com/home/en/qa/16023 (accessed on 17.08.2019).

Germann, Nadja, "Al-Farabi's Philosophy of Society and Religion," published online: Edward N. Zalta (ed.), *The Stanford Encyclopedia of Philosophy* (Summer 2018 Edition), https://plato.stanford.edu/archives/sum2018/entries/al-farabi-soc-rel/ (accessed on 04.08.2022).

Ghafour, Hamida, "The *Fatwā* Hotline: 'We Have Heard Everything'," published online: *The Guardian*, 20 August 2016, https://www.theguardian.com/world/2016/aug/20/heard-everything-women-fatwa-hotline-abu-dhabi (accessed 18.08.2019).

Ibn Musa, Marwan Hadidi, *Tafsir Al Qur'an Hidayatul Insan*, vol. 4, fn. 1264, www.tafsir.web.id (accessed on 04.08.2022).

Imam Ali Foundation (ed.), *An Enlightening Commentary into the Light of the Holy Qur'an*, vol. 17, https://www.al-islam.org/printpdf/book/export/html/29731 (accessed on 22.07.2019).

Indonesian Ministry of Religion, "*Tafsir an-Najm* (53) Aya 31," published online: *Kementerian Agama*, 2017, https://quran.kemenag.go.id/surah/53 (accessed on 04.08.2022).

Islamic Verdict on Contraception, https://www.facebook.com/Shariah4Mauritius/posts/islamic-verdict-on-contraceptionintroductionthe-issue-of-birth-control-and-famil/2002265896722278/ (accessed 04.08.2022).

Islam Question & Answer, "Ruling on Cloning of Human Beings", https://islamqa.info/en/answers/21582/ruling-on-cloning-of-human-beings (accessed on 04.08.2022).

Johnson, Alan, "Hamas and Antisemitism," published online: *The Guardian*, 15 May 2008, https://www.theguardian.com/commentisfree/2008/may/15/hamasandantisemitism (accessed 10.08.2022).

Kamali, Mohammad Hashim, "Human Dignity in Islam," published online: International Institute of Advanced Islamic Studies (IAIS) Malaysia (ed.), 2007, https://iais.org.my/publications-sp-1447159098/dirasat-sp-1862130118/media-articles/item/36-human-dignity-in-islam (accessed 29.05.2022).

Maguire, Daniel C., "Contraception and Abortion in Islam," *Patheos*, August, 6th, 2009, https://www.patheos.com/resources/additional-resources/2009/08/contraception-and-abortion-in-islam?p=2 (accessed 07.08.2022).

Maudūdī, Abū al-Aʿlā, *The Meaning of the Qur'ān, Commentary on Sura 72*, http://www.englishtafsir.com/Quran/72/index.html (accessed 04.08.2022).

Melbourne School of Theology, *Qur'an Tools*, https://qurantools.mst.edu.au/auth/login.php (accessed 04.08.2022).

Mozaffari, Mohammad Hossein, "Human Dignity: An Islamic Perspective," *Hekmat Quarterly Journal* 4 (2011), https://www.researchgate.net/publication/327237458_Human_Dignity_An_Islamic_Perspective (accessed 04.08.2022).

Al-Muhajiroun, "Islamic Verdict on Contraception", http://www.almuhajiroun.com/Islamic%20Topics/Islamic%20Fiqh/Contraception.htm. Reproduced at https://www.facebook.com/Shariah4Mauritius/posts/2002265896722278 (accessed 11.05.2023).

Al-Munajjid, Shaykh Muḥammad Ṣāliḥ, "Are the Monkeys and Pigs that Exist Nowadays Humans who Have been Transformed?," published online: *Islam Question & Answer*, https://islamqa.info/en/answers/14085/are-the-monkeys-and-pigs-that-exist-nowadays-humans-who-have-been-transformed (accessed 05.08.2022).

Al-Munajjid, Shaykh Muḥammad Ṣāliḥ, "Permissibility of Contraception," published online: *Islam Question & Answer*, http://islamqa.info/en/answers/587/permissibility-of-contraception (accessed 04.08.2022).

Al-Munajjid, Shaykh Muḥammad Ṣāliḥ, "Ruling on Aborting a Pregnancy in the Early Stages," published online: *Islam Question & Answer*, https://islamqa.info/en/answers/42321/ruling-on-aborting-a-pregnancy-in-the-early-stages (accessed 05.08.2022).

An-Naysābūrī, Muslim b. al-Ḥajjāj, "Ṣaḥīḥ Muslim, Book 19, Ḥadīth 22," published online: *Sunnah.com*, https://sunnah.com/muslim/19/22 (accessed 15.08.2022).

Rakhmat, Jalaluddin, "Tentang Syariat, Islam Fundamentalis dan Liberal," *Tempo Interaktif*, 11 December 2000, http://media.isnet.org/kmi/islam/gapai/Syariah.html (accessed 15.08.2022).

Rosenthal, A.M. "Management by Arafat," published online: *The New York Times*, August 5, 1997, https://www.nytimes.com/1997/08/05/opinion/management-by-arafat.html (accessed 10.08.2022).

Sachedina, Abdulaziz, "Islamic Perspectives on Cloning," published online: *Ummah.com*, https://www.ummah.com/forum/forum/general/the-lounge/13596-islamic-perspectives-on-cloning

Sachedina, Abdulaziz, "Human Clones: An Islamic View", *The Fountain*, 1999, n. 26. https://fountainmagazine.com/1999/issue-26-april-june-1999/human-clones-an-islamic-view (accessed 11.05.2023).

Singh, Jasbant, "Malaysia's Islamic Decision-Making Body Bans Human Cloning," published online: *Associated Press*, 13 March, 2002, http://cairunmasked.org/wp-content/uploads/2009/12/CAIR_Alerts_501-600ed.htm (accessed 15.08.2022).

Tahir-ul-Qadri, Muhammad, "Islam on Human Personality," *The Nation*, 28 August 2007, https://www.minhaj.org/english/tid/667/Islam-on-human-personality.html (accessed 23.07.2019).

At-Tirmidhī, Abū ʿĪsā Muḥammad, *Sunan at-Tirmidhī*, published online: *Sunnah.com*, n.d., https://sunnah.com/urn/635420 (accessed 01.06.2019).

Usmani, Mufti Taqi, *Islamic Fiqh Academy: Deliberations of the 97 Meeting*, 28 June–3 July, Mecca, https://islamqa.org/?p=22327 (accessed 09.08.2022).

Al-Wahhāb, Muḥammad Ibn ʿAbd, *Kitāb al-Tawḥīd*, selections at http://islamicweb.com/beliefs/creed/abdulwahab/KT1-chap-21.htm (accessed 05.08.2022).

Al-Wahhāb, Muḥammad Ibn ʿAbd, *Kitāb at-Tawḥīd*, http://islamicweb.com/beliefs/creed/abdulwahab/KT1-chap-21.htm (accessed on 05.08.2022).

Az-Zamakhsharī, Abū l-Qāsim Maḥmūd, *al-Kashshāf*, published online: Aal al-Bayt Institute for Islamic Thought, https://www.altafsir.com/Tafasir.asp?tMadhNo=0&tTafsirNo=2&tSoraNo=51&tAyahNo=56&tDisplay=yes&UserProfile=0&LanguageId=1 (accessed on 04.08.2022).

Suggestions for Further Reading

Fadel, Hossam E. "The Islamic Viewpoint on New Assisted Reproductive Technologies," *Fordham Urban Law Journal* 30 (2002), published online: https://ir.lawnet.fordham.edu/ulj/vol30/iss1/8 (accessed 05.08.2022).

Hamdy, Sherine, *Our Bodies Belong to God: Organ Transplants, Islam, and the Struggle for Human Dignity in Egypt*, Berkeley: University of California Press, 2012.

Kamali, Mohammad Hashim, *The Dignity of Man. An Islamic Perspective*, Cambridge: Islamic Texts Society, 2002, 147–157.

Khan, Wazir, *Wakf Publication: Islamic Perspective on Human Dignity and Wellbeing*, Independently Published, 2018.
Vöneky, Silja/Wolfrum, Rüdiger, *Human Dignity and Human Cloning*, New York: Springer, 2013.

Ghassan El Masri

Epilogue

1 What Is a Person?

"What does it mean to be a 'person'?" is a fundamental question of philosophy and theology, and one, of immense complexity. The present volume can merely offer select facets of the many different answers that this question can have. Three authors, represent the three monotheistic traditions, each in their own, personal way. In this epilogue, I will very briefly outline the main premises of what an answer might look like and will explicitly state the implicit knowledge, underlying the answers of the different authors. In a way, I will be stating the obvious, which is not always a simple task. To begin to deal with the question of what personhood is; an object of ongoing philosophical and theological debate, legal negotiation, and psychological enquiry, one must survey the broad intellectual trajectories in which this concept developed, that is philosophy, theology, and jurisprudence and distil from them, the essence of the matter. We notice that personhood is essentially bound to three elements: consciousness; relationality; and the ability to act and therefore moral responsibility. Each person, we also notice, having its unique consciousness and relation to the world as well its distinct set of acts and responsibilities has a value that is incommensurable to anything or anyone else. Dignity, and sacredness, therefore, become the only proper values that can be assigned to a person. Finally, temporality, while the human person is temporally limited, it is intimately bound to other persons of various time-spans, and to an eternal person of great power and significance. I shall go through these elements, briefly, in the pages that follow, before I turn back to the religious dimension of being a 'person' and complement the picture drawn by the three authors with additional knowledge that I feel must be included for a fair overview.

2 Consciousness, Relationality, Activity

Consciousness, relationality, and the ability to act – responsibly – become palpable when we ask the questions: What makes an entity a person? What distinguishes it from a thing? and, what is the difference between a subject and an object? We encounter these questions in philosophical, theological and legal debates of various kinds, ranging from the most general question of what it is to be human to specific debates pertaining to abortion and the liminality between the fertilized egg and

https://doi.org/10.1515/9783110756715-005

the human person. We equally identify these three qualities in questions regarding animal rights, and of late, the rise of artificial intelligence, and the 'personhood' of machines, that are able to take decisions and implement them. Whether we identify personhood with 'mental properties' actual or potential, or by association with a group of beings that possess such properties; consciousness, relationality and ability/responsibility will always be part of what personhood is. Speaking of what a person is, another distinction is also necessary, that is between the mundane human person; the incorporeal person that is constituted by humans (e.g. firms, corporations, states), and the incorporeal person that transcends humanity such as reified abstractions like demons, angels, and above all: God.

3 Consciousness

However one understands or imagines personhood, it is always assumed to be aware of the world; in the case of human beings, this awareness is literal and direct. In the case of incorporeal entities, it is assumed is figurative and indirectly; it is, however, legally binding. Suffice to say here, that whenever talk is about a 'person' then this warrants the assumption that the entity described is able to perceive the world and form an epistemic relation to it. A human person is epistemically engaged with the world through sense perception and mental abilities that allows it to cogitate the contents of its perception as well as reflect on its own ideas and other mental contents and inner states. An incorporeal person, such as a corporation, can be blamed, in a court of law for example, and even be punished, for not showing enough awareness of the effects of its products on the environment, for example. As for transcendental and incorporeal entities, their consciousness is a matter of great complexity, especially when we talk of the all-knowing, all-seeing God or His angels that observe, register and react to, human behaviour. The epistemic consciousness of God, is undeniably affirmed in the three faiths here consulted. The personhood, or as some say – erroneously I will argue – the personification of God, is a matter of great significance, which will be dealt with separately below.

4 Relationality

We can imagine, for the sake of argument, a *homo sapiens* born in isolation and growing up without contact with conscious beings. It may survive and have a long life, but what survives is the physical body only. A person, however, can never exist in isolation. What I am referring to here is the distinction between human beings insofar as they are physical entities, made out of material substance, thus the *homo sapiens*; as opposed to the human being as a conscious, relational, moral agent. Without an encounter with another person and the recognition of that personhood, humans cannot transcend their material features and physical natures. Mutual recognition, between persons, is essential for the inception of the new person. Consider how the new-born child realizes the other, and then itself. It begins with the child realizing that some *things* around them purposefully interact with them. At first, the child does not distinguish between persons and things; indeed, they are born, partially blind. For the child, to see that others respond to them and interact with them comes as matter of discovery. In other words, when the new-born realizes that the moving face in front of it sees it as it itself sees the moving face, the process of communication starts, and with it the identification of the other person, and of oneself. Neuroscientists may call it the mirror neuron, 'learning through imitation' is the more mundane expression. By whatever name one calls it, this is how the new-born starts to become conscious of the other human person, which is part and parcel of becoming conscious, ultimately, of oneself. It is in that sense that a person can never exist in isolation, and that personhood is essentially a relational quality. Bodies beget other bodies, and persons create other persons.

Through this essential relationality, the personhood of every human, is created, and later on, develops. As the person develops, on the way to adulthood, the relational aspect becomes indispensable for realizing even the most basic aspects of humanity. Through communion with other persons, the person is created and through the community, it is perfected. For that reason, interpersonal relations are not societal luxuries, but are essential to human fulfilment.

5 Moral Action

The third mark of personhood is the ability to act and with it, moral responsibility. Personhood, ascribed to a human being, an incorporeal entity, or a transcendent being, means that this being or entity is able to initiate an act, influence the world, and is therefore either morally responsible or ethically significant in its action. The moral accountability of human beings is a social given, although, to be sure, it has been questioned by various philosophical streams. The moral accountability of incorporeal entities, such as corporations or states is derivative from them being run by humans. However, this is not the case for transcendental reified entities; that the actions of demons, angels and gods, are ethically significant, and the very ascription of purposeful action to such beings has been the subject of great debate in modern times, as well as in the past. In the same way that the moral responsibility of the human person was debated, on the grounds that humans have a physical nature, by virtue of which they become subject to physical laws and thus determined in their behaviour; the morality, and the very agency of transcendental powers were equally questioned. The claims of physicalism and determinism, that applies to the individual, equally apply to the gods. The universe, according to certain brands of atheism, is merely a complex machine that serves no ulterior purpose, it is morally blind, and senseless. One can read both forms of determinism, of the human agent and of the world, as denials of personalism, on the human and the cosmic levels respectively. Whatever position one may take regarding the personhood of man, or of other entities, it remains the case that to speak of a person is to speak of an active and thus morally relevant being.

6 Human Dignity and Divine Sacredness

Being unique, conscious, interactive, and responsible puts the value of the person above any material object no matter how treasured that object may be. If the value of a physical object is measured by its worth, economic or otherwise, the value of the human person is measured by their dignity. Philosophers often grounded dignity in the autonomy of the person and their ability to excercise the three personal qualities we listed above. Yet not all persons excercise them in the same manner, or to the same degree of success and therefore they cannot be said to possess dignity to the same extent. The honour, rank, esteem, regard or even reverence that persons can receive vary due to a number of reasons. Not least, their conduct in relation to others. Another reason, is their integrity, or their ability to live according to the social principles while guarding their personal standards. The most praiseworthy source of dignity is the ability to maintain one's autonomy, in the sense of freely enduring in one's action while continuously assuming moral responsibility, despite adversity. The autonomy of the person grounds their dignity, and steadfastness and endurance confirm their integrity. It is not, however, the greatest source of dignity in the monotheistic traditions. It is their consciousness of the world, their awareness of its complex orders and endless implicit meanings that is the source of the highest honour for a human person. This is the honour of the prophets and their distinction among humans. It is also what honours humanity above the rest of the creation, in certain cases, even above the angels.

7 Personification

In the case of the human person, these three elements ground our faculties, the epistemic, the social and the moral, respectively. Incorporeal mundane persons, manifest these qualities as well, however differently. A corporation or a sovereign state can have the legal status of the person, they can take decisions, be aware or ignore certain facts, and be held morally responsible, even punished through fines, embargos or wars. The personhood of incorporeal transcendent beings, such as demons or angels, and above all of God, the universe or time, manifest the three elements in a fundamentally different way. God in the monotheistic tradition is all-seeing, and relates to the creation in every detail of its life. God also acts and intervenes in every aspect of our livelihood. How this happens, is the fundamental narrative of these faiths, it is the main meaning of religion, to say the least. To worship the living God, in that sense, is nothing less than to partake in His personhood, and from this perspective it would be a grave error to speak of the personification of God as if it was bestowing upon Him, a quality that He lacks in reality. For personification often implies that the entity involved, is in reality lacking life or vitality, but has been ascribed the quality of a person for some purpose or another. The personhood of God, unlike anthropomorphic qualities metaphorically ascribed to Him, is real, it is thought to be ontologically founded.

Plato personified the laws in the *Republic* to interrogate them. The Four Horsemen of the apocalypse are, arguably, personifications for illustrative reasons. Poets have personified almost every imaginable object, from the lily to the stone, passing by the stream and the breeze. Yet God, the monotheistic faiths would insist, is a person, and not a personification. Being a person, is not to be mistaken with being an anthropomorphic entity. To speak of the personhood of God is not intended to mean that the almighty, transcendent being, is like man, but, rather, the other way around: that the personhood of man, his consciousness, relationality and ability, are derivative from the personhood of the absolute being. God is a person in the sense that the creation is aware of itself, that it stands in conscious relation to itself, and that what ensue from this relation, is morally significant, and ethically consistent. The universal power that is behind this creation is God, who, because of the nature of His creation that is sentient/conscious, relational, active/moral must himself be a person. If one may pun on language: it is not man who 'personified' God, it is God who 'personalized' man.

8 Becoming a Person

How does this act of 'personalization' occur? The allegorical act begins with God breathing His spirit into the clay-creature, Adam, making him in His image. This spirit, and the image, are the carriers of personhood, transmitted from the universal to the particular. Some traditions leave the 'image' element out of the narrative, but Judaism, Christianity and Islam agree on the fact that the spirit of man derives from God and that this spirit is the seat of human ability, dignity, freedom and distinction. One finds the personalization account, narrated, piecemeal, in the monotheistic scripture through the various accounts of the conception, birth and development of the human being. Upon birth, we come to the world barely sentient. Our cognitive abilities are minimal, arguably non-existent. But the newly born creature will become a fully-fledged human being, fed from the bosom of its mother, and made conscious of the world through her word, and through the word of the father. To the screaming child, the world is infinitely mysterious and complex, yet through the word, the vehicle of the spirit of God, the world will become familiar and mundane, even simple and predictable. Eventually, the insensible scream becomes a word, and a meaning; the barely sentient beings, once ignorant of their very names, become self-reflective and creative moral agents that are cognizant of the world and are able to explore and change it. Personhood is thus transmitted. The Word, the traditions of Judaism, Christianity and Islam, teach us, is God's most special gift to humanity and its mark of distinction among the rest of the creation. Some say, the Word is God himself, or His most precious manifestation, at least. That the screaming inarticulate child develops into a cognizant and eloquent person is an instantiation of the act of creation though the Word. God creates the human body from earth and from water, while the human person, the 'spirit', is communicated through the mouth, the divine breath, that gave humans the freedom and the power of knowing all the names (Genesis, 2:20, Quran 2:31).

9 Community and Divine-Human Communion

One is tempted here to make an overarching generalization: all images of God drawn in the scriptures are personal interpretations that empower the human being to forge ahead through life despite the obstacles and the challenges. God, wants to make a mighty person out of the weakest of His creation. The three monotheistic scriptures are vividly concerned with the elemental forces of the world that ravage the human being, and with the endless cycles that turn the life of each and every. Reality, be it in the form of a natural physical world, or a transcendental metaphysical God, struck humans as an inescapable given, and above all, confronted humanity in the guise of a person. In their engagement with the world, humans assume the word to be an acting person, "the world *did* this to me" says man, or "time *stole* that from me!", "God *knows* how much I care" claims another. What religion offers is knowledge of what is real and how things will evolve. Whether we consider the main actor to be the cosmos, or God, we assume, in the way we speak, that it reacts to human actions like a human person does. To believe in God, is to consider that the creator is cognizant of what we do, that He interacts with us and that the interactions are morally significant, even consistent. This moral interaction grounds the belief that we cannot sow the seeds of thorns and harvest sweet grapes, or persist in good or in evil and assume that the memory of the world will not persist, or that God will forget. The interactive, morally consistent relation between man and world or man and God, deeply strikes us as an inter-personal relation. That through knowledge we can predict the world and design some of its elements according to what we need, confirms the impression that we are dealing with a transcendent person. Religions and Philosophies offered humans outlooks and practices that enabled them to live in the right relationship with themselves, each other as well as with the world. Religions, according to this reading, are schools of inter-personal relations, with the human and the incorporeal alike. Personhood, from all of this, emerges as the figure on the throne, that runs the show: for the atheist it is human, for the theist it is divine or angelic. The school of religion teaches us to recognize a 'sentient', 'active', 'moral' power in the cosmos. One might want to call it 'fate'; but 'God', the believer believes, is the richer and more empowering name. Through this transcendental personhood, humans realize the power of their own persons, and through it, they situate themselves morally in the world and latch on to it epistemically.

10 One's Soul and the Other

According to the three faiths, all were created in the same image decided by God, although, every person will follow a unique course of life. Even if the general course of life is determined, starting by birth and ending with death, and even if it shares other general existential features, each will follow her particular course and meet her own destiny. As a complex being with myriad intricate connections between the physical and spiritual aspects of her individual life, the life of a human being is decided by the different choices she makes … within the situation that has been pre-determined by divine powers. Actions will always yield consequences that are beyond the control of the actors, but in the interplay between the human person, and the personhood of the world is one's margin of freedom. The soul is also knowable, through the institution of prophecy. The soul, shared by all humans, and reflective of the singular universal order, is central to the power of personhood. The eternal and divine being, the soul, that exists within every individual, powers the person's higher consciousness, innermost feelings, and moral and ethical consciousness, and guarantees the individual's communication with other human persons, as well as her epistemic connectedness to the world. It is the source of the affinity between the human person and the divine person, and despite the categorical difference between the mortal human and the immortal divine, understanding God and knowing oneself are bound to each other in the three monotheistic religions. In Judaism, for example, the most secure understanding of the concept of a person and of human nature ensues from 'probing and exploring the concept of God'. Christian and Islamic mysticism offer detailed knowledge and intricate cognitive techniques to explore the divine person and identify with it through exercises of self-knowledge and self-denial.

It is not only the divine-human relation that is essential for the perfection of the human person, but humans, too, are a great blessing to one another. Being a relational entity, personhood implies that we are bound to engage in community-life and develop social connections. The monotheistic traditions have taught us that love and knowledge are the focal points of inter-personal communications. They increased when they are shared, and enrich the life of those who offer them. The salvation of the individual is nearly impossible without the community, this is the opinion of the majority of scholars, across the traditions. It might be the case that the immediate community be an erring lot, in which case other measures apply, but that humans depend on each other for perfecting their lives is rarely disputed. This means that individuals are not only shaped by personal values and beliefs but are essentially dependent on their relationships and on other members of society for their own personal salvation.

11 The Soul, Its Identity, Persistence and Extension

One of the perennial questions of modern philosophy has been that of personal identity: What makes a certain person the same across time, despite all the changes that she undergoes? This question amounts to asking: what is the substance of 'personhood'? What sort of object, metaphysically, is a person? In the case of the human person, the sort of question develops into the interaction between the mind (or soul) and the body of the person, and yields a number of conundrums regarding the physical and as well as meta-physical extension of the person. Physically, a human person ends at the perimeters of their bodies, but the reach of the person, extends much further, both physically and temporally. Some 'persons', say, like Socrates, Homer, or Alexander the Great, have existed since millenia, others, that were born and died very recently were forgotten and are almost no more. Questions regarding the persistence of the person through time; the substance of personhood and its physical and metaphysical boundaries are collectively answered in reference to the soul.

The soul, the seat of personhood in the monotheistic traditions, is individuated through different particular bodies at different times. All humans share the same soul, just as they are all composed of the same physical substance. That the human person is composed of an actually limited body and a potentially limitless soul, has determined his condition through worldly existence. It is the predicament of the human person to aspire to the divine person, while struggling with the confines of its own materiality. Struggle, in the path towards God, is the human destiny; and that man will meet God or see the consequences of his struggle, is his fate (Q 84:6). Therefore man, should not await redemption within his lifetime, nor would it be appropriate for the divine breath in him to accept 'passive withdrawal'. The contribution of Aryeh Botwinick reminds us that, although we can neither fulfil our aspirations or overcome our limitations we must accept the struggle. Humans will forever err, sin and backslide on their principles and objectives, but they have the God-given power to continually reinterpret where they are and redirect themselves to where they ideally would like to be.

12 Sin, Repentance, Redemption

To err is in the destiny of every human. Error, even recurrent error and sin is inevitable. Through the institution of repentance, the human person has the power to readjust her course of action and reinvent herself. Muslim scholars advise those who became addicted to sin, to become addicted to repentance. No matter how often a person relapses into error, the door of repentance remains open and should be returned to without hesitation. Scholars agree, that the volition of the person, the determined ability to act morally, if true, will prevail, and this is key for salvation. The self-consciousness of the person, through the faculty of memory will assist the act of repentance. For, in the same way that the repentant amends her sinful habits by re-establishing herself into new ones, her memory will reinterpret her past in line with how she imagines her future. The human recollection of past events is a highly dynamic process; a person is constantly reshaping her past and reordering her perception of her present and her imagination of her future. Events, recall, are ontologically fluid objects; 'what they are' very much depends on how one interprets, describes or recalls them. For example, a divorce or the loss of a friend today, might be perceived as a disappointment or a failure, but it can be recalled, years later, as an emancipation or a new-beginning. Winning the lottery, they say, had detrimental effects on the winners' lives, although the event is joyfully celebrated at the time of its occurrence. Were these events blessings or curses? They were both, and neither. The answer is likely to change, and change again, several times, in the course of a lifetime. The person's power over their memory is tremendous, albeit indirect, and the power of memory to (re)shape personal identity is equally great.

We certainly cannot alter our memories through direct will, or immediately change how we recall past events. Yet we do know that how past events will be recalled will change radically and continuously in light of changes of habits, preferences and new realizations we make and resolutions we take in the course of our lives. If the institution of repentance changes the person's habit, their memory is best changed through the institution of prayer. The physical act of relinquishing an old habit, and the verbal act of wishing for a new one, are tools in the hands of every person to reinvent herself in the course of time. Time, recall, is itself a manifestation of the divine person, "I am time (ar. *anā d-dahr*)" declares God in a sacred hadith. He is the master of remembrance and oblivion. God's favourite creature, He asserts in another hadith, is *al-ʿaql*, the nearest equivalent to the Greek *nous*. God explains that *nous* is His instrument for giving humans and for depriving them, for rewarding and punishing them. God's ability to cause to forget and to force a memory to persist despite a person's wish otherwise is asserted numerous times in the Quran and Hadith. The manipulation of history and memory is one of God's greatest retributive powers on the day of judgement.

13 Temporality

A human person, as such, is a temporal entity, in the sense that she is constantly reshaped by the person's choices and by the nature of personhood as such. Being born, growing, knowing, sinning, aging, repenting, forgetting again, recalling, forgetting, recalling, redeeming, relapsing, dying, being born again, and so forth is testimony to the temporal essence of humanity. The great Muslim scholar al-Ḥassan al-Baṣrī quotes the great Mystic Rābiʿa, she says: "O, son of Adam, you are but your days", asserting the temporal substance of humans along with the physical and the spiritual substances that constitute their natures. We are not only composed of flesh and blood, but of days, years and moments. The temporality of the human person, does not only carry implications for the body that is generated and is caused to perish, but on their immaterial personhood. For personhood equally regenerates itself and perishes, through the person's actions, their memory and their oblivion. Socially, our person can outlive the destruction of the body through its effects on the world and through the memories of others, it can be praised or cursed, or even sanctified, its destiny, is decided well after the physical human is gone.

14 Worship

The relational qualities of the person, brought to the fore through communication and love are so paramount, indeed, that they are established as the justification of creation in the Islamic tradition. God created the world for recognition: 'I was a hidden treasure, and I wanted to be recognized', speaks God, in a sacred hadith, "for that, I created the world". Recognition, has two senses here. One, is the epistemic sense of 'knowing' God through His creation; the other, is the moral sense of 'acknowledging" His grace and providence. These two acts, knowledge and gratitude, are the primary purposes of mankind from God's perspective. Worship, is the highest act of recognition, in both senses I just mentioned. For that purpose, the world as such, is designed like a woven tapestry of divine signs (ar. *āyāt*, Q 41:53, 17:44) and an endless panoply of divine grace (ar. *ni'am*, Q 14:34, 16:18). God's signs and his providence, are meant to bring the human person to enter into a relation of recognition and love with others and with the universe, transcend the limitations of the human person, find comfort and solace in society and better, in union with the cosmic person.

15 Mysticism

The institution of Sufi mysticism is premised upon the idea that the path towards the cosmic person, to be near to it, even to have union with it, is knowable and that this path is open for everybody. Union, often referred to as annihilation (ar. *al-fanā'*) is the ultimate reward of the mystic. Short of annihilation, rising through the various states and stages to attain a higher state of consciousness is the purpose of every mystic, be they Muslim, Christian or Jewish. To that end, the human person must depart from the confines of the flesh and the fears and desires of the soul. The path is not entirely intellectual, it cannot be achieved through reason or meditation alone, but requires training the entire human person, body and soul to relinquish its fears and abandon its earthly habits and desires. This is achieved through 'bodily exertions' against the calls of the flesh, as well as through noetic and spiritual training.

During the annihilation of the human in the cosmic person, or the absolute reality, the adept will no longer sense their personal ego, nor will they realize the passage of time but will experience the now as an infinite moment and a blissful sense of 'permanence in an absolute reality'. This ensues from the 'annihilation of the will' in a 'union with God' or through the experience of the 'unity of existence'.

Pirkei Avot (2:4) teaches us to

> make that His will should be your will, so that He should make your will to be as His will. Nullify your will before His will, so that He should nullify the will of others before your will".

This wisdom is equally shared, by al-Ḥallāğ

> I have a beloved, whose love is in my heart //And when He wishes, He can walk on my cheek
> His spirit is my spirit, and my spirit His Spirit // Should he desire, then I desire, should I desire, then He desires!

These are also the meditations of John of the Cross, in his *Spiritual Canticle* where the bride speaks to the bridegroom (the soul speaks to Christ) in an interplay between the anxiety of loss and the joy of reunification:

> "My will is yours,"
> the Son replied,
> "and my glory is
> that your will be mine..."

Once the adepts of the Sufi way realize and understand the possibility of 'loosing oneself' in sublime experiences of divine beauty, goodness and truth, they can train themselves by climbing a ladder of seven states that start with repentance and ends with contentment. These states should lead them to direct experience of divine recognition. This experience is the state of the human person, detached from the confines of her humanity. This is the euphoria of someone who forgot herself, her troubles and needs, and experienced, even if for few fleeting moment, a timeless, endless joy. This experience, the Sufi school teaches, can be reproduced through experiential knowledge, and be lived and relived regularly through spiritual training.

16 Restoring Personhood

One may feel uneasy, at first, with the strongly realist position that Edward Alam, assumed regarding the ontology of personhood. Through and through, Alam spoke of person as a real entity. Yet his position, must serve as a wake-up call for those hypnotized by system-oriented philosophical theories. Emmanuel Mounier's brand of personalism is a reminder of how 'impersonalist' structures of thought have dehumanized the living, and turned them to 'passive elements' in vast philosophical systems. Personalism forces the realization, that analytical philosophy is guilty of reducing the human to any one of a set of objects such as sensory perceptions or a cogitative mind, as in the case of epistemology. In metaphysics and ontology, the human contribution is little more than to offer 'false witness' to realities that are often beyond human epistemic reach, or to admit to scepticism that demolishes every epistemological foundation. One cannot help but wonder at the sort of philosophical path that has led some modern philosophers to consider solipsism as a defensible position. The reminders, from the rich schools of personalism, of the fundamental relationality of the person, is a broader version of Wittgenstein's response to solipsism based on the idea that language, a rule-following activity, somehow guarantees the existence of other minds. The *logos*, the mediator between persons of all sorts, human, angelic and divine, gives humanity a stable foothold in the world, ontologically and epistemologically.

We live in an age of terrible individualism and suffer from alienating philosophical systems that puts emphasis on the human, but only to disempower it. The human being has become a mere phenomenon in these systems, often detached from reality. If the human is ever to be included in the reality of the world, then it is a reality that she constructed and that lacks epistemological justification and ontological support. If the reality is asserted, such as nature in a deterministic physicalist system, then man is assimilated into this reality and is forced to cope with being reduced to a morally insignificant and powerless automata. The principles of idealism might be able to save man from the determinism of nature, but it detached him epistemologically from all that is real. Philosophical systems, more often than one would wish, analyse the human person vis-à-vis systematic forces and contexts that reduce the human person to an insignificant element in a vast cosmic scheme. The human person, according to these systems, is epistemically blind, ontologically outcast, morally nutralized, captive and incapable, with no significance, really, to the system that is determining his life, and his very worth and meaning. The observation made by personalists, from different schools, that the person is the only ultimately real, is strikingly simple and elegant. As the claim that the individual is the only existent was strikingly frightening. The mirror effect between the extreme scepticism of solipsism and the confident awareness of personalism is very telling, and speaks for an entire era in the history of philosophy and theology. The mirror of personhood may be held in front of systematic philosophy, for hopefully it will yield a deeper reflection and more balanced image of the human state today.

List of Contributors

Aryeh Botwinick received his Ph.D. from the Inter-Disciplinary Program in Political Philosophy at Princeton University in 1973. He teaches regularly within the Department upper-class electives and graduate courses in the philosophical foundations of religion and medieval Jewish philosophy. He received the College of Liberal Arts Award for Excellence in Teaching in 2008 and a Senior Fellowship to the Maimonides Center for Advanced Studies at the University of Hamburg in 2017. Since the publication of his book, *Skepticism, Belief, and the Modern: Maimonides to Nietzsche* (Cornell University Press, 1997), he has been working to reconfigure and rearticulate the relationship between Western monotheism and Western secularism. He has tried to highlight a continuity of logical structure between key interpretations of monotheism and key readings of philosophical liberalism.

Peter G. Riddell is Professorial Research Associate in History at SOAS University of London and Senior Research Fellow of the Australian College of Theology. He is a Fellow of both the Australian Academy of the Humanities and the Royal Society for Arts, Manufactures and Commerce (RSA). He has previously taught at the Australian National University, IPB University (Indonesia), the London School of Oriental and African Studies, and London School of Theology, where he served from 1996–2007 as the founding Director of the Centre for Islamic Studies and Muslim-Christian Relations and Professor of Islamic Studies. From 2008–2019 he served at Melbourne School of Theology, first as Director of the Centre for the Study of Islam and other Faiths and from 2012 as Vice Principal Academic. He was invited as visiting fellow at *L'École Pratique des Hautes Études/Sorbonne* (Paris) in May/June, 2015.

Edward J. Alam teaches in the Faculty of Humanities at Notre Dame University-Louaize, in Lebanon, where he holds the Benedict XVI Endowed Chair for Religious, Cultural, and Philosophical Studies. He is Consultor on the Holy See's Dicastery for Catholic Education and Culture and an ordained Cantor in the Syro-Maronite Catholic Church. He lives in Lebanon with his wife and family and is the proud father of four children.

Ghassan El Masri is expert in Islamic faith and culture, has authored several works on the Qur'ān, contemporary Arab-Islamic political-theology and modern inter-religious engagement. He provides formal advice to Arab and European civil and political institutions, and works in German universities as a researcher and teacher since 2011. He is currently research associate at the Bavarian Research Center for Interreligious Discourses at the Friedrich-Alexander University of Erlangen-Nuremberg.

https://doi.org/10.1515/9783110756715-006

Index of Terms

Abortion 97, 110n41, 130n76, 138n96, 139–143, 139n99, 141n104+105, 150, 151, 153
Active Intellect 106n31, 122–124, 132
ahl al-ḥadīth 107, 110, 121n53 and 151
Akeidah 13, 15
– the Limits of the Relationship to God
Analogia Entis 63, 63–64n43, 70, 93
Apophatic Theology 59, 70

Breirah 32, 32n47, 33
British Empiricism 77, 78n71, 80
Burning bush 20

Cairo Declaration on Human Rights in Islam (1990) 136
Christians 125, 137, 146
Christology 54, 70, 86
Cloning 97, 142n112, 143–145, 144n116+118, 145n122, 150–155
Contraception 97, 110n41, 137–139, 137n93+94, 138n95, 138n98+99, 150, 152–154
Council of Chalcedon 53, 55
Council of Ephesus 53
Creation 6, 9, 11–13, 20, 21, 34, 36

De-personalization 148, 149
Determining the Veracity of Prophets 22
Dignity of Person 97, 134

Faith 19, 25, 26, 41
Fatwā 115, 137, 138, 138n97, 140, 141, 142n110 +111, 144, 147, 149, 152, 153

Ḥadīth 97–104, 99n5, 100n13, 101n17, 102n22–26, 107, 107n35, 109–112, 118, 119n42, 1211n53, 124, 136, 136n90, 139, 140, 140n101, 141, 144, 144n117, 151, 152, 154
Hebrew Scriptures 6, 7, 39
– Foundational Text 7
– Monotheistic Religions 7
Holiness 27
– Horizontal 27
– Vertical 27

Hope 17, 24, 28, 32
Human Theorizing 19
Hypostatic Union 54, 72

Insān/an-nās 98, 99, 104, 119n46, 125, 153
Insurmountability 1
Islamic *Fiqh* Academy 115, 143n114, 154

Jacob's Ladder 9, 17, 18
Jews 125, 137, 146–149

Knowledge of the Unknowable God 68

Literalism 108–110, 109n39, 117, 119, 120, 122–127, 129–132, 137, 138, 140, 146, 147
– Hobbes, and Weak Messianism 36

Mechanical Philosophy of the 17th Century 75, 77, 78, 78n71
Messianism, Weak/strong Messianism, and Marx
Metaphor 3, 4, 9, 14, 17, 20, 23, 24, 30, 34, 36, 37
Midrash Rabbah 11n21, 13, 16n26 feature
Monotheism 13, 16, 19, 24
– Metaphysical Middle 6, 8, 12, 22, 27, 41
Mu'tazila 106, 108, 110, 112, 119

Naaseh V'Nishmah 21
Nafs/anfus 98–101, 101n18, 104, 106, 109, 120–122, 121n52, 122n57, 124, 129, 136, 151, 152
Negative Theology 3, 4, 8, 9, 11, 13, 20, 23, 24, 30
– Monotheistic Religion 1, 7, 13
– Pantheism 16
– Gnosticism 8–11, 17, 23

Olam Habah 34, 57

Paradigms
– of Emulation 1, 7
– of Avoidance 1, 7, 21
Personality 58, 81–82n78, 82, 91–93
Personhood 59, 70n56, 80n75, 91

https://doi.org/10.1515/9783110756715-007

Philosophical Personalism 77, 87
Prayer 30, 31

Qur'ān 97, 98, 98n2, 99, 100–104, 100n11 +12,107, 109–112, 116, 120n49, 122n54, 125n63, 124, 125, 135, 137, 139, 142, 144, 146, 149, 149n133, 150–153

Rajul/rijāl 98, 101, 102, 104, 117
Reformation 46, 46n3, 75, 76, 79
Relationality 45, 46n2, 58, 65, 66, 74n64, 76–79, 94, 95

Shakhṣ 98, 99, 103, 129
Skepticism 3–5, 19, 26, 33n49, 35n52, 36n53, 43, 44
Sh'ma 18
Sin of the Golden Calf 9, 24–26

Tafsīr al-Jalālayn 112, 121n51, 127, 128n71, 151
Teshuvah 8, 24, 28–33, 29n42, 30n43, 35, 41
Transgression in the Garden of Eden 23, 24, 26
Trinitarian Relations 51–55, 57, 64, 66, 69, 70, 72, 72n60, 74–76

wajh/wujūh 98, 103, 104

Index of Names

Abdel Haleem, M. A. S. 98n2, 150
Abdulaziz Sachedina 114, 139, 139n100, 142, 142n112+113, 143–145, 145n119, 152, 154
Abraham 7, 12–15, 19, 27, 41, 67, 81n78, 90, 93
Abu-l-Kalam Azad 108
Abu-Saud, Mahmoud 113, 131, 131n78+79, 150
Adam and Eve 11, 12, 12n22, 23, 24
al-Ash'arī, Abū al-Ḥasan 107
al-Baghawī, Abū Muḥammad al-Ḥusayn b. Mas'ūd b. Muḥammad al-Farrā' 111, 118, 118n43, 121, 122, 125, 125n62, 128n72, 152
al-Baṣrī, al-Ḥasan 111, 119
al-Fārābī, Abū Naṣr 67, 106, 106n31, 109, 111, 122, 123, 125n58+59+60, 124,124n61, 125, 132, 151, 153
al-Ghazālī, Abū Ḥāmid 65, 65n46, 67–68n52, 94, 109, 121n52, 125, 136
al-Jawziyya, Ibn Qayyim 112, 121, 121n53, 122, 136, 151
al-Kindī, Abū Yūsuf Ya'qūb b. Isḥāq 105, 105n29+30, 111, 124, 125, 150, 151
Andresen, Carl 50n11, 74n63, 93
Aquinas, Thomas 50n13, 51, 61–69, 63n41, 68n53, 71, 72n61, 74, 83, 88n86, 93–95
Aristotle 51, 51n16, 58, 61–63, 63n43, 65–69, 66n47, 67n48, 71–75, 74n64, 80n75, 85, 86, 93, 94, 105, 106, 111
al-Ṭabāṭabā'ī, Muḥammad Ḥusayn 113, 135
al-Ṭabarī, abū Ja'far Muḥammad b. Jarīr 111, 120, 120n50, 121, 122n54
Augustine 51, 57, 58, 58n29, 63, 66, 79, 79n63, 91n93, 93, 94
az-Zamakhsharī, Abū l-Qāsim Maḥmūd b. 'Umar 112, 119, 119n48, 154

Basil the Great 51
Beit Halevi 24, 25n35, 43
Benjamin, Walter 36n54, 43
Betz, John 88n88
Blake, William 78, 79
Boethius 66
Buber, Martin 87
Butterworth, Charles 67n48, 93

Cavadini, John C. 58n29, 91n93, 93
Clement of Alexandria 50
Corbin, Henry 64, 64n44, 65, 65n46, 93
Cosgriff, M. J. 90n91+92, 93

Davidson, Herbert 67–68n52, 93, 95
Descartes 77n69, 78, 79, 79n73, 94

Ephrem the Syrian 60, 60n34, 94
Eran, Amira 67–68n52, 94
Esau 14, 16, 17
Eve, see Adam

Fazlur Rahman 113, 125, 139

Goethe, Johann Wolfgang 78, 79
Gordon Tucker 12, 12n22
Grillmeier, Aloys 54n24, 94, 95

Harold Bloom 9, 9n15, 43
Heidegger, Martin 60, 81, 81n77, 88n88, 88–89n89, 93
Hippolytus of Rome 50
Hobbes, Thomas 14n25, 20, 43
Husserl, Edmund 88, 88–89n89, 94

Ibn Rushd 61, 65–67, 65n46
Ibn Sīnā, Abū 'Alī al-Ḥusayn b. 'Abd Allāh 60n35, 61–65, 67, 72, 106, 112
Ibn Taymiyya 112, 125
Ingarden, Roman 88
Ismā'īl al-Fārūqī 109, 113, 116

Jacob 14
Jalaluddin Rakhmat 115, 126, 126n69, 127, 154
Jamaat-e-Islami 113
Joseph (Son of Jacob) 19, 20
Justin Martyr 49, 50, 54, 64

https://doi.org/10.1515/9783110756715-008

Kant, Immanuel 45, 78, 79n74, 81n78, 88–89n89
Kierkegaard, Søren 80, 80n75

Laban 14, 16
Lahbabi, Mohammed 87n87
Leibniz, Gottfried Wilhelm 79
Luther, Martin 76, 77, 88n88, 94

MacIntyre, Alasdair 48n5, 80n75, 94
Maimonides Moses 7, 7n11+12, 8, 11, 13, 23, 24, 29–32, 29n42, 30n43+44, 35–41, 35n52, 36n53, 37n56+59, 40n66+68, 41n69, 43, 44, 61, 67–71, 67–68n52, 68n53+54, 69n55, 73, 93–95
– Theory of God 7
Marcel, Gabriel 89, 90, 90n91+92, 92, 93
Maritain, Jacque 89
Marx, Karl 80
Maudūdī, Abū al-Aʿlā 113, 119–120, 120n49, 125, 126n66, 153
Meister Eckhart 56, 72, 72n59
Meyendorff, John 55n25, 94, 95
Mohammad Hashim Kamali 114, 134, 134n84, 135, 135n88, 136, 136n89, 153, 154
Moses 7, 9–11, 22, 35n52, 36
– vs. Korach 7–10
Mounier, Emmanuel 58, 58n31, 59, 59n32, 89, 92, 94, 95

Newman, John Henry 78n72, 80–87, 84n81, 85n83, 87n86, 88–89n89, 94, 95
Nicolas of Malebranche 78, 79, 79n73
Nietzsche, Friederich 80

Origen 50

Pasnau, Robert 66n47, 94
Pegism Anton 62n39, 94, 95
Pharaoh 7, 9, 21
Pieper, Josef 70n58, 94
Plato 50–52, 56, 58, 60n35, 61, 62, 66, 67, 71, 74n64, 78, 105, 105n28, 123n60, 124n61, 151, 153
Polkinghorne, John 46n2, 94, 95
Powers, Richard 45n1, 94
Prophet Muhammad 97, 104, 147
Pseudo-Dionysius 66, 70

Rashi 10, 11, 11n20, 13, 13n24, 17, 17n28, 23
Ratzinger, Joseph 50n9+11, 51n14+17, 89, 94, 95
Rav Dessler 34, 35
Riffat Hassan 110, 114
Rubio, Mercedes 68n53, 94

Scheler, Max 88
Schelling, Friedrich Wilhelm Joseph 80–82, 81–82n78, 82n79, 94
Shahid Athar 114, 140, 141, 141n103, 150
St. Paul 68, 90, 92, 93
Stein, Edith 88

Ṭahir-ul-Qadri 115, 132, 133, 133n80
Tertullian 49–51, 54, 64, 69, 74

Volozhiner, Chaim 18, 18n29, 24, 34, 34n50, 44
von Balthasar, Hans Urs 50n12, 52n18, 88, 89, 93, 95
von Hildebrand, Dietrich 89

www.ingramcontent.com/pod-product-compliance
Lightning Source LLC
Chambersburg PA
CBHW021709230426
43668CB00008B/777
9783110756647